The Collector Today

Challenges of District Administration

अ अक्षर
प्रतियोगी पुस्तकें

The Collector Today

Challenges of District Administration

Alok Ranjan

RADHAKRISHNA PRAKASHAN

ISBN : 978-81-19092-77-2

The Collector Today

Challenges of District Administration

Revised Edition : 2023

Price : ₹299

Publisher

Radhakrishan Prakashan Private Limited

G-17, Jagatpuri, Delhi-110 051

Branches : Ashok Rajpath, opposite Science College, Patna-800 006

First floor, Darbari Building, Mahatma Gandhi Marg, Prayagraj-211 001

1, Anmol Building, Sorabji Santuk Lane, Marine Lines, Dhobi Talao, Mumbai, Maharashtra, 400 002

Printed at

B.K. Offset

Naveen Shahdara, Delhi-110 032

Contents

Foreword

The administrative supremacy of the British Empire in India was established in large measure through the Indian Civil Service officers working as sub-divisional and district officers. The district collector emerged as the principal agent for consolidating the British rule by maintaining law and order and by effectively controlling and collecting the revenues for the state. He became the symbol of imperial authority and at a time when communications were not so well developed, he almost single-handedly decided government policies and reacted to extraordinary situations of law and order. Even our nationalist leaders were so impressed with the steel frame of the Indian Civil Service, especially in a country with such diversities, that the Indian Constitution and nationalist administration continued with the same administrative network.

At the same time, independent India saw the establishment of welfare state and strong democratic institutions at all levels. The district magistrate today is much more involved in the overall development of the region and his coordinating functions in respect to government programmes are endless. Education, literacy, community development, rural sanitation, poverty alleviation programmes, employment generating and asset creating programmes, and family welfare are only an illustrative list of the programmes that receive his guidance in some form or the other.

Simultaneously, the aspirations of the political executive have also been on the ascendancy, and sometimes narrow partisan interests overweigh the long term interests of the people. Even the choice of officers for a posting in a district may get decided on sectional considerations, as the political elite perceives the district officer as someone enjoying enormous powers to make or mar the emerging political aspirations of a political party or a leader. This often vitiates decision-making at the local level. In our endeavour to seek favourable postings, we often lose sight of the mandate provided to us by the Indian Constitution. In a democracy, it is a bounden duty of the bureaucracy to give a patient hearing to the elected people's representatives; but following their advice must always conform to the rule of law.

At a time when district administration is becoming very complex and taxing, it is refreshing to find someone like Alok having served as a district officer in five districts of Uttar Pradesh: Allahabad, Agra, Ghaziabad, Banda and Ghazipur. As his experiences in the district reveal, he has used tact on many occasions to diffuse a crisis situation and has been able to withstand the pressures which most Collectors face. He has been able to put together some very useful experiences in the five districts covering most facets of district administration. The title of the chapters are well chosen and cover nearly all aspects of a Collector's work schedule. Law and order, revenue administration, and development works are the priority areas. These are also the areas where a Collector has to continually innovate. Decisions are required to be taken at the spur of the moment under pressure and one wrong decision could mean many human lives especially in an extreme law and order situation, besides causing immense damage to the reputation of the officer. Very rarely do the decisions of one person have such far-reaching consequences and Collectors cannot afford to take their job lightly.

It is only appropriate that Alok has chosen to deal with the issue of handling of the press and the politicians in one chapter. In a democracy, the political elite does have a very special position and Alok is absolutely right in concluding that we must accord utmost respect to them. They have a right to be heard and many civil servants develop the wrong notion that whatever a political person says is bad. Alok has rightly pointed out that most politicians are willing to see reason only if you communicate with them with respect. Alok's analysis of the role of the press is also very perceptive. We must appreciate the great role of the press as an opinion builder. At the same time, we cannot afford to hanker after petty personal publicity as it often boomerangs.

A chapter is devoted to the handling of public grievances. The people are a very good feedback regarding government programmes or impending communal tensions and it will be foolish for any Collector to ignore them. A Collector has to be accessible all the time and there is no substitute to personal knowledge. Alok stresses the need for building systems rather than to take piecemeal action against corruption or in other matters. Alok has also cautioned against the middlemen as visitors who claim to be well-connected. His emphasis on meeting the unprivileged and poor is very correct as the accessibility of the Collector to the poor sends the right signals to the people and helps in building the credibility of the Collector. We must also ensure that appropriate follow up action is taken on the public grievances. Our job is not to say yes to everything. All that is required is that we must be willing to look into a grievance in all sincerity.

The role of the Collector as the leader of a team is equally important. A very large number of functionaries in a district look up to the Collector for guidance. In a government set up, the only way to improve performance is to improve the motivation of the personnel working directly or indirectly under you. Example is always the best precept. Similarly, in a law and order situation, a Collector must lead from the front if he expects his police constables to look up to him. The morale of the police force and their mental attitudes can be conditioned by the way the Collector chooses to interact with them. We must begin with trust and personal ways of living are always the greatest motivations. It is very difficult to be a good motivator if you yourself have double standards.

It is useful to caution fellow officers about tact as very often tact means a total surrender to the whims of the political executive. Principled stands must always be taken and our impartiality must never be under a cloud. There is a rule of law that binds all of us and it is definitely an unfair practice to let a criminal roam scot free simply because he is well-connected. Such soft peddling leads to the breakdown of law and order and sends very wrong signals to the people. Our practice must conform to published principles of working if we wish to retain credibility. If the authority of a Collector has been eroded, it is our own colleagues who are to blame for it. We made deviant political masters feel that there was nothing legal or illegal that could not be done. It is not absolutely wrong to say that on many occasions Collectors have preferred to crawl, even when they were only asked to bend. When the quality of politics is on a decline, when corruption has become a way of life, it is undoubtedly going to impinge on the efficiency of the Collector.

The best way of understanding district administration is through case studies and anecdotes. This is the approach adopted by the author. The book is based on his practical experience and offers pragmatic solutions. On the whole, I very much appreciate the trouble that Alok has taken to prepare a detailed account of the changing role of the Collector.

Dr. N. C. Saxena
I.A.S, Ex. Director, Lal Bahadur Shastri National
Academy of Administration,
Mussoorie.

the people. Our practice must conform to published principles of working if we wish to retain credibility. If the authority of a Collector has been eroded, it is our own colleagues who are to blame for it. We made deviant political masters feel that there was nothing legal or illegal that could not be done. It is not absolutely wrong to say that on many occasions Collectors have preferred to crawl, even when they were only asked to bend. When the quality of politics is on a decline, when corruption has become a way of life, it is undoubtedly going to impinge on the efficiency of the Collector.

The best way of understanding district administration is through case studies and anecdotes. This is the approach adopted by the author. The book is based on his practical experience and offers pragmatic solutions. On the whole, I very much appreciate the trouble that Alok has taken to prepare a detailed account of the changing role of the Collector.

Dr. N. C. Saxena
I.A.S. Ex-Director, Lal Bahadur Shastri National Academy of Administration, Mussoorie

Preface

The cutting edge of the functioning of the government is the district. The common man relates with different wings of district administration regarding his day-to-day problems and grievances. It is to the district administration that he looks for the safety and security of his life and property. He comes in contact with the police station, block development office, Municipal Corporation, office of the state electricity board, etc. The kind of response he gets from them and the sensitivity shown by the government departments towards his problems shapes his opinion about the government and strengthens his faith in the democratic system.

The focal point of this district administration is the Collector and District Magistrate. He represents the government at the district level and it is his job to solve the grievances of the people and also to take the policies of the government to the people and ensure that the policy does not remain on paper alone. He has to lead, coordinate, push and harmonise various departments and diverse aspects of government functioning at the district level.

This book is based on the challenges that a district administration faces. There are daily conflicts, strains, pulls and pressures. These have to be resolved and equilibrium maintained. All this requires a mature mind, a problem-solving approach and sensitivity to the woes of the common man. The District Magistrate is also a professional but his vision has to be much broader and higher. His actions bring him into constant contact with the society and the people. He has, thus, to learn to deal with situations with the knowledge that his actions shall affect people. Yet, he cannot function in an adhoc manner. He cannot say, let a situation come and I shall handle it. He has to have an approach. He should think about the various alternative approaches to solving a problem and that he should always work in an analytical framework. The administration at the district level is an art but an art which can be learnt through sharing of experiences and enunciating certain general principles which can be applied.

There are many books on district administration but most of them give the rules, the procedures, the law and government schemes, policies and orders. They do not talk about how the district has to be handled by a district officer. When I became a Collector I looked around in vain for such a book, and realized that this need felt by me would be shared by others also. I realized the need of such a book.

Coincidentally, one after another, I got a series of district postings and every assignment gave me a wealth of experience. I did not want these experiences and the lessons that they threw up to remain embedded in my subconscious. I wanted to share this with others and this was the inspiration for this book.

More than twenty-five years have passed since I wrote this book. Much has changed yet the basic principles of District Administration have remained the same. This new addition has some additional chapters and I have added some new insights and experiences to the existing chapters to make the book relevant to the modern day Collector/District Officer.

It was difficult to find time to write this book along with the demands of my job. Yet the years of distilled experience came readily to the mind and the book was born.

It would be only fair at this juncture to acknowledge my indebtedness to my wife, Surabhi, whose patience, understanding, support, companionship and sharing of problems and immense sacrifice helped me handle my districts well and gain experience which has come on to the pages of this book. She taught me how to look at my own administrative style and constantly analyse it to improve. She reacted to my actions on behalf of the people and as such always kept the prism of reality before me.

Thanks are also due to Mr. Niaz Uddin and Mr. Ram Kailash Yadav who worked with great sense of devotion to type and retype the book. I would also like to thank Mr. Rudra Srivastava and Mr. Salil Kumar for spending so much time in typing this new updated version of the book.

Last, but not the least, I would like to express my gratitude to Dr. N. C. Saxena, IAS Retired, Ex. Director, Lal Bahadur Shastri National Academy of Administration for agreeing to write the 'Foreword' to this book. The few words expressed by him have given me a tremendous sense of satisfaction and encouragement.

Alok Ranjan
IAS, Retired
Ex - Chief Secretary, UP Govt.

Introduction

Many brilliant young men and women nurture the ambition of being selected for the IAS. A great sense of euphoria takes over the moment one is successful. At this stage, and in most cases, the job is invariably and exclusively linked in one's perceptions to the post of a District Magistrate. In fact, most people think that the person has become a 'Collector' right from the time of his selection.

Though one becomes a 'Collector' (and a District Magistrate or District Officer) at a relatively junior stage of one's career, it is one posting that every IAS officer looks forward to and the one posting that he always remembers. You meet any senior officer and very soon you find him narrating anecdotes of the days when he was DM of so and so district.

There is no doubt that this is one of the most challenging and rewarding assignments that one can get. There is tremendous responsibility, accountability and also opportunity, attached to the post of a Collector. Most of us have ideas on how things should be runt–this post gives an opportunity of trying them out. General administration at the district level is directly linked to the personality, approach and competence of the DM. This is not to say that things would not move if a DM does not do anything. They would, but the DM could make things move in a particular way and in a specific direction.

The assignment is very enriching on account of the diversity of the challenges that are thrown up every day and most importantly, the DM gets an immediate response to his actions from the people. Praise as well as criticisms are very immediate and very infectious.

In smaller districts with a large rural concentration, the personality and style of the DM are one of the main topics of discussion. It does not take long for people to know his likes and dislikes, habits and preferences. He does not have anything remotely akin to a private life–everything is for public consumption–what he eats, with whom he dines, who are close to him, etc. So significant is the post that people feel that the three most important people in government are the DM, CM (Chief Minister), and the PM (Prime Minister). If you want any scheme or project to be implemented then it is these three whose will and leadership makes it possible. I just read a book by Parmeshwaran Aiyyar, Ex Secretary Govt. of India and the architect of the immensely successful Swatch Bharat Mission which made India ODF (open defecation free) in October 2019. He clearly says that the mission was successful because it had the political will of the PM behind it and he directly approached the CMs of the States and the DMs to implement it. The PM, CM, DM route ensured the success of a very difficult mission.

On a lighter note, I may recount an incident mentioned by an IAS officer in an article talking about his days as DM. He says that one afternoon while he was taking a nap after lunch a call came from Delhi. His orderly (peon) picked up the phone and bluntly told the caller that it was not possible to talk to DM Sahib as he was resting. Later in the afternoon when the officer reached his office the orderly nonchalantly told him that some PM wanted to talk from Delhi but I told him that Sahib was resting! I too had a similar experience when I was DM Ghaziabad in the early nineties. There was a communal riot in the District and I had worked along with my team without rest for a week to control it. Once things were normal I tried to get some sleep and I also had a terrible throat and could barely speak. The Chief Minister's office rang up saying that the CM wanted to speak to the DM. My orderly without batting an eyelid said that this was not possible as the DM Sahib had a bad throat and was resting. The very same evening the CM came to Delhi and I went to call on him. Imagine my consternation and embarrassment when the CM casually said that he wanted to talk to me in the afternoon but could not get through as presumably I had a sore throat! These two stories go to show that for the officers, staff and citizens of a District there is no equal to the DM anywhere in the Government. He is virtually the King of the District.

The institution of the District Magistrate as well as the concept of district administration was introduced by the British. Even today, when one gets posted to a district, one will find a list of Collectors on the board in one's office, and feel a sense of history as one reads the names of incumbents dating to more than a hundred years ago.

Things have changed. In the British days the DM was virtually the unquestioned head of his district and his main responsibilities were the maintenance of law and order and the collection of revenue. It was within his jurisdiction to dispense justice on a variety of issues. He also organized relief at the time of natural calamities. Today, the role and responsibilities have changed. In a democratic and welfare state the DM has to be accountable to the peoples' representatives. He has to take the lead in the development of the district and in implementing the schemes of the government. No longer can the DM feel that his word is law. His actions are open to scrutiny and it is his job to listen to the people and understand and accommodate their aspirations.

The system of *mulaqati* or meeting people existed during the British days too but the visitors often used to be a select few. They would wait outside and the Collector would meet them when he had the time. Today, anybody who has a problem comes to the Collector. There is no definite time for this–it could be late at night also. The Collector is expected to, and does, meet them. It is his job to take up their grievances and attempt to resolve them.

Many officers resent this and talk of how wonderful it must have been to be Collector in the days of the British. They resent the constant interference in their working. Nothing is achieved by romanticizing the bygone era. The present day District Magistrate has to alter his attitudes and behaviour if he really wants to make a success of his job. There should be no regrets about this change as the fact is that the job of a Collector today is far more diverse, complex and challenging. There is a tremendous scope for use of creativity and if a

Collector really applies himself, his presence does make a discernible difference to a district.

Though the Collector today does not have direct authority over the police and other departments, sufficient authority is still vested with him to make all the key players agree and accept his leadership. The Collector is made responsible for implementation of any scheme formulated by the government. He could, at any point of time, be the Chairman of almost a hundred committees. Though it is conceded that in a short term of about two years the DM will not be able to change the face of the District but he can always make a significant impact as almost everything 'flows' through him. The government also makes him responsible for anything that happens in a district.

The structure of district administration was conceived by the British and it has stood the test of time. Even a modern management guru like Peter Drucker has applauded this system and has analyzed it and put it up for the modern managers to follow. According to him this is a perfect organizational system of delegating authority and responsibility on one person and holding him accountable. This system delivered the results it was expected to. The system was designed to maintain status quo and it did a wonderful job. The very same institution has adapted itself wonderfully to democracy and to the needs of a State committed to development. The basic principle is that the DM represents the government at the district level. The State government communicates with him. He gets the work done through a team of officers at the district level. He has sufficient independence to choose his course of action and his personal style makes the difference. So, the first principle behind the district set-up is that of unity of command which is very necessary for any organization to succeed.

Another important concept is that of decentralization. There can be no greater example of decentralized decision-making than this. The DM is left free to resolve law and order problems and other issues in any manner he wants. He is given responsibility and is accountable for the consequences of his decisions. Even in development programmes only policy and general guidelines are indicated. It is now up to the Collector to plan out his strategy. He is free to devise his own system of information and monitoring. The task is to achieve the goals and he is held responsible for that.

If it weren't for this, one can imagine how impossible it would become to govern. If, for instance every small matter or issue were to be resolved at the state level, the top-heavy system would certainly have failed to deliver.

It is sad commentary on the present-day system that attempts are being made to dilute the institution of the DM. Today the government is always ready to make a scapegoat out of a DM if anything goes wrong. Political interference has reached a stage where the DM is expected to shuffle his team of officers in accordance with the wishes of public representatives. His independence is getting reduced as he is increasingly asked for reports on issues and then told what he should do. Instructions coming from the state level have increased, curbing the autonomy of the institution. Even if there is a small law and order problem, the state government wants to know whether DM personally visited the site.

This goes against the grain of district administration. SO's, SDM's and ADM's not withstanding, the DM is persuaded to reach the spot himself. More so, it leads to the DM getting too exposed which leads to a reduction in his authority. It has also become common to call for an explanation from the District Officer regarding the State development projects. Worst still even before an officer can settle down in a district he gets transferred. The average span of a Collector's posting in UP would not be more than one year.

DM, as an institution, is reeling under a concerted attack from all sides. The people in police department want to take away his authority in law and order. The technical departments want to be totally independent. Another concept that is being floated is that development should be entrusted to another officer of the same seniority. The politicized executive is now selecting DMs on the basis of their 'acceptability' and 'adjustability'.

Things have reached a stage where people have started talking in terms of an elected person being a DM. They feel that such a person would be much more responsible towards the aspirations of the people. They suffer from a grave misconception. One can turn around and see that an elected Mayor of Municipal Corporation has not done any better than official administrator. Moreover, an elected person, on taking over can never be neutral or impartial. Hence, the very foundation of this institution is being dug up.

It is the public at large which actually invests the DM with his authority and status. Even today, for any problem they would approach the DM. Some Collectors try to escape the responsibility by saying :

"This problem relates to police, go to SSP" or "This relates to electricity, please approach the concerned executive engineer" and so on. But this is not proper. The public feels let down and the institution of the Collector suffers. The DM has both a right and a responsibility to look into public grievances of any nature.

People recognize the DM and even come to him with problems which could be called personal in nature. It is this immense faith in the institution of the DM that makes the system work. People feel that at least at the level of a Collector some action would be taken.

To preserve the primacy of the post of DM it now devolves upon officers to do justice to the aspirations of the people. As long as they are perceived as being neutral, impartial and aboveboard, the people will continue to go to them with respect. If they work sincerely towards solving people's problems then the faith in this institution would continue. This is the only mechanism by which he can control his district, and make a significant, complete and lasting contribution.

The Collector Today

Challenges of District Administration

Evolution of the Role of the Collector (District Officer)

The role of the District Officer has evolved over time. Some powers and responsibilities have been added while a lot of the aura of power has diminished. Yet the institution remains as vibrant and relevant as before. Actually, its role has become far more important and he is at the centre of the development paradigm of the state. It is the foundation on which the entire edifice of public governance is built. His performance determines the impact of the government on citizens. Despite evolving over the years the constant factor has been the centrality of the District Officer. He was, is and shall remain the Chief Administrator of the District. Times keep changing and so also does the structure of governance. The office of the District Officer naturally cannot be immune to this. The institution cannot remain static. It has to be dynamic–constantly responding to the changing nature of the state and administrative requirements.

The post of the Collector was created on 11th May, 1772 by the Governor General Warren Hastings (East India Company). At that time Bengal generated revenue amounting to 50% of the British Public Revenue. The office of the Collector and District Officer was responsible for public order, swift administration of justice, prompt payment of taxes, maintenance of land records and preventing property disputes. Soon two models of District

Administration evolved. The Munro School was prevalent in Bombay, Madras, North Western Provinces and United Provinces. The other was the Cornwallis Model which was applicable in Bengal. The former carried the Mughal legacy of a strong area administrator in whose office was concentrated the role of Revenue Collector, Civil Judge and Magistrate. Cornwallis Model separated the revenue and judicial functions and the District Officer was positioned as a coordinator of activities at district level. However, in 1780 Civil Judges were established in districts of Bengal and in 1787 Collector was also made the Civil Judge and Magistrate. Gradually, he became representative of governing power and head of general administration. In 1790, the company took over the administration of the District Magistrate.

Again in 1793, Cornwallis separated the powers of the Magistrate and Collector. Judge Magistrate post was created. In 1793, after observing some short-comings in the system Cornwallis divested the Collector of judicial authority in revenue matters. But by 1820 magistracy, revenue, judicial functions and general administration all unified in the Collector. By 1857 there was complete movement from Cornwallis School to the Munro School and all the powers were then concentrated in the District Officer.

The second half of the 19th century saw the creation of the office of Superintendent of Police (SP), Public Works Department and Health. Direct executive administration of these departments was withdrawn from the Collector but he continued to exercise the power of general control and administration.

The period from 1857 to 1919 was one of the commanding role of the District Officer. It has been called the era of triumphant bureaucracy. The development role of the District Officer was secondary. The aspect of the development was always secondary to the colonial regime. Development work was sporadic and "extra- curricular". Welfare activity depended upon the predilection of the concerned District Officer. The British started building irrigation systems and the District Officer would often be involved in work related to dams, embankments, wells and tanks. Some officers gave importance to schools and roads also. From 1919 to 1947 was a trying period for the District Officer. The nationalist movement was gathering steam and the District Officer had to deal with them according to the dictates of the colonial masters. Just before World War-II Provincial Congress Governments were formed and it was a new experience for the Collector to work under them.

In his remarkable book *The Ruling Caste* David Gilmour has sketched out the experience the ICS (Indian Civil Service) officer had in a district and how he learnt the ropes. The ICS officer arrived in either Calcutta or Bombay from London and was given a letter from the Chief Secretary directing him to report to a district which was often chosen on the basis of the personality of the Collector. The idea was to send a young officer to a district where the Collector would be able to train him. More often than not the young officer stayed at the residence of the Collector and learnt administration by constantly observing the Collector at work. There was no scientific training schedule laid out. It was haphazard and dependent upon the capabilities, whims and fancies of the Collector. Even today the situation is very much the same in reality despite the formalized training apparatus. The Collector then, as now, would give the young officer some experience in court work, magisterial duties and revenue work, besides attaching him to the district treasury. Little effort was made to teach the young officer the principles of administration and coordination with other departments. All this, the young officer had to fathom on his own. Of course, there was a lot of formality on social occasions–who would sit next to whom and also in the ICS days they were very particular about the warrant of precedence.

Lord Curzon once said that India may be governed from Shimla or Calcutta but it is administered from the planes. The planes he was talking of were around 250 districts of British India. Districts were huge having an average area of 4430 square miles. Smaller districts used to have about half a dozen British officials whereas in bigger districts the district judge and other magistrates were also from the ICS. Even in those days, the powers were concentrated in the District Officers and the Commissioner merely had a supervisory role to play. The District Officer was responsible for almost everything–police, jails, forests, roads, canals, etc. The common man had immense faith in the institution and a Collector's day was never complete without listening to petitioners. Of course, there cannot be any comparison between the accessibility expected of officers today compared to the British rule. The District Officer supervised his District by his tours and inspections. The ICS were great at building systems and when I was posted to the districts I found that inspection manuals had been prepared during the British days for a detailed inspection of tehsils and courts and police stations.

The District Officer was expected to protect the people in case of any natural calamity or emergency. Depending on the characteristics of a district the profile of the District Officer would be different in terms of focus and priorities. But by and large, the job content and responsibilities of the District Officers were the same throughout India. Law and order was a major responsibility especially in later part of the 19th century when communal flare-ups were on the rise.

The District Officer was very much the monarch of all he surveyed but increasingly over time, the secretariat officers began to encroach upon his time by asking him for numerous reports and statements. The interesting thing is that the District Officer, just like today, treated these directions from the secretariat as a nuisance and always had a healthy contempt for them. Even today most District Officers would tell you that officers in the secretariat do not have a proper appreciation of ground realities.

There were no elections to be conducted at that time but the District Officer was the officer responsible for conducting the census operations. There was tremendous variety in the job of a District Officer. This must have been a major solace and motivating factor for the District Officers to spend quiet, lonely lives in far-away districts with only a handful of fellow officers for company. The powers were huge but the work was onerous and the working conditions taxing. The authority vested in them was commensurate compensation for the life they had left behind in England.

We have all seen the romantic photographs or paintings of that era depicting the District Officer wearing his hat, formal clothes, sitting under a tree in a village and dispensing justice. The concept of winter touring has come down to us from those days. We are now expected to do winter touring for 45 days in a year but no District Officer really fulfills these targets. The ICS District Officer of the colonial era had no option but to tour extensively. In those days when there were no other means of communication, touring and camping was the way to control the district and subordinate officers. Currently, District Officers stay in guest houses during tours but in those days the District Officer used to travel with his entire camp and retinue and put up tents and spent the nights in the interior. I recall that as an SDO and District Officer I also pitched tents in the village and spent nights there but these tours have now become a rarity. The District Officer has to be in constant touch with his district headquarters and also the whole process of camping in the interior has become cumbersome. Still, I am of the definite opinion that if a District Officer spends nights in camps in remote areas he would be able to appreciate the people and the problems better and in general the quality of administration would improve.

The collection of land revenue was a high priority task and many ICS officers worked as settlement officers who laid down the mechanics on the basis of which land revenue would be assessed. By and large the maintenance of land records was much better at that time as the District Officer gave a lot of time to this work. Undisputed cases of succession/mutation would be often carried out sitting under the tree by the District Officer.

The District Officers criticized the secretariat officers for increasing the paperwork and restricting the movement of the District Officer amongst the people of his district. They found the approach at the secretariat too theoretical and restricted to paper knowledge. It was felt that India was too diverse a country for any one policy or government directive to be uniformly applicable across all districts. David Gilmour in his book *The Ruling Caste* quotes Harcourt Butler ICS as saying that India could not be governed by general principles. He felt that the growth and stylization of the bureaucracy had got it out of touch with people.

This was a period when India was slowly moving towards self-governance. The District Officers, often, resisted the fact that there were district boards to run schools and congress members working as ministers. It was a situation of government versus those demanding more autonomy or independence. The District Officer often had to take strong measures on behalf of the government even though his heart could be elsewhere. The powers of District Officers were becoming less and less. He had to now work through systems and processes where earlier he had the freedom to appoint people, distribute patronage and licenses. The municipal boards also had an elected Chairman where previously the District Officer used to look after this work. Naturally, there were areas of conflict. The Congress government also looked at the civil servants with suspicion. This was natural as many District Officers had arrested them and sentenced them.

The institution of the District Officer has been one of the lasting legacies of the British Rule. Viceroy Lord Wavell in an informal speech after he left India said that the English would be remembered not by this institution or that but by the ideal left behind of what a District Officer should be. The District Officer was a symbol of justice and sympathy for the common man of India.

The ICS and the District Officer came under fire as soon as the country became independent. It took all the persuasive power, firmness and wisdom of Sardar Vallabhbhai Patel that enabled the survival of the civil service rechristened now as the IAS. The IAS has tried to live up to the standards set by the ICS. It is a question of debate to what extent it has succeeded and how it has responded to the changing political and social scenario. I have dealt with this in a separate book but here I am concerned with the District Officer. The institution has evolved continuously and still retains its place in the scheme of administration and implementation of policies. It is now an instrument of public service and the first ARC (Administrative Reforms Commission) while examining its role commented "This system has stood the test of time and even though it was basically designed to meet the colonial needs of the British it can continue to serve the needs of a welfare state also."

The relevance of the institution of the District Officer is in the faith that the people have in it. For any problem in the district a person would like to meet the District Officer who is the representative of government and recognized leader of the administrative structure. Line departments have proliferated after independence and each one of them have their offices at the district. There is the District Inspector of schools, Basic Education Officer, Executive Engineers of PWD and Irrigation, Chief Medical Officer, Divisional Forest Officer, Superintendent of Police, District Development Officer amongst others. They report to their superiors in the department and the District

Officer is not involved in their day-to-day working. However, District Officer remains the principle coordinator. The skills now required of the Collector are that of collaboration, team building and communication. The government still relies upon the Collector to implement any scheme or project which seems to be falling behind. For instance I recall as Chief Secretary monitoring the construction of new transmission substations. The work picked up only after I started having regular video conferences with the Collectors and made them responsible for the progress. In the same vein the public approaches the District Officer in the event of power break downs or water shortages or potholed roads. The District Officer takes up the issue with the department at the district as well as state headquarters and his intervention always begets a response.

Whereas, the success of the District Officer as a leader depends on how well he is able to forge a team spirit, the attitude of the secretaries sitting in state headquarters also goes a long way in empowering the District Officer. In U.P. we found that letters written by District Officers to departmental secretaries were not being given due importance. It was, hence, mandated that any letter of a District Officer should be responded to within a week by the Secretary and positive action taken in the matter. This helped the District Officer to exercise his authority at the district level. There is also a mechanism whereby the District Officer gives an annual remark in the performance appraisal of line officers with respect to their contribution to flagship development schemes. Of course, the District Officer is not the unquestioned leader of yester years. In the earlier days any officer visiting a district, irrespective of seniority, was expected to call on the Collector. Nobody does that now. When I was a Collector I remember if I made any reference to the secretary of a department the secretary concerned would ring me up and discuss the issue over the telephone. This linkage between the District Officer and the state secretariat leads to effective governance.

However, the departments concerned should not fix all responsibility on the District Officer and let their own officers go scot free. I found a disturbing trend in government orders saying that for any slippage the District Officer shall be personally responsible. This is just not right. The District Officer is a coordinator. He cannot get into all aspects of a department. Then there are a lot of financial approvals which the District Officer has to give without having access to all the relevant information which is available with the departmental officers. There was a case in U.P. where the District Officer approved the rate for mid-day meal schemes and the matter later on became a subject of CBI enquiry. I witnessed some excellent and honest Collectors undergoing the trauma of a CBI investigation. I feel the District Officer should be protected against such allegations and investigations. He does not have the time to go into the details of each and every matter put up before him. The responsibility must be that of the departmental officer.

It is also true that several departmental officers resent the intervention of the District Officer. There is an undercurrent of hostility and some even try to ignore the District Officer. There have been cases of the District Officer writing to the state headquarters against certain officers. The position of the District Officer becomes untenable if no action is taken on his letter. Unfortunately, this happens in several cases.

In the early years of my service I was given charge of a district as my Collector went on long leave. He had antagonized officers of other departments by his strictness with them and his propensity to review their working on a detailed basis regularly. Things came to a pass when an officer of the Power Department was transferred and new incumbent came. He tried to move into the house vacated by his predecessor. The prerogative of house allotment is that of the Collector who allotted the house to the District Panchayat Raj Officer. It became a major issue and the entire Power Department became a party to this resentment. I took charge when this problem was at its peak with hot words having been exchanged by my predecessor with the Power Department officers. The issue came up before me. The officer of the Power Department had also made an effort to forcibly enter the house. Further, they were not interested in talking with me and spurned my offer for a discussion on the issue and threatened to cut off the power supply of the district at mid-night if I did not relent. Now the battle lines were drawn. I did not budge and they switched off the power to the district headquarters at mid-night. It was a remote hill district in the early 1980's and the communication with state headquarters was very difficult. I responded by ordering their arrests. Officers and employees of the Power Department were arrested and sent to jail. Meanwhile, I got through to state headquarters. They responded by sending some additional teams and power supply was restored by noon next day. For me, it was a real baptism by fire. However, I learnt an important lesson. The District Officer has to literally walk on the razor's edge in trying to get work out of line departments. He has to lead by the force of his personality and should never be over-bearing, rude or abrasive. I held charge of five districts after that but never faced any problem with line department officers and we all worked as a team. The Collector today has to be the leader of a team but his powers flow not from some laid down hierarchy but from his role as a coordinator who leads by his professional competence and ability to handle people.

The District Officer has to work along with elected bodies in urban as well as rural areas. The panchayats have now been greatly empowered getting a lot of funds directly from the Central and State Finance Commissions. The Chairman of the Zila Parishad (District Council) is also a figure of great political importance. In many states there is a separate officer serving as Chief Executive of Zila Parishad under the Chairman. District Officer has only a marginal role in development. It could be as a member of the district planning or development council. Even in Uttar Pradesh which has the Chief Development Officer as the IAS officer in charge of development the role of the District Officer is getting restricted in matters related to development. However, in the Uttar Pradesh model the Chief Development Officer (CDO) is invariably junior to the District Officer and so the latter is able to assert himself in the field of development. I personally feel this model is better than the one where the CEO of Zila Parishad is senior to the District Officer effectively eliminating the District Officer from development projects. The faith that the people have in the institution and the powers that are vested in him in his capacity as District Magistrate make him invaluable to the development process.

Similarly, in urban areas the elected Mayor or Chairman assisted by the Municipal Commissioner or Executive Officer is responsible for all aspects of urban governance. However, once again the expectations of the people are only from the District Officer and there is no restriction on his involvement or intervention in areas of urban development in municipalities which are small in size and are headed by an Executive Officer of the municipal cadre. However, in larger cities where normally an IAS officer is posted as Municipal Commissioner the role of the District Officer in urban governance is limited.

The role of the Collector has changed with the evolution of elected urban and rule local bodies but still his role as a coordinator continues. The overall mentoring role of the District Officer remains and should remain. He now has to guide the democratic bodies to fulfill their role in the mandated manner for the benefits of the citizen. The District Officer has to play the role of a principle change agent. He has to steer as well as row.

Then after independence, came the elections to assemblies and parliament on a regular five year basis. The District Officer is the District Election Officer and during the time of elections, once the elections are notified, he is vested with immense powers to conduct the elections in a free, fair and transparent manner. Similarly, it is the District Officer who conducts the census and livestock census where once again he coordinates the activities of all departmental officers. In times of natural calamities it is the District Officer who is responsible to save people, provide relief and give an assessment of the damage. Once again he has to play the role of a leader.

The use of information technology has greatly strengthened the District Officer. Every district now has an IT based Grievance Redressal System. Many young District Officers are engineers and I have seen them creating Apps to provide faster and better services to the people.

The authority of the District Officer is such that if the state government wants anything to be done on priority it looks to the District Officer to make it happen. I have described later in this book how I could implement total literacy campaign in the district Agra of Uttar Pradesh as District Officer. Similarly, one can see how the District Officers have performed in taking leadership in special programmes like Pulse Polio to eradicate the disease of Polio and which has been a huge success. No development project can proceed without land acquisition and here once again it is the District Officer who declares the award and distributes compensation. It was the Collectors who negotiated and acquired the land of Lucknow-Agra Expressway which we were able to build in a record time of 23 months. Similarly, when as Chief Secretary we built the Lucknow Metro it was the District Magistrate who was made responsible for removing encroachments along the alignment and he did a wonderful job.

The role of the District Officer has evolved over time. Yet he remains the principle figure in the district administration through whom all major programmes are facilitated and coordinated and schemes are implemented. His role has changed from that of control to bringing about positive change and service delivery.

In a conference on the role of the District Officer the then Prime Minister of India Mr. Manmohan Singh very appropriately defines the importance of the institution of the Collector. He said, "The role of the Collector has been transformed into a more powerful one of coordinator, facilitator and a person who is responsible for intersectoral coordination of various activities." Needless to say, the institution has stood the test of time and will certainly evolve further to face the new challenges of district governance.

Law and Order

Law and order is the 'be-all' and 'end-all' of district administration. A district officer may be doing well in development, court work, or in collection of revenue, but if he fails in law and order then he has failed to run the district. In the eyes of the government also, the maintenance of law and order gets the highest priority. And the same is true with the people of the district. Without doubt, this is the most important function of the government. If people are secure, they will develop. Naturally then, law and order is given the highest priority by the district magistrate.

There are various theories about law and order but what measure will succeed is always a situational variable. One of our teachers at the Mussoorie Academy of Administration, after several sessions on law and order theory, summed up by saying that success in a law and order situation was always a matter of chance. If you succeed, you are praised for your presence of mind and promptness in decision-making. If you fail, the whole thing recoils and everybody finds fault with your decision. In law and order, nothing succeeds like success.

This does not mean that it is only a matter of fate. A lot of planning, personal qualities of leadership and knowledge of people and places goes into success. However, the main point is that there is no definite solution to a law and order situation. Each problem has to be tackled in a unique manner.

The qualities required most of all are the presence of mind and coolness at the time of crisis.

Case Studies

To put things in the right perspective, I would like to illustrate with two case studies.

The Rickshaw Puller

District 'G' was a small, backward district having a district headquarter with a population below one lakh. It was an underdeveloped district where caste factors played an important role in the life of people. The DM, Mr. A, joined the district taking up his first charge and was immediately struck by the fact that this was a neglected district. He plunged headlong into the process of development. Despite its backwardness the district was full of politicians. Not major politicians or significant leaders, but it seemed that every unemployed youth would sling a *jhola* on his shoulder, collect a couple of applications and present himself before the DM regularly. Though kowtowing and timid when in the office, these Netas were gossipy by nature and totally unreliable.

On a fine December morning at about 8 am when the DM's driver came on duty he told him that there had been some incident of a Sub-inspector (SI) of police beating up a rickshaw puller who succumbed to his injuries. The people were agitated. The DM promptly spoke to the SP and SDM of the area. They both assured that they would look into the matter. The SDM (sub-divisional magistrate) and CO (circle officer police, also known as DSP) were asked to go to the spot immediately.

At about 9:45 am, the SDM and DSP came to the DM. They were looking tense and worried. A long stream of visitors was moving in and out of the DM's office. The SDM, on old man, very politely suggested that the matter was urgent. The DM moved to the inside chamber and heard their story. Evidently a SI of the Kotwali was driving his motor-cycle early in the morning when he collided with a Rickshaw. The SI promptly got off his motor-cycle and started beating up the rickshaw puller in full view of people. The beating was so savage that the rickshaw puller started vomiting blood. He was rushed to the hospital where he died. Word spread like wild fire and soon an agitated mob collected and moved towards the Kotwali. It grew till about a thousand people were surrounding the Kotwali and raising slogans against the police. They had carried the dead body to the gate of the kotwali and kept it there. They wanted the lodging of an FIR and the arrest of the Sub-inspector on charges of murder.

The DM spoke to the SP over the telephone. The SP admitted that a crowd was gathering. There had been some incident but he was inquiring whether the Sub-inspector was responsible. He was sending the additional SP to the spot. The SDM and CO were also sent back. About 45 minutes went by and then SDM called up the DM from the Kotwali. He informed that an attempt at talks had made no headway. The crowd was swelling and shouting violent slogans, demanding that the DM and SP come to the site. Sensing the seriousness of the situation the DM decided that they must go. Both of them left for the Kotwali around 11:00 am.

On the way the, DM suggested to the SP that if the SI was involved in the incident there was a case for lodging an FIR against him and suspending him. The SP said that the facts had not yet been verified and this demand was being raised by those who were against the police. He felt that only an inquiry into the matter should be ordered and emphasized that it was a question of the morale of the police force.

It was with difficulty that the vehicles of DM and SP could reach the Kotwali. Immediately people started shouting anti-police slogans. They were demanding that the SI be handed over to them. There were about 3000 people there.

A hurried meeting was held inside the Kotwali. The police story was that the SI had only slapped the rickshaw puller. The unfortunate man died because he had TB and they also had a doctor's certificate to prove this. They also alleged that the leadership of the mob was in the hands of criminals. However, it was agreed to invite the leaders for talks.

The talks revealed that the leaders were in an intransigent mood. They told horrifying stories of how the SI had thrown the rickshaw puller on the ground and jumped on top of him. Their demands were that a case of murder be registered and the Sub-inspector be handcuffed and handed over to the people.

Long protracted negotiations went on. The formula offered was an inquiry by a Magistrate, to be done within a week and action taken accordingly. This was not accepted. Finally, on sensing the situation it was agreed that a case be lodged under section 302 of IPC and the SI be suspended. However, there was no question of handcuffing the SI in public or handling him over to the crowd.

The leaders went back to consult the crowd. Long speeches were made. But one could hear that the crowd was getting violent. It had swelled to about 5000 and had been joined by college students who had formed a procession under a vitriolic student leader and had come to the Kotwali. The SP had toyed with idea of blocking the routes to the Kotwali but then decided against it.

It was past 2.00 pm and the crowd was still baying for the blood of the SI. The leaders came back and said that the people would settle for nothing less than handcuffing of the SI in public. The administration refused. All of a sudden it became clear that these so called leaders did not have the capacity to make the crowd see sense. The DM decided to directly address the people. A makeshift stage of a rickshaw was set up and a mike provided. Despite advice to the contrary, the DM got on to the rickshaw and made a speech. He promised full justice to the people. Most of the people seemed to be pacified with the decisions taken but one section of the crowd kept shouting that the SI be handed over to them. The DM used all rhetoric possible to swing the public opinion away from this unreasonable demand. He stressed that the SI was being given the same treatment as any other citizen and that the people should repose faith in the administration.

By and by the situation abated and some of the leaders came into the Kotwali and congratulated the DM on his speech. Some of them even said that tea should be prepared while they went out to finally disperse the mob. A great feeling of 'crisis averted' prevailed among the officers and they all sat relaxing in the Kotwali.

All of a sudden there were sounds of commotion outside. People were running and shouting. The DM, SP and others rushed to the Kotwali gate to find police vigorously lathi-charging a mob on the run. They tried to stop the police and find out what happened but there was too much confusion. The students in the crowd gathered bricks, stones and started hurling them at the police. A battle ensued. The police force was outnumbered and pushed back. They moved into the Kotwali and the mob surrounded the inner gates of the Kotwali. Bricks and stones were flying furiously into the courtyard. A couple of policemen got hit. Another attempt at a lathi-charge was made but it was beaten back with injuries to the police force. The DM, standing in the courtyard, found bricks landing all round him. He then saw a lot of smoke in the sky. It was confirmed that a police truck and two official jeeps had been set on fire by the mob. A situation was reached where the Kotwali main gate was being unhinged and the mob would enter the premises at any moment. Violent bloodshed would result.

The SP came close to the DM and requested for firing orders. The DM stood thinking for a moment. He wanted to avoid firing but sensed the situation. He gave the orders but seeing the anger on the faces of police he expected them to be indiscriminate. He thus advised the SP to ask the additional SP to lead the squad and use minimum force.

Three teams, one under the SP, the other with the additional SP and the third under a DSP were formed. They left from the back gate. A few minutes' later sounds of gunfire resounded. There were shrieks and screams and then a stampede. More shots were heard. It was all over within minutes. Somebody told the DM that the crowd had dispersed and that the police was chasing it.

Three policemen entered the Kotwali. They were holding the leader of the mob. As soon as they entered the Kotwali they flung him to the ground and started beating him with their lathis. The DM shouted asking them to stop but they would not listen. He had to physically intervene and make them stop. The DM had barely recovered from this when two policemen entered carrying a boy of about 18 years of age and threw him on the ground. He had a bullet wound through his stomach and was bleeding profusely. The policemen hurled the choicest abuses at him and laughed. The DM was horrified. He immediately called his SDM and had the injured boy taken to a hospital nearby. The Chief Medical Officer was called but the boy was declared dead. The score was one dead and dozens injured.

Later, as they sat in the Kotwali, the full story came out. Evidently the SP had asked for a particular CO over the wireless to come to the Kotwali with tear-gas. By the time the CO came, there was no way he could reach the Kotwali from the front because of the crowd. A back entrance was available. This was around the time when the leaders had gone back to the crowd and were trying to persuade them to disperse. He blew his siren horn and waded through the crowd in his vehicle and reached the Kotwali. Many people in the crowd started thumping the jeep's bonnet as it passed. The CO asked them to lay off. Some people started abusing. The CO got off his vehicle. Suddenly someone in the mob started pelting stones. The CO looked at the police personnel standing nearby and commanded them to lathi-charge. The rest followed.

The issues that get raised in the above case study reveal that there is no one solution to any situation. Things could have been handled differently by different people. Some would feel that firing was not necessary while others would say that it was essential. In any case a number of questions can be posed.

1. Would the situation have been averted if the police had registered the FIR in the morning itself? Should it have done so? It could have nipped the issue in the bud. At the same time this could have possible led to further demands from the mob who would have perceived the administration as weak.
2. Should the DM and SP have gone to the spot earlier? Their going could have led to an early resolution before the mob swelled. Alternatively, their early exposure would have diluted the authority of the subordinates and also committed them to a stand from which they would have no bargaining point left.
3. Should the DM and SP have not gone to the site and called the leaders for talks at a different place. It could have worked had the leaders agreed. They, on the other hand, could have resisted and not left the site.
4. Did the talks take too long?
5. Should they have realized that the mob was leaderless and ordered a lathi-charge earlier?
6. Should the police not have cordoned the area? Why were the students allowed to reach the spot?
7. Could the CO not have used discretion and entered the Kotwali through the back entrance? Should he have ordered lathi-charge or kept quiet?

These and many other questions shall always be there. *There is no such thing as a unique solution to a law and order problem, and much depends upon the early assessment of situation and understanding the psychology of the people. Decisiveness is always better than dithering. Use of force at the right time is often the best solution to prevent a larger tragedy. I would like to illustrate the latter point by another case study.*

The Holy Idol

This relates to a tehsil headquarters in district 'G'. It was a commercial and prosperous town but known for caste tension in its extremely volatile form. It all started with routine information coming in via intelligence reports that some people were claiming that an idol of Lord Shiva along with snakes had emerged of its own from under a tree. This tree was in a private property and the situation could cause trouble. The SDM and CO were asked to look into the matter. They reported nothing serious and ensured that the idol would soon be moved to a temple. A few days later, further intelligence reports came in and people met the District Magistrate. It transpired that there was a large piece of land right in the centre of a locality which was inhabited by Jatav Hindus. A Muslim had purchased this land as a colonizer and had done the plotting work and was now selling it. Evidently, he was selling only to Muslims. This was not acceptable to a Hindu leader of the locality who also claimed that this property belonged to his ancestors and moved the court. The court proceedings were going on when this idol of Lord Shiva and the snakes appeared. The Hindu leader was now spreading the news that the God had made an appearance and people, particularly ladies, had started visiting the tree to offer water, flowers and perform pooja.

The SDM and CO talked to the parties. Initially, the Hindu leaders agreed to shift the idol to a temple. They look three days time from the administration. Thereafter, they went back on their word. Their contention was that since people had started offering pooja the idols could not be shifted. Indeed, they wanted the administration to persuade the opposite party to give some land for building a temple. The Muslims colonizer was inclined to agree but on the condition that thereafter no dispute about property would be raised. A couple of days went by with no solution. Both the parties were trying to get the maximum in the deal. Meanwhile the crowd of worshippers at the tree increased.

Sensing that the situation was being allowed to drift, the DM and SSP send the ADM and SP of rural areas to the spot. They were asked to camp there and resolve the problem. After a full day's negotiations, the ADM informed the DM that some headway had been made and a compromise solution would be worked out. But the negotiations on the second day didn't bear any such results. The main issue now was the amount of land that should be given to Hindus. They were demanding more and more and it was clear now that they wanted the administration to pressurize the Muslim colonizer to leave the land and go. They wanted the land to be attached under Section 145 of the CRPC (criminal procedure code) by the state.

The ADM and SP warned the Hindu party that if it did not agree by 11:00 am on the next day to shift the idols to a nearby temple then they would come with force and do the needful. The leader said that there was no need for this and that he would himself ensure that the idols were taken to the temple. After that the administration wanted to attach the land under Section 145, CRPC and direct the parties to the civil court to resolve their dispute.

The DM was sitting in his court the next afternoon and was hearing arguments in a case when his PA discreetly entered the court and asked him to attend to a very important telephone call. The caller was a political leader of eminence who informed the DM that the police had opened fire killing several Hindus and that the position was serious. The DM got in touch with the SSP who informed him that this was true and that he was coming over with full information. Within 15 minutes the DM and the SSP left for the tehsil headquarters. On the way, the SSP confirmed that the police had opened fire—they had gone to remove the idols and people had blocked their way and pelted stones and bombs at them. Two people were reported dead.

As soon as they entered the tehsil headquarters and reached the Thana, the report was that four people had died. The DM immediately sensed that the situation could get communal as one community would take out their anger on the other. Accordingly, immediate curfew was clamped and force from all over the district was called in. The DM and SSP visited the site. It was cluttered with brickbats, stones, empty bottles and remnants of petrol bombs. As many as dozen policemen had sustained injuries. The ADM and SP filled up the gaps in the story. It so transpired that the leaders had agreed to shift the idols voluntarily by 11:00 am They had not done so. When the police searched for them they kept asking for some more time, and around 2:00 pm they went underground. Meanwhile, the news of idols being shifted spread around and a crowd of worshippers, mostly women, thronged the place. The police cordon stopped them. They became restive and were soon joined by others. At this point the ADM and SP reached the spot. They started making preparations to shift the idol. They had also brought along a priest for this purpose. But the moment the idol was lifted the women started wailing and shouting. They tried to forcibly break the police cordon. They were pushed back. Immediately, they started pelting stone at the police. From all the sidelines hordes of people emerged as if they were lying in wait. People went up the rooftops of their houses and petrol bombs and brickbats were hurled on the police. The policemen sustained injuries and had they not opened fire in self-defense they would have been lynched.

A wave of anger was sweeping through the city and it was directed mostly against the police. People were coming out on the streets. The first priority was to impose the curfew properly. The DM and SSP themselves moved through the city warning people to go indoors, and at a couple of places the lathi had to be wielded. Within 30 minutes the curfew has been effectively imposed.

Immediate attention was now given to the deployment of force. Sensitive areas were identified. Additional force under able officers was posted in these areas. Force from adjoining districts was called in. Just as the DM has apprehended, news came in that one member of minority community had been stabbed and his body found. Another body with stab wounds was found a few minutes later. A communal situation was at hand.

The strategy was clear–to ruthlessly enforce the curfew to prevent a major communal riot from erupting. For three days no negotiations were held with anyone. Curfew was rigorously imposed and large-scale arrests were made. The spirit of the rioters appeared broken. On the fourth day, curfew was relaxed slightly and talks were resumed with the leaders. It took another three days to resolve the issue. The idols were removed to a temple. That particular piece of land was attached and the dispute referred to a civil court. A very serious communal situation developed but very tough handling after the firing led to its effective control.

A very important thing to keep in mind while enforcing a curfew is to manage it in such a manner that the ordinary peace loving citizen does not face any undue hardship. Provision of essential services like medical facilities, milk supply, food and vegetables etc have to be managed in such a manner that despite the curfew the public does not suffer. Essential municipal services like sanitation and water supply also need to be ensured and there should be no disruption in power supply. The DM has to put all the resources at his disposal in the action mode because without the coordinated efforts of all this management will never be possible. It is thus clear that handling a law and order situation is much more than filing cases, deploying police force, taking legal action and use of force.

This case study, like the previous one, throws up several issues.

1. Should the idols have been removed the day they were installed?
2. Should so much of time have been spent on negotiations?
3. Should the DM and SSP have personally gone and negotiated?
4. Was it wise for the ADM and SP to try to remove the idols after talks failed? Should they have operated clandestinely by the night?
5. Was firing necessary?
6. Could not the property have been attached earlier?

There are as many answers as there are questions. These are various ways in which the above crises could have been resolved. But the fact remains that there is no definite formula that can be applied. Any given solution could have succeeded or failed. The central issue is that law and order dealings require presence of mind, constant sizing up of the situation and of the people involved and a judicious mixture of firmness and tact.

This is not to say that resolution of a law and order problem is merely a matter of chance or that the solution is merely a shot in the dark. There are certain well-accepted principles which must be borne in mind.

The lessons to be learnt from the above two case studies are that a seemingly innocuous looking situation can turn into a serious law and order problem. It is important to anticipate this possibility and act fast and promptly to defuse the situation. In the first case, had the district administration acted swiftly against the station officer, lodged an FIR against him and suspended him then the situation would never have developed into the ugly one that it did. The second incident shows that the removal of idols was always going to be a tricky situation and perhaps more tact was required or else the removal should have been done on the first day itself.

The DM has to maintain his cool in such situations. The entire team looks up to the DM and SP to provide leadership. Their demeanor should re-assure the team that everything is under control. Coolness and calmness is a pre-requisite for keeping your presence of mind and common sense intact and these two are the basic qualities required to handle a law and order crises. I remember that in the second incident I had a quick meeting with my officers and since my attitude was calm we could do intelligent planning and also attend to all possible details. Effective strategic planning and execution are the essence of controlling a law and order situation.

The entire police and magistracy should function as a team with a uniform goal in mind. For this, the example has to be set by the DM and SP who should clearly give the signal that they are on the same wavelength. Any discord or difference between the two could gravely endanger the peace-keeping effort. Perfect coordination is the essence. In addition, the entire team down to the constable needs to be briefed in great detail about what is expected of them. Each member of the team shall perform up to expectation only if he knows his role properly.

The subordinate officers must have faith in the DM and SP. They should not be apprehensive that their bosses would sacrifice them in the event of any inquiry or action process initiated by government. In a second case in district "G" the ADM and SP rural were very that they might be held responsible for the breakdown of law and order and face disciplinary action. The SSP was also of the view that the two officers could have shown more tact. However, the DM released that he needed these officers to control the situation and as such nothing would have been achieved by doing anything to lower the morale of these officers. The DM patted the two officers on the back and said that he was proud of them. They have done their best possible and the DM said clearly that in the event of an inquiry he would take the responsibility of having ordered firing. This assumption of leadership role by the DM uplifted the spirits of the two officers and they worked round the clock to bring the situation under control.

The most important thing is to keep one's eyes and ears open. The District Magistrate must collect intelligence from all possible sources. Information is knowledge. Regular reports from the local intelligence unit are submitted–these are not always exhaustive or even very correct. The other genuine source is the people. The DM should be accessible and have the capacity to hear people. Lots of information is gathered during the daily meetings with the public. Collection of intelligence through lekhpals and other revenue officials is also a very good method. However, the principal is that any bit of information which the DM feels can create a problem should be attended to immediately. Nothing should be brushed aside as routine Very often, if at the initial stage of a dispute the concerned officer acts, the problem is nipped in the bud. Delay can cause major problems.

Linked to this is the issue of appropriate time for talks and for the use of force. Many veterans of law and order rely on the panchayat approach–holding long, elaborate discussions This can often be counterproductive. It is best to call all parties concerned for talks right at the beginning but if their attitude is not proper than action such as lodging of cases and arrests should be taken without much delay. In a situation where a problem has arisen and mob is collecting, it is best to reach the spot and take a quick decision resolve the matter. If force has to be used it should be used at a time when minimum force would achieve the objective. If one allows people together and spends too much time in negotiations than it boils down to the resorting to the use of maximum force which could have averted.

At the same time there is a situation where a mob has collected–like a farmer's dharna in the Collectorate or at the Thana. The people are emotionally surcharged over some issue. Use of force in these circumstances can snowball into widespread riot situation. Here, the best strategy is to negotiate–to wear down the opposite party to finally come to terms to share exhaustion! I remember an ADM of mine who was a master negotiator in such situations. He would keep talking endlessly without relenting and keeping calm. There was an occasion when he kept having talks for more than 36 hours. Ultimately, fatigue set in and the protestors gave in unconditionally. It is sometimes an excellent strategy in a law and order situation to keep talking and engaging the leaders across the table to prevent them from inciting their followers to violence.

In order to highlight the above point I would like to narrate an incident which took place when I was DM Ghaziabad. A very powerful farmer leader gheraoed the Collectorate with the long list of demands and started making speeches which were crude and abusive in nature. Despite advice to the contrary from my officers I went to the office and sat there for the entire day. The city magistrate and his counterpart police officer with trying to talk with the farmers and convince them to hand over their memorandum and disperse. In the process there was a scuffle and a mild lathi-charge followed. This infuriated the agitators and they continued the dharma for three days. On a third day, their patience started to wear out. They wanted the DM to come out apologise for the lathi-charge and assure them that their demands will be met. I refused to go. They then requested that any other officer may come. I again did not agree and instead ask them to send their representatives to talk with me. They came but kept insisting on some representative of government coming in their midst and apologizing. I did not agree and eventually they gave in and moved out saying that they would march to Delhi and give the memorandum to the Prime Minister! Their agitation had been worn out by sheer fatigue. So, the tactics of a good law and order negotiation is not to be too aggressive, not to be in a hurry, where out the opponent by sheer attrition and by applying continuous gentle pressure.

One principal who is very important is that there should normally not to be any delegation of authority. The DM and SSP should not rush in where SHO would be sufficient. The local officer should be asked to attend to the problem. If required, the person above him should then be sent. Each level must be given full autonomy in consonance with general policy of administration to resolve a problem. It must be borne in mind that in a district the DM is the final authority. If he and SSP get involved directly with a situation then there is no arbitrator left. They will then be committed to a stand. The people, finding that they cannot go to anyone else will resort the violence Moreover, an element of flexibility should always be intrinsic to a law and order situation. There should always be an escape route if things get thick. This is only possible if the DM does not get directly involved from the very beginning. He should stay away to function as a Court of appeal.

For this reason the DM should never personalize a problem. It should never become DM versus the people. The impression always has to be that the DM is impartial and open to all suggestions. Even if he has to take action like ordering firing, it should be impersonal. The people respect him for that. At the same time, even if a tough decision has to be taking the DM should never leave his sense of compassion behind. His attitude should always be that of parent towards his offspring. In the second case study a young student died. The DM ensured that he was rushed to the hospital. He had even stood by his side to ensure proper medical treatment. A few days later the DM visited the family in a village and shared their sorrow. The family forgot their bitterness and almost accepted the DM as the guardian and of their family. They were overwhelmed. The DM has refused to take any police force with him and went as the head of the family genuinely sharing their grief. Compassion and empathy are very important qualities for a DM. Even if firing have been ordered by the DM he has done it in his professional capacity and he should not bear any ill-will towards anyone. He is then seen as a real leader and he gets a lot of public support.

Use of Force

How much force should be used and when? It is clear that force should be the last resort when there remains no other method to protect life and property. At the same time one should not compromise discipline and never accommodate anti-social elements for short-term gains. Logically, and as per the books, tear-gas should be used first. However, this does not happen in practice. One reason is that tear-gas is not always available. However, this is one of the most effective methods of crowd dispersal. Whenever there is a demonstration or an unruly mob collecting, lathi-charge, if done effectively, can dispose mobs. If done at the right time and forcefully it ensures that the firing option does not rise. In a particular district during the elections the DM and SSP visited a polling booth in the interior of a village. A young boy was caught impersonating. He was pulled out of the queue and beaten up. Immediately, the people surrounded the DM and SSP and their force. They were gesticulating angrily and shouting. The young boy happened to be the son of the Pradhan. People emerged from the by lanes and a hostile crowd started swelling around. Sensing the situation the DM and SSP resorted to a lathi-charge. The SSP let it himself it was fast and determined, and the people were chased right up to their houses. The Pradhan and village elders immediately called for peace and held talks with the DM and resolved the matter. Had the lathi-charge been delayed, the crowd would have thrown stones and brickbats at the police and a situation of police having to open fire and arisen.

One thing, however, is important. There should be sufficient police force available before you resort to a lathi-charge. Because if the lathi-charge fails and the police force is beaten back then you have the worst possible situation at hand. The morale of the mob rises while that of the force crumbles. The force also gets angry and feels humiliated and very often opens fire even without orders from the senior officers.

Firing is unpleasant but one should not hesitate to order it if the situation gets out of hand. Use of firing at the right time can often prevent a measure riot and many more details. When used, it should be effective but restrained. That is why it should always be done under the supervision of senior officer. One the mob starts running, firing should be stopped. Firing in the air is never a good principal but efforts should be made to fire low. One method advocated by many is that the targets should be picked and short. It sounds almost like murder but makes sense when you realize that often the real instigator escapes and innocent people get killed. This, however, is not always possible as the leader disappears at such times and also the police force is not very cool and calculating at a moment fraught with such tension.

Broadly speaking, the law and order problem can be classified under four categories. (i) Communal, (ii) caste-based, (iii) student unrest, and (iv) level trouble. Each of them is unique and demands different approaches to control and resolve.

Communal Tension

Communal tensions emerge when two communities get polarized on religious lines and start interpreting ordinary disputes along these lines. There are any theories for the exercise of communal tensions. Very often, it is found that a communal riot takes place after a seemingly innocent incident like a boy of one community beating up a boy of another community. This, however, is only the manifestation of simmering tension and distrust between the two communities. A small incident just lights the fuse and an explosion occurs.

There are some patters behind communal riots. They predominantly take place in cities and urban conglomerations rather than in villages. The tensions of city life, the unemployment, an also the non-existence of a community set-up, as also the anonymity of urban life are factors responsible for this. More often than not, in riots the cause is economic. There several illustrations of riots in cities where most people are involved in a particular trade, e.g. weaving of cloth. One community is involved in the weaving while the trading is in the hands of another community. The income differences between them widen. One sees the other as the exploiter. Normally this should break out as a class struggle but not so in our country. The two communities start falling back on religious differences. They make it a point to show that their religion is different–in the way they dress, speak, in their method of salutation and through a public display of prayers and religious festivals. Since religion is an emotional factor the communities start giving vent to their emotions and a situation ripe for a communal riot comes into being.

One of my colleagues had an interesting way of putting it. He saw it all like pyramid. Initially the communal tension is widely distributed but not very specific. It starts narrowing and focusing on certain issues. Slowly, tension builds up and reaches the top of the pyramid where tensions are intense between two small groups and the smallest of incidents leads to an explosion.

However, you may like to describe it, the fact remains that the district administration has to watch carefully and not allow tensions to build up sufficiently to reach a flash point.

If a district has a mixed population in almost equal percentage (40:60 or 50:50) and has had a history of communal riots then the DM will have to view any situation in its communal aspect and gear up his responses accordingly.

The best thing to do about a communal riot is to prevent it. To achieve this end the DM, on taking charge of a communally sensitive district, should study the reports of previous riots and ascertain the local factors and people responsible for communalism. He should open links with four types of people– those who are incite communal feelings and those who can be used by the administration to control situations. The idea is to have a regular feedback on what is going on in the minds of the people. If any dispute occurs that can take a communal tenor, it should be dealt with decisively, promptly and firmly. At the same time a continuous drive should be launched against anti-social elements on both sides and action against them under various acts should be vigorously pursued. This gives the impression to the people that administration means business. Moreover, 'the anti-social elements would then go into hiding thereby ensuring peace in the district.

Peace communities for each Thana must be formed. The normal practice is that these peace committees are not properly constituted and become active only after a communal riot takes place. It is much better to form these committees beforehand– the lists of people should be scrutinized by an officer of the rank of an ADM or Additional SP. These peace committees should be kept active in times of peace also. Regular meetings help in bringing simmering issues out into the open, they serve as for giving vent to feelings–the responsibility and the recognition given to them can make them do wonders. Some of my colleagues have felt that peace committees should not only consist of respected and good citizens but should also include some of the troublemakers. This helps in keeping an eye on them, bringing them into focus in front of general public and this in turn, does have an effect of keeping their activities under check. In any case, the peace committee, to be effective should consist of active people and not dead wood.

In a communally sensitive town the people have their minds occupied with communal issues and, as such, a constant state of tension is maintained. A unique method adopted by some administrations is to divert the minds of the people. This is done by launching a drive or a campaign, or even an event which involves all the people. Municipal issues are at the forefront in cities. There is the case study of a DM in a communally sensitive town who started a large-scale revision of house tax. This involved everyone in the city. As notices of increased house tax assessment went around, people became agitated. They talked and discussed amongst themselves, met the DM, took out processions, held public meeting. In short, their collective minds became obsessed with house tax and communal issues took a backstage.

Similarly, an anti-encroachment drive can capture the attention of people. A major sanitation drive can also help. It also helps if a major sports event like a hockey or a cricket tournament is organized. In fact, organizing sports activities throughout the year helps in diverting the youth and providing a constructive, channelization of energies. Organizing cultural activities on a large scale also helps in diverting the attention of the people.

Whenever a situation becomes potentially communal, either due to an incident within the district of due to the repercussions of an outside event, immediate preventive action like imposing a curfew and arresting of anti-socials is often the best answer. Administration can prevent a major riot by taking preventive actions at the right time. A clear example of this is a study of districts after the December 6, 1992 incident. Wherever the district imposed a preventive curfew on time, restricted the movement of anti-socials, carried out arrests and raids, and formed peace committees, it succeeded in preventing a riot. Wherever there was a delay in appreciating the situation, a riot resulted.

A few words must be said about the curfew. It is an unpleasant but necessary measure which the administration has to adopt to control an explosive situation. The first thing about a curfew is that it should be imposed strictly. For this a proper planning of police deployment and briefing of the personnel is necessary. Senior officers have to be mobile to ensure that curfew is not violated at will. No quarter should be given to influential persons.

However, the DM must realize that a majority of citizens are peace-loving and a curfew can hamper their normal life. There are also the sick and the needy. For this purpose a curfew should be effectively managed. All the personnel on duty should be briefed to be firm but polite with ordinary citizens, and to help a person out if he or she is in genuine trouble. Passengers stranded at railway stations can be escorted by the police to their houses. The sick should be taken to hospitals. In fact, mobile medical teams with medicines can be allowed to move around so that people get medical attention at their door. Supply of milk, sanitation services and even supply of essential commodities can be ensured. Mobile vans carrying milk and essential provisions can move in the area under police protection.

A curfew has to be handled firmly but it must be ensured that the essential needs of the people are catered for. At the same time, the trouble-makers must be made to feel the heat. This difficult task is only possible if the senior officers are personally involved and the entire district works as a team.

A very important decision is about lifting the curfew. It should neither be too early nor too late. In fact, effort should be to normalize things as fast as possible. A preventive curfew where no incident takes place can be relaxed faster than a curfew which is imposed after a riot. Relaxation has to be for a limited time and the time increased gradually. However, maximum vigil has to be kept by the administration at the time of curfew relaxation. A recurrence of incidents is possible which can further deteriorate the situation. Intelligent barricading, mobile patrolling, significant police present at nodal/sensitive areas as well as frequent reassurances through special radio bulletins, flag marches and megaphone speeches, are all very essential in curfew management.

Caste Disputes

The method of assessing, preventing and tackling a caste dispute is similar to the communal one. Normally a district would have a history of caste tensions and the administration has to keep collecting all possible information. The one difference is that violence based on caste can occur more often in rural areas–in backward villages. Social transformation is taking place slowly due to development of infrastructure, spread of education, job opportunities for the lower castes, contact with the outside world and due to the breakdown of the feudal system. A static equilibrium in village life has been disturbed. As the search for a new equilibrium goes on caste tensions increase. The historically dominant community resents any change in age-old social mores attempted by the lower castes.

An apt illustration is the major caste riots in district 'A'. There was a sizeable population of lower castes in that village and many members of these families had gone to a nearby city to work in an industry. A couple of members of their families had become active social workers. A young boy of the community got a decent job outside and came back to the village to get married. He decided to ride on a horseback as a bridegroom. This amounted to breaking the caste norms as only bridegrooms of upper castes rode on a horseback. The result was that the marriage procession was attacked by the upper castes and a major riot resulted.

This shows that resentment between the castes is constantly brewing due to the breakdown of the traditional social structure. Any chance event can trigger off a clash. Another incident which substantiates my point is that of District 'G' where a fight between children of two castes led to a large-scale attack, counter-attack, arson and looting.

It is difficult of forecast the above tensions, and as such, a problem to prevent them. However, if villages with caste disputes or tensions are identified and a constant vigil maintained, then a major eruption can be controlled. If the people realize that the administration is impartial and tough they do not resort to violence as they fear the consequences.

In many villages, caste disputes start from land and keep simmering for some time. In such cases the administration should collect intelligence, react promptly, resolve the dispute firmly, and also make a show of force. Normally, an eruption would not occur after this.

Collection of intelligence through the revenue officials network i.e. the lekhpal or patwari is very useful in this. They have the best knowledge about a village and in matters of land disputes they are the people who can best resolve the issue. Caste violence should be dealt with firmly. Use of force is necessary and large-scale arrests of leaders and anti-social elements should be taken up immediately. Caste has its tentacles in district administration and police also. Thus, it is important to project an image of caste neutrality in administration.

Village life is an example of mutual co-existence in a community and each individual is identified with the community. Further, despite the caste consciousness there is never any great feeling of hostility towards each other in village. Also, the pace of life and community support keeps the pot from boiling. If, and when, under rare circumstances a communal riot spread to villages then it is very difficult to contain it as one cannot possibly deploy adequate police force everywhere. In 2013, in Muzaffarnagar, UP their communal riots which spread to the villages with serious consequences. Several people left their village homes and there was a deep communal scare on the face of the community living there. A DM must always take steps to avoid a communal conflagration from spreading from urban to rural areas.

Land disputes are an extremely common occurrence in rural areas and are often the main reason for crime against the human body–murder, rape, molestation, grievous injury etc. The District Officer must evolve a system of resolving these land disputes. Most of the applications received at the Thana and the Tehsil relate to land disputes. A register should be prepared at both the Thana and Tehsil level where such complaints should be registered and categorized according to their seriousness or intensity. Thereafter, a join team of revenue and police officials should visit the village, call the concerned parties and resolve the matter. In low intensity cases the lekhpal and the police sub-inspector can go; in more serious matters the Naib Tehsildar/Tehsildar along with Station House Officer (SHO) of the Thana can go; then SDM and SDO police can attend to matters of a more serious natures. A dispute which could attain a more serious dimension should involve the DM and SSP who should themselves visit the village. This system, if implemented properly will ensure that disputes are not allowed to fester and reach a stage where any of the parties may resort to violence. The DM should not restrict himself to applications received. Officers should jointly visit villages and try to ascertain if there are such issues and resolved them. This method can be hugely successful and I have personally used it in several districts. It leads to reduction in crime rates and law and order disturbances.

Students' Unrest

This kind of law and order disturbance is more likely in university towns which have a sizeable college-going student population. Every university has a politicized students union and the relation between them and the college management is never very critical. There is always agitation on some issue or the other. However, it is not the job of the administration to intervene in any internal matter concerning the university. Most of their problems have to be solved bilaterally by the vice-chancellor (VC) and the student union. In fact, administration should enter the campus only when the college management asks them to do so.

They can also enter at times of emergency in the light of violence and arson in the campus.

Rivalries amongst unions, politicization of unions, rising unemployment, general decline in values, suppressed anger against a process of social change which is leaving them as by standards, are some of the principal reasons for student unrest. Over the years violence in the campus has increased and has also over flown into the streets. It is the latter situation which concerns the administration directly.

Very often, agitated students leave the campus and block main roads, stone vehicles and resort to arson on the streets. That administration has to move in to protect life and property and to maintain the peaceful daily tempo of life.

Handling of student problems has to be different from that of communal disturbance or caste riot. Here one is dealing with young boys and girls, and therefore, one has to avoid use of force till the very end. Use of tear-gas, and in serious cases lathi-charge, can be resorted to but one should not open fire. Of course sometimes a situation can become so serious that police has to fire but this should be only under extreme compulsion. If a student gets killed due to police firing or a lathi-charge then the administration loses the support of the people. The administration is criticized as brutal. Even otherwise, students are of an age when they are immature and need counseling more than violence. Hence, handling of a students' problem has to be deliberately softer than other disturbances.

The basic issue to be kept in mind is that the problem should not become students versus the administration. The efforts should be to keep the problem within the campus and use one's good offices to amicably resolve the dispute. One should, however, keep track of the *goonda* element which merges with the students on such occasions.

Very recently we have witnessed large scale student disturbances in Delhi, Aligarh and some other cities as part of the stir against CAA (Citizenship Amendment Act) and NRC (National Register for Citizens). There were serious allegations against the police for entering the Jamia Milia campus library and beating up students. Then again there was violence insight JNU (Jawaharlal Nehru University) and the police were accused of inaction. Similar was the story in Aligarh. Actually the police cannot and should not enter a university campus without the permission of the VC and at all times use minimal force. In districts which have universities it is an important part of the job of the DM to meet the VC of the university and maintain cordial relations with him. At the first hint of a students' unrest the district administration should prevail upon the VC, Dean and Registrar to resolve it at their level. Giving them an adequate security cover is the responsibility of the administration. The DM should also network with important students' leaders so that they listen to his counsel at the time of unrest.

Labour Troubles

In cities where there are a large number of industries, this is a major source of law and order disturbance. Labour and management in most industries see themselves as opposed to each other. This is changing with the advent of participatory management and techniques of Human Resource Development but the age-old attitudes linger on in most units. This situation of conflict leads to a breakdown of collective bargaining and incidents of *gherao,* violence, strikes and lockouts.

There are a number of labour unions in industry. This leads to union revelries. Moreover, outside political elements make themselves president and secretaries of unions. These leaders do not understand the dynamics of the industry and want to perpetuate a situation of conflict for their own political gains. With this attitude in mind they create an issue of wages, bonus, overtime, uniforms or even suspension of employees. This is not to say that the demands of unions are not genuine but they can be resolved by talks across the table. A predetermined attitude on both sides leads to making this resolution rather difficult at times.

Labour unions, when they go on strike, send a copy of their notice to the district administration. This is just sent to the labour office and the administration does not interfere. However, if management and labour fail to resolve their problems, both sides move the district administration. The labour unions want the administration to intercede on their behalf. The management demands protection and posting of police force around the factory. The strategy has to be to encourage resolution by conciliation. The representative of Labour Commissioner in the district has to be pressed into attempting conciliation. Police presence around the factory is necessary to ensure that there is no damage to life and property.

Normally things are settled by negotiations excepting for issues of taking back suspended or terminated workers. Here the stalemate starts. This results in a declaration of a strike. The administration has to move in when the strike continues for long and threatens to damage industrial peace. Tripartite talks are held and very often a compromise solution effected.

The management always feels that the district administration is taking the labour's side. Actually, in a situation of stalemate a compromise is the only solution, and thus, labour often gets more than the management is prepared to concede. Labour also alleges that the administration is siding with the management–it points towards presence of police, banning of their meetings under Section 144 of CrPC. The administration has to walk the tightrope and act fair and resolve the conflict. This is potential area for a law and order problem where a lot of time has to be spent on negotiation and it should be seen that talks never reach a dead end.

Use of force should be resorted to only if labour turns violent. Maximum effort should be made to control the situation through a show of force. However, anti-social elements among the labour unions should be singled out and dealt with severely. This, by itself, will ensure your industrial peace. The administration has to keep the larger dimension of impact of productivity and economic development in mind. A short-term approach should be jettisoned in favour of a long-term vision.

The above were the main areas of law and order disturbances. However, wherever a group of agitated people collect, a potential law and order problem exists. This could be spontaneous–a reaction to a murder, crushing of a child by a truck or death in police custody. The crowd collects on the road and resorts to pelting of stones and arson. Often it is deliberate, for political gains, a group collects people, shouts provocative slogans and forms a procession. A group clash often results in these cases.

Blocking of main roads, squatting on railway tracks and gheroaing officers are the main forms of protest that are generated almost every day in a district. The administration should not allow inconvenience to the ordinary citizen, at the same time it should be sensitive to the genuine grievances of the people. An active, alert and responsive administration with a reputation for honesty, fairness and toughness is the solution to any kind of law and order problem.

Criminal Administration

The DM is directly concerned with law and order but he is also the head of the criminal administration of a district. It is true that he does not get involved in day-to-day matters of criminal investigation and the working of thanas but he remains responsible to the people on all matters. It is not uncommon to find the DM being gheraoed if a murder takes place or a kidnapping for ransom incident is reported.

A high incidence of crime completely puts the district administration into disrepute. The time-honored method is to take effective, preventive steps. List of history sheeters and anti-social elements is available with each thana. These needs to be constantly updated and reviewed. The local Station Officer (SO) must keep a close watch on the movements of these people and if they try to indulge in mischief, action should be taken against them immediately.

The Criminal Procedure Code has Sections 107/116, 109, 110, 133 and 145, which if used effectively, can definitely control crime. Section 107/116 is one of the most potent weapons but over the years this measure has been losing its sting. The main reason is that cases keep pending and are automatically dropped after six months. Since no one is bound down, people realize that futility of this measure. In fact, very often the SO is just satisfied by saying that he has reported 'X' number of cases under Section 107/116. Thereafter he doesn't take interest in even serving the notice issued by the Executive Magistrate.

It is my concerted opinion that if used effectively Section 107/116 is a very powerful measure. The first thing is that the SO should genuinely satisfy himself before sending the report of Section 107/116. People should not be included in the list indiscriminately. Very often you find that the old, children and physically handicapped people are included in the list. Before issuing notice the Executive Magistrate must also satisfy himself that it is a fit case. Very often, the SOs send their report just to protect an increased level of preventive action. The Magistrate must peruse the content of the report. It is neither mandatory nor advisable to issue notice in each and every case reported by the SO.

Once the notice has been issued the service should be insured by the SO. It has been my experience that most of the notices are not served at all while some are served after inordinate delay. Even after service, in more than 90% of cases no evidence from the police is made available and the case is automatically dropped after 6 months. This greatly reduces the efficacy of an otherwise very powerful measure. From the police end, they have a genuine problem–there are far too many cases and it is not possible for the SO or SI to appear in every case. However, this problem can be solved if one day of a week can be fixed for a particular thana by the Executive Magistrate. Then it is possible for the SO to come on that day and record his evidence in all cases relating to his thana. If this is done and over 60% of people under Section 107/116 bound down to maintain peace, then this Section can actually control crime and law and order disturbance in the district.

Section 110, CrPC is also a very effective tool. This is used against habitual offenders who escape conviction but keep creating problems. They can be arrested and then bound down with heavy surety.

Goonda Act which allows externment from the district for a period up to one year is very effective against anti-socials. Here again, the crucial thing is that the police report should be as per the provisions of the act and police evidence should come forward on time. Even if a couple of people in a district get externed the impact is salutary all over. There have DMs who have used this act to control crime in their districts.

Modern day criminals are getting brazen. They have a lot of contacts and money power. They terrorize the people to an extent where nobody comes forward to give evidence against them. They are a threat to a society and the only method to control them is via the National Security Act (NSA) and the Gangster Act. To make a case under NSA succeed, all the necessary documents should be available and all the essential instructions followed. The District Magistrate must apply his mind before using the NSA against anyone. Many people argue that there are enough provisions in the ordinary law of the land. They feel that acts like the NSA are draconian and should not be used. But the fact is that when a DM or SSP sees a criminal moving around freely, acquitted in all cases due to lack of evidence, and terrorizing the society, they are left with no option but to invoke the provisions of the NSA.

The position of crime in a district is reviewed on the basis of crime statistics for every three years. Generally, a decline in figures is taken as representing a control on the criminal situation. However, this can often be misleading. In an effort to show better statistics, Station Officers tend not to register FIRs. This tendency has to be discouraged by the District Administration. An FIR must be lodged. The DM of a district gets several complaints that reports are not being lodged. These should be taken seriously. If the DM is satisfied the prime facie should order an FIR to be lodged. Alternatively, he could direct a senior officer to inquire and lodge an FIR. It is also to be borne in mind that the tendency of not reporting cases works against the interests of the minorities and oppressed classes.

A case of a district comes to mind where crime was curbed, criminals on the run, and the writ of the administration was running large. Yet, the crime statistics showed a marginal increase over the previous year. This was because both the DM and SSP had insisted on filing of FIRs. The crux of the issue is that FIRs must be lodged to instill confidence in the people of deliver justice.

My view is that crime is curbed if the police is seen by the people as determined to restrain the criminals. The criminals normally lie low or leave the district when such an administration takes charge. The most important thing is that action has to be taken against big criminals, mafia dons and also the otherwise powerful people. This gives the administration a lot of support from the people and the firm grip over the law and order situation of the district.

In 1991, I was posted as DM Ghaziabad and I had a very brilliant officer, Shailaja Kant Mishra as my SSP. We were given the mandate by the Chief Minister, Kalyan Singh, to curb the mafia menace in Ghaziabad and take action against high profile criminals. Ghaziabad, at that time, was notoriously known as the wild west where crime was the way of life. We coordinated the efforts of the magistracy and the police, used all the preventive sections of the criminal procedure court, special acts like Arms act and Excise act and made generous use of Goonda act, Gangster act and the National Security Act (NSA). We posted the best inspectors as SO's of thanas and provided leadership to the team. We treated a criminal like a criminal irrespective of his affiliation to the ruling party. In this we had the tremendous support of the Chief Minister. Once a member of parliament began to pressurize the SSP to release a criminal he had arrested on the grounds that the person was an important functionary of the ruling party. Together the SSP and I briefed the Chief Minister about this on his next visit to Delhi. The very next day the CM called the MP in front of us and gave him a severe tongue-lashing. The MP cringed, apologized and literally disappeared from the scene after that. Naturally, with such support we went hammer and tongs at the criminals. Some very prominent mafia leaders were evading arrest. We got orders for attachment of their property and went about it ruthlessly. The result was that criminals and mafias left the district of Ghaziabad and move to the adjoining states. Residents of Ghaziabad who had left the city returned to their homes and property prices went up. All of a sudden the district of Ghaziabad once again began to be a vibrant progressive district. This illustration shows what a DM and SSP team can do with political will behind them and if they take action against criminals without bothering to consider the status, connections or political affiliations of such people.

In fact, law and order suffers most due to political interference. This tendency has unfortunately increased overtime and often the ruling party politicians considered the police as their private army to be deployed against their political rivals. I recall that when I was DM Allahabad elections were held and a new political dispensation came to power. Soon a very powerful minister from the ruling party gave a list of his political rivals to the SSP and asked him to book them either under NSA or Gangster Act. The SSP was perturbed as these people did not attract the provisions of these acts. We decided to put up a united front and did not carry out the instructions of the minister. He was severely put off but then DM or SSP cannot frame ordinary persons as criminals irrespective of their political leanings. Most DMs and SSPs in districts now routinely face this predicament. Many buckle down to retain their district postings but in the process their grip over law and order is considerably weaker and ultimately the society suffers.

A deplorable trend visible these days is the DM or SSP not taking action on the spot and consulting the home ministry or even the office of the Chief Minister. This is especially pronounced when certain caste based parties are in power and criminal happens to belong to the "ruling caste". This gives a bad name to the district administration as they are not viewed as being neutral or impartial by the citizens. Also, it allows criminals a free hand if they belong to the right caste. This is against the very basic tenet of administration. The man at the spot–the DM or SSP–knows the situation and can decide whether to use force or otherwise. I found, to my dismay, in recent times certain district officers trying to consult state headquarters before deciding on use of force. Several such cases came to my knowledge when I was Chief Secretary and I made it a point to admonish such officers.

One measure which helps is the quick arrest of the 'named' people in FIRs. Normally, one would find that a large number of people are named but have never been arrested. A drive can be launched or getting hold of all the wanted people. The SO must be made personally responsible. The result can be electrifying. I recall the case of a district where law and order was bad. Over 1100 wanted people were there on the police records. Within two months 900 had been arrested. The entire law and order situation changed.

The key player in the law and order situation is the SO. He is the most powerful person in his area. He lodged reports, arrests people, take preventive action and patrols the areas. On his personality depends the law and order situation of a thana. He gets all intelligence about his area and knows all about the movement of criminals. But the tragedy is that many of them don't deliver the goods as motives other than good work guide their minds. Corruption is a frequent complaint made by the public.

However, the district administration cannot just sit back and let each SO act as per his will and interest. The crucial task for a DM and SSP is to make an SO perform. This is not difficult. First, it needs honesty at the top. If the top administration is corrupt then it can never control the SO; second it has to be ruthless in punishing where the job is not being done well.

For a Sub-inspector the be all and end all of his career is to hold charge of a thana. There is no more belittling punishment to him then being sent to the lines (line hazir). Frankly, I have never been able to understand why an SI take this as a severe punishment. The police lines have a good atmosphere and an officer can stay with his family and also do useful work. However, there is a stigma of incompetence and a feeling of being deprived of power attach to such a posting. This then is the tool in the hands of the district administration to control the SOs. The task has to be clearly outlined to them, they have to be made responsible for law and order and crime in their area. If they fail they have to go to the lines. Rigorously enforced, this ensures that the best person remains in charge of a thana and delivers results.

The post of the SHO is prone to a lot of political interference. Ruling party representatives and ministers want officers of their choice to be posted and exert a lot of pressure on the SSP and DM. Often ruling parties also expect officers of certain castes to be posted as SHO things in UP have come to such a pass that some SHOs in a district are more powerful than the SSP and have the capacity to have him transfers. I have seen several bright officers buckling down to this unhappy situations just to retain their postings in a district.

Once when I was secretary to the Chief Minister of UP a powerful minister kept approaching the Chief Minister to transfer an SHO out of his district and replace him with a particular person. The CM past him on to me and the minister kept mounting pressure on me. Ultimately, I asked him one day as to how an SHO is so important for him. I told him that I shall speak to DM and SSP and they will be responsive to his issues. The minister than frankly told me that his election depended upon the SHO. The current one was fair and so was of no use to him. He wanted a particular person because then this SHO will take action against his political opponents and never take action against his supporters. This will build up his image and the district and people will gravitate towards him sensing his immense power. I finally worked out a compromise. The current SHO was transferred but we did not give the minister the replacement he sought. The district administration posted another upright officer in his place. The minister was peeved but kept quiet as the CM had been adequately briefed by us.

The district officers have to use their tact and communication skills to handle this political interference which can wreck law and order. Besides, if all the district officers behave in a similar fashion then the politician would give up. He succeeds when one DM is willing to accommodate him in everything even if it leads to poor governance.

It is also a matter of fact that a strong and effective SO can curb crime in his jurisdiction and put the fear of God in the criminals. But he needs the backing and support of the DM and SSP. I recall that when I was DM Allahabad there was an SO who was absolutely honest, very strong and efficient. In his jurisdiction there was a very famous mafia leader owing allegiance to the ruling party. This SO took action against the mafia leader and registered several cases against him and his team. However, the mafia used his political connections and money power to pressurize the DIG and IG of that area to have the SO transferred. The SSP was the brilliant, smart officer who refused to relent and shared his predicament with me. I too supported the SO and we put up a united front against the senior officers. We were successful in saving the SO and the result was that the criminal activities of the mafia leader came to a halt for some years. There are enough teeth in our laws and sufficient powers vested in the SO to have the criminals on the run. The DM and SSP must extent their full support to such officers.

Law and order or crime situation in a city, district or state is a matter of perception. It is not a question of crime statistics or data. It is how people feel. Small incidents of violation of law, petty crime, eve teasing, molestation of women, extortion from shopkeepers and businessmen create a huge negative impression on the psyche of the people. There is no denying the adverse impact of a sensational crime like daylight murder, gang-rape, kidnapping but an administration which can control small violation of law can prevent major crimes because of the perception amongst criminals and reassure the citizens about their safety. One of the biggest indicators of law and order is whether a woman can venture out alone in the evening without feeling threatened. Flagrant violations of traffic and municipal laws show that people are not generally law abiding unless they fear penal action. I have noticed in India people jumping red lights with impunity but the same person is extremely scrupulous in adhering to traffic laws when he goes abroad. The district administration has to ensure that a law abiding culture prevails in the districts.

In recent years and especially after the Nirbhaya incident there has been an upsurge in incidents of crime against women coming to light and because of an extremely vigilant media such crimes attract nationwide uproar. The district officer and his SSP must sensitize the entire police about the seriousness of this. Prompt FIR should be registered and investigation started immediately and the culprits should be arrested at the earliest possible. Having women in the police force would help. Crime against women is the most pernicious and deplorable act and in-effective response by the district administration can tarnish the image of the district officers forever.

Much of the impact of law and order is psychological. The people should feel secure. Figures don't matter. This is ensured by police patrolling, quick police action and action against visible and local goondas. In big cities, if incidents of chain snatching, eve teasing and realization of goonda tax, go unchecked, then the people feel insecure no matter what outstanding work is done in any other area. Hence, if strong action is taken against this, people can lead their daily lives peacefully. Goondaism in the marketplace, on the roads and public places must be dealt with severely.

The System of Criminal Justice

Law and order and crime control depend to a large extent on the law breakers getting punished. However, as a District Magistrate, when one reviews the criminal cases it is clear that percentage of conviction is always less than 10%. This makes the criminal act in a brazen manner. They are quite confident of getting away scot free.

I recall being visited by a Pradhan whose son was an accused in a murder case. I thought he had come to see me to convince me that his son was innocent. He, on the contrary, accepted that his son had committed the crime. He wanted two things– one was that the police should not a arrest his son, and that he be allowed to surrender in the court as he was afraid of the police beating up his son, the Other was that the State should not vigorously oppose the bail application. I was taken aback but decided to probe this further. I asked him whether he was not afraid of his son spending his life in jail. His answer was simple, "I shall hire a good lawyer and the case will linger for years and then my son shall be acquitted for want of evidence."

The above attitude is not unique but has become widespread. This has reduced the fear among lawbreakers. This is not to criticize our system of criminal justice. In fact, it is based on the western law of jurisprudence which says that not even one innocent person should get convicted. The state will have to prove in case beyond reasonable doubt to ensure conviction. This system ensures the liberty of the individual, protects his fundamental rights, and is indeed laudable. In fact, those who criticize this should imagine a situation where one of their close relatives is wrongly accused and then convicted without fair trial. I am sure that they would thereafter agree with the philosophy behind this system.

However, it cannot be denied that in actual practice the system has reached a point where criminals are going scotfree and the law and order situation is getting adversely affected. At the district level the District Judiciary (DJ), police and the DM are the three main people associated with administration of criminal justice. An excellent mechanism of coordination through monitoring cell meeting has been created. The DJ is the Chairman and the DM and SSP are its other members. This monitoring cell is expected to meet once in a month and review matters. If held in the right spirit these meetings can be very fruitful. Very often the Judiciary and police keep putting the blame on one another. However, the idea should be to evolve methods of ironing out the deficiencies. The forum has to be used to appreciate the problems that each wing faces. The police would say that on a particular day the state witnesses came but were not examined. The reply would be that on several dates the states witnesses had not come and on this date also, they came late. Hence, adjournment. Be it as it may, I still feel that many useful day-to-day problems are thrown up and solutions found during such meetings. This monitoring cell institution, if properly used, can certainly improve matters.

In my experience, I have always found the monitoring cell an invaluable institution. In every district I made this an informal affair where every aspect could be discussed freely. We would meet for dinner either at the residence of the district Judge or SSP or DM along with families. The discussion then would go beyond the rigid boundaries of the agenda and all three would have a free and frank discussion on the law and order and the criminal situation in the district. Extremely useful information was exchanged and all three came onto the same wavelength. In fact, these informal meetings and social get-togethers often resolve the trickiest of matters of issues in a district by creating harmony and team spirits. In recent time, I have seen incidents of tension and conflict between the district judiciaries and the executive magistracy and the police force. So much so that often cases came to light where CJM (Chief Judicial Magistrate) or Additional

District Judge ordered registration of FIRs against officers belonging to the team of the DM and SP. This creates a lot of bad blood and adversely impact the law and order situation in the district. If the DM can maintain excellent relations with the DJ then this kind of situation would not arrive. On joining a district I made it a point to call on the DJ both officially and socially. This went a long way in ensuring a harmonious relationship.

Most importantly the state case should be properly put forward. A mechanism exists at the district level to monitor this, but is getting neglected. On every case of acquittal a report has to be submitted by the District Government Counsel (DGC Criminal) stating reasons for acquittal. These reasons should be perused and put up before the DM. If the police have failed in its duty then the matter can be taken up with the SSP. If the case has not been properly contested then the State Counsel could be held accountable. However, I have found that in most districts these reports have stopped coming and even if they do come nobody bothers to analyze them.

The crucial factor is that proper people should be appointed as DGC and as ADGC. There is a perfect procedure for this in which a report on their performance is taken to the District Judge for considering their overall suitability. If done impartially, it would ensure that the best candidate is selected But unfortunately, there has been almost total politicization off the post of DGC. The State Counsels hold charge on the will of the State Government in power. This degeneration has to be corrected.

The police machinery also gives investigation a low priority. The SO and his team are often busy with VIP duties. They get very little time to investigate a case. This results in cases lying with them for a long period of time. Most often, the right person is not arrested and proper evidence not accumulated. Once the case starts in a court, the SO treats it as a burden to go to the court and have evidence adduced. In fact, he does not even bother to serve notices on State Witnesses.

A solution recommended for this is to have separate investigative machinery at the district level or even at the thana. Cases are to be investigated only by them. The SO and his force should be left free to deal with VIP duty and law and order. Theoretically, this suggestion is good as it ensures that investigation will get priority and the state case will be properly prepared. However, it is felt that the overall fallout of such a measure is not beneficial. If the ISO is not involved in investigating crime and arresting people then the authority that surrounds his post diminishes. He would then cease to be a major force in his area and this would hamper his ability to prevent crime and even maintain law and order. The institution of the thana, which has stood the test of time would eventually suffer.

The DM and SP should monitor the performance of thanas by not only analyzing the number of FIRs lodged and arrests made but they also monitor the number of charge sheets filled or investigation closed and the time period within which this has been done. The status of the cases in courts should also be monitored with the prosecution wing and district government counsel (criminal).

The only way out seems to be to strengthen the thana. More power will have to be given, including to the Additional Sub-inspectors. The SO would be in overall charge but would have a bigger team with him. This would enable him to spare SIs from other duties for investigating crime. The thana would have to be better equipped in terms of vehicles, communication, and also modernization in maintenance of records. Use of computers would certainly help in investigating a crime better.

Death in Police Custody

A very relevant point to be discussed is that of death in police custody. This is fallout of the discussion above. It never ceases to surprise me that even in this age of only method that the police have of investigating a crime is to arrest suspects and anti-social elements and to take a confession out of them through physical duress and even by resorting to third-degree methods. No system of detection, analysis and nabbing of a criminal through the use of investigative techniques is followed. Institutes of the science of criminology have been set up at the Central level, and also in some states. I feel all police officers should be extensively trained in Forensic Sciences and techniques of investigation. The set-up at the thana and district has to be modernized and equipped with equipment, aids and investigative devices. This can certainly help in logic replacing the brutality of the police station.

However there is another reason for beating up of suspects/ criminals at police stations. As outlined above, the rate of conviction is less than 10% the criminal is almost sure of not getting convicted. This means that he does not have to go to jail. There is no fear of law–no deterrent force. The criminal is only worried about what happens to him in police custody. Thus, the major deterrent today is the beating at the police station. In a district where SSP and his team indulge in this in a big way, crime unfortunately tends to get controlled and a psychology of terror is created.

But the above does not justify use of such measures. This brutality has to be done away with. We have to improve our investigation and ensure that the criminal justice system operates in a manner such that no innocent person suffers.

Besides police brutality leads to death in police custody. This is very serious matter. It is a question of violation of human rights and should be dealt with very severely. As a DM the immediate action to be taken is to lodge an FIR for murder against the SO and have him arrested. Many police officers oppose this measure as they feel that the force shall get demoralized. But it's a question of moral of the force versus

Human Rights. In fact, it is not a question of morale of the force also. No force can be allowed to indulge in mindless brutality as a morale booster. Hence, a case of death and police custody has to be dealt with severely.

In the same vein the police should not be given a free hand to encounter to criminals. The due process of law has to be followed. Besides allowing encounter makes the police trigger happy and you often find them chasing targets of conducting encounters. More often than not it is the small time criminal who gets shot while the big fish get away. However, in heinous crimes you find that there is often very great support from the citizens in the police encountering the criminals. Just recently there was the case of a ghastly rape in Andhra Pradesh where the police officers resorted to encountering the alleged convicts. The entire nation and media applauded them. However, this is a debatable issue and encounter should be used as a extreme weapon. The fault actually lies with the criminal justice system where matters get unduly delayed. Very recently the rapists of Nirbhaya got hanged after more than seven years of trial which had exhausted the patience of the nation. The legal system allows appeals and right to be heard and to be legally represented. This is how as it should be but in heinous crimes the matter should be fast-tracked. Recently, in a state, a rapist was convicted within two months of the crime. Speeding justice will greatly enhance the faith of the people in the criminal justice system.

Relations between Police and Magistracy

This is the issue which is uppermost in the mind of officers taking charge of a district. In more specific terms, it boils down to a question of relationship between the DM and his SP. The fact of the matter is that the relations are not always very good. The disturbing thing is that these differences trickle down to all the levels of the police and magistracy. They result in a lack of coordination, cooperation and consequently affect the proper handling of law and order issues.

Worse still is the impact of the public and the advantage that unscrupulous elements try to take out of this. In fact, the moment one joins a district, efforts are on by such elements to sow seeds of discord between the DM and SP. They will create stories, misinterpret situations and responses, and try to influence the officer. If the officer concerned has a habit of reacting without verifying or has a tendency to believe everything that is told to him, then misunderstanding starts and soon snowballs into a major controversy.

Some years back the DM used to write the annual entry of the SP. This naturally meant control and ruled out the possibility of both functioning as parallel centres of power. Now this system has been changed. Most DMs argue for a return of this power as they feel that they are thrown into an unenviable situation of responsibility without authority. The Police Act says that the DM is the head of the criminal administration and the government also fixes full responsibility on the DM for any law and order disturbance. We see so many situations everyday where in the event of a riot the DM is transferred out first. Hence, the arguments that DM should be given authority over the SP.

Naturally, the magistrate and police have their own arguments on this issue. I too cannot fully claim to be free from bias on this issue as I belong to the magistracy. The police people argue that the powers of the DM be taken away as they can run the law and order on their own. They feel that as it is they who do most of the work. On the other hand, there is the view that we don't want a system where we can give the police unfettered powers–we cannot have a police state, and hence, the powers to Executive Magistrate to maintain the checks and balances. These issues have to be decided by an independent body. But the point to be emphasized is that a solution has to be found if deterioration in handling of law and order has to be checked.

The discord between the DM and SP is often the result of a clash of egos. Relations begin to get strained over petty issues. If both the officers have a broad-minded way of looking at things then a conflict can always be avoided–it all starts from day one. On joining a district the DM expects that the SP would call on him officially and then call at home, socially. Many police officers tend to avoid this and would at best talk over the telephone. Tensions are born. I, for one, see no reason why the issue of calling on should be seen as one of subordination. It can be done in a spirit of friendship and camaraderie. There was a classic case where the SP did not call on the DM for several days. The DM announced over the wireless that he was coming to meet the SP and proceeded. By the time a surprised SP could gather his wits the DM arrived at his office. In the novel with the DM made his point and thereafter the SP also did not stand on his ego on other issues. The position is clear–the DM is head of administration at the district level. The convention is that if the District Judge is in the district before the DM then the latter shall call on the former. The other offices of the district shall call on the DM.

The next round of conflict starts with the DM's staff meeting. The DM expects the SP to attend in person. The SP always finds an excuse for not coming. He sends his representatives. There is no shortage of people who could come to the DM and say: "The SP does not even come for your greetings. You have no control over the police." Instantaneously, the DM reacts in two ways–he either shouts at the representative of SP in the meeting, demanding from him the reasons for the SP not coming, or he shoots off an angry letter to the SP. The SP responds with an insolent letter from his side and the battle lines are drawn.

The fact of the matter is that the DM's staff meeting is held once in a month. Criminal case work, the work of state counsels, acquittal percentage and issues of law and order are discussed. The date is normally fixed. Hence, it is not difficult for the SP to plan his time and come for the meeting. It brings him closer to the problems of magistracy and helps him in better managing his police force. On the part of the DM, he should have the issues concerned with the police discussed first and then let the SP go. The latter should not be made to sit out unnecessarily while the DM peers over the figures of the revenue court work.

There could be occasions when the SP is genuinely busy. He could just make a telephone call and tell the DM and the letter should accept it gracefully. Additionally, the SP should send his second-in-command for the meeting. Sometimes the SPs send a very junior officer for the meeting. The DM naturally tends to feel humiliated. It is in the interest of work that a person senior enough to contribute to the deliberations be sent.

The above applies to any meeting of the DM. However, the DM should talk to the SSP over the phone and fix up a mutually agreed date for the meeting. In fact, if the communication lines are open between the two then the possibility of a conflict recedes. More stress should be laid on oral communication than written. Letters always tend to add to complications.

In fact, I worked out a system of having a separate meeting on law and order where only the DM and SP and their team were present. There is no need to call the SSP for a meeting where all other officers are present. Besides, law and order and crime control have a lot of confidential issues which cannot be discussed in the open. Moreover, a separate meeting gives an opportunity to discuss all issues at length and also helps in building a spirit of comraderie between the executive magistrate and the police.

The next major tussle starts with the issue of posting and transfer of SOs. It is provided for in the police act that the approval of DM shall be taken. The SP normally does not like this, he feels he is the head of the force and it should be his prerogative. The DM points to the provision in the police act and naturally feels insulted when he is not consulted. It is not uncommon to find a situation where the SP passes the order and DM comes to know of it through the press. In retaliation, the DM shoots off a letter, very often demanding that SP's orders to be cancelled and the issue goes out of hand.

Some SPs pass the orders and send a copy to the DM (not on the original) stating that these orders have been issued with the consent of the DM. Some don't even do this. Almost no SP takes approval in writing.

The fact of the matter remains that the police act provides for the approval of the DM in the posting of SOs. An SP should not make a prestige issue out of this. It may be true that it is the SP who monitors the day-to-day working of the SO but this tool is provided to the DM to enable him to perform his duty as the head of the criminal administration. The SO is the pivot around which the entire criminal administration revolves. If the DM has no control over the SO then he cannot possibly ensure maintenance of law and order.

Most experienced and mature SPs find a very neat way of resolving this issue. They talk to the DM over the telephone or in person, and tell him about the proposal of transfer of SOs. Normally, the DM agrees to the SP's proposal. The order is then passed and it is mentioned in the orders that it has been issued with the prior consent of the DM. As a very experienced SP told me, he had yet to come across a DM who disagreed with his proposal!

Conflict between the DM and SP erupts over childish and immature things. It can start from the ladies club, who attends the phone first, whose car goes ahead, where is the chair of the SP placed in a meeting, etc. If the DM starts with the assumption that the SP would not listen to him and give him due respect, then he becomes paranoid and tends to view every action in a negative light. The way out for the DM is to be to broad-minded and open. Communications–social and official, should be open and frequent. This helps in building up team spirit.

The police force even now listens to and pays respect to the DM. However, the problem is much more complicated for the SDM and other magistrates. The local SO does not even call on the SDM. The origin of this is in the 1973 Amendment to the Criminal Procedure Code where the power to try Special Acts like Gambling Act, Excise Act, Arms Act, etc. have been taken away from the Executive Magistrates and given to judicial magistrates. Hence, except for law and order duties, the SO has little to do with the SDM. I strongly feel that this issue needs to be debated and resolved. The Special Act must be returned to the Executive Magistrates.

However, even today the SDM can use the powers available to him to be effective in his area. It is not mandatory for the SDM to issue notice in every case of Section 107/116 that is reported to him. It depends on his satisfaction and if he is not convinced then he can return the report back to the SO. He should also fix a date for each thana and insist upon police evidence. Surely someone from particular thana can come once in a week. If no evidence comes forth then he is at a liberty to drop the proceedings. That gives the SDM control over his thana. He is not meant to be a rubber stamp.

The SDM is expected to inspect thana in his jurisdiction. It is done casually, it is advisable for the SDM to carry out a thorough inspection of the thana. This also enables him to have a grip over the police.

However, everything flows from the talk. If the DM and SP are not getting along then this message goes down the ranks and you find no coordination existing. The system as it stands today needs maturity of outlook on the part of the DM and SP. They have to realize that only if they complement and supplement one another, can effective administration of law and order be ensured. The ego bag has to be locked up in the trunk.

An overt display of fraternity on the part of the DM and SP would serve to be mutually beneficial. This has a very good impact. The DM and SP should insist that all magistrates and police officers complement and supplement each other. The ADM and Additional SP, SDM and CO would forge close links amongst themselves if they move together. The DM and SP would then send the message that law and order is a shared responsibility.

I found that at least one official meeting in a month, of all police officers and magistrates, helps in coordination. Moreover, social get-togethers can play a major role in bringing people together.

The issue of relationship with the police is one of the most crucial aspects of a DMs job. He is the leader and if there is lack of coordination then the DM gets a bad name in the public and is considered tactless by the government. A delicate balance has to be maintained all through, between the aspirations and rights of the people and the morale of the police force. The DM has to assert in just the right quantity–if he does not assert at then police can become unfettered and dominate every; if he asserts too much, discord sets in. The system as it stands today demands a lot of fine balancing on the part of DM. Much depends upon his personality and the outlook of his counterpart.

I would like to relate my experience of 6th December, 1992 after the demolition of the Babri Masjid to illustrate how effective law and order handling can be if the magistracy and police work in tandem. I was posted as DM Agra and had a very competent SSP in Arvind Jain. Around noon on that fateful day news started filtering in of the Babri Masjid being demolished and within a few hours the deed was done. Agra was an extremely sensitive district which had witnessed severe communal riots just a few years ago. Both communities had mischievous leaders who could mobilize their community and create violence. I immediately got in touch with my SSP and we began to patrol the city. People were congregating at places and we stopped to talk to them in order to gauge their mood and make a plea for peace. We called a meeting of influential leaders and asked them to move within the communities to maintain peace. The peace committees consisting of members of both the communities were immediately activated. Police deployment was done at all sensitive spots. The executive magistrate and their police counterparts were formed into teams for patrolling. We called in the force from the local provincial armed constabulary battalion and moved them around the city to make a show of force. This patrolling went on till midnight and we decided not to impose a curfew and wait for the next day. However, I got independent feedback in the night that there was tremendous resentment amongst the minorities and a major incident could take place anytime. At about 1 am in the night we decided to impose curfew in nine police stations of Agra. Arrangements were made during the night. The police force deployment was drawn up and detailed briefing given to them. The trouble-makers of both communities were arrested under preventive sections during the night. Our efforts paid dividends as Agra remained an oasis of peace as violence irrupted in adjoining districts the next day.

My SSP and I worked together to see that the police force did not resort to unnecessary force to enforce the curfew. At the same time I, along with my entire team of officers, worked out a system of ensuring supply of milk, essential commodities and medicine to the people. The sick were escorted to the hospitals or doctors visited them in their homes. These measures created an environment of mutual trust with the common citizens and we got their support as well as that of the media. An atmosphere of peace was created which was not disturbed even when all the top political leader from Mr. Adwani, Mr. Joshi, Ms. Uma Bharti and others were sent to Agra jail. At that time the presence of these people in Agra was a potentially explosive situation but we were able to maintain peace as the people had faith in the fairness and neutrality of the administration. This successful management of the situation was possible only because the DM and the SSP and their entire team worked together as one to control the situation. My view is very clear that if the DM and SP worked in close coordination then there is no situation which they cannot tackle.

Recently in UP, the Police Commissioner system has been introduced in Lucknow and Noida. Many big cities of India have this system. IAS officers generally oppose the move whereas the IPS officers support it. The farmers see it as a dilution of their powers while the later sees it as making them more powerful. It gives a lot of senior and powerful posts to the police but there is no doubt that it greatly erodes the authority of the institutions of the District Magistrate. I, for one, feel that instead of looking at it from the coloured lenses of the IAS or IPS officers it should be examined from the point of view of the citizens. As it is, the crime aspect is almost exclusively looked after by the police. The DM comes into the picture only in matters of law and order. The proponents of the Police Commissioner system argue that it gives the police a uniform integrated command which will enable them to handle law and order better. This argument, in my opinion, is fallacious as there is a rare occasion where a DM does not give permission for imposing curfew or ordering views of force or taking action under preventive sections if the SSP recommends. If the relations between the DM and SSP are good then there is never any problem. Besides, the institution of the DM puts in place a system of checks and balances which is essential in a democracy. The citizen must have and alternative remedy if he is unhappy with police action. Moreover, a citizen is more comfortable going to the DM and Magistracy with a problem rather than the police which has a command structures and force oriented mindset. The example of foreign countries is given but this is not strictly applicable as there is no parallel to the institutions of the DM in these countries. Moreover, even in cities like New York or London, the Police Commissioner works under the civilian control of the mayor.

I guess there would be different views in this matter. I am all for upgrading the level of policing in large urban towns. Let there be Police Commissioners of senior rank and more police officers posted. A big city needs to be policed in a very different manner from a district headquarter which is semi-urban. The police force needs to be equipped better, modernized, given more vehicles and equipments and better living and working conditions. However, the institution of the DM should be allowed to continue to have a voice in matters of law and orders. This can be done by letting the DM and Magistracy continue with its powers under the various acts like excise act, entertainment act, arms act, goonda act, gangster act and national security act. The citizen must get better crime control, law and order and security. It is his interest that should be uppermost in the minds of the policy-makers rather than making it an issue of one service versus the others.

The level of policing definitely needs a lot of improvements in states like UP. First, the sanctioned posts of the constables and sub-inspector should be filled up in a fair and transparent manner. Our police always suffers from a critical shortage of personnel and the police to population ratio in India is very much on the lower side. Above this the problem is compounded by the culture of providing VIPs (ministers and important political functionaries) with gunners, shadows, escort and securities. A whole lot of police force is wasted in these duties which mainly cater to the ego of the VIPs and is taken as a status symbol. Maximum police personnel should be deployed on active duty.

Another point that I have noticed that after being with the VIP for sometime the police officers lose their policing instincts and often become lazy and corrupt.

The police is often blamed for being rough and rude with people and intimidating in their behaviour which is the result if the citizens are afraid of visiting the police station. This can be remedied by proper training of the police force. Currently, the new recruits are often sent directly to the field without any training because of the shortage. Naturally, their behaviour and performance would leave a lot of gaps. Also, it is important for the SSP and other police officers to act as true leaders of their force and genuinely look after their personal and official problems and give them humane treatment. Recently in Delhi, the police revolted against their own seniors because they did not expect fair treatment from them. This is a failure of police leaderships. In addition, the welfare of the police personnel should be a priority issue and each commanding officers should be concerned with the living conditions, barracks and police lines where the police personnel live and train. These are hygiene factors but essential to bring out the best from the force.

Technology is a game changer. The DM and SSP can use technology to genuinely improve tracking of criminals, working out crimes and handling cyber crimes. But at the end of the day there is no substitute for basic policing like the revival of the system of the beat constable who knows everything about the area of jurisdiction. In UP recently, we implemented the UP-100 system which is now called UP-112 in which a UP-100 vehicle with police force would reach the scene of a crime or disturbance within 20 minutes of getting of call. Close co-oporation between the DM and SP is required to make this technological intervention successful as it is opposed by none other than the police thana.

Ultimately, the DM must realize that the SSP is the captain of his force. The DM should not do anything to interfere with the authority of the SSP and give him all possible support. Mutual trust, respect and camaraderie between the DM and SP is a best way to control crime and law and order.

To sum up, law and order requires the presence of mind, appreciation of situation, knowledge of people and a sense of timing about action to be taken. The DM should never get personally involved in any issue. He should always be projected as a fair and impartial observer. Rigidity is never the answer. An open, flexible approach is required. Above all, the one quality that is really required is coolness–a clear-head at the time of a crisis.

Development Administration

One of the prime tasks of the District Officer is to oversee and manage the implementation of development programmes. In our system of a welfare state the government actively intervenes in the planning of resources, designing programmes for eradication of poverty, generation of employment, providing facilities for education and health care. The policies are formulated at the state level but the cutting edge of its implementation is the district.

Crores of rupees are being spent on schemes for rural development. If utilized properly they can bring about a total change in the rural scenario. However, a large number of people –both official and unofficial–develop vested interests. The schemes do not reach those for whom they have been designed. Corruption has spread its tentacles at every step. The net result is that the return on investment in rural development is very poor. The challenge before the district administrator is to plan, organize and physically implement the project in a manner to provide maximum benefit to the target group.

Organization Structures for Development

The Collector is an extremely busy person. A survey on the time of a Collector showed that he spent the maximum percentage of his time on meeting people, law and order, VIP duties and holding meetings and coordinating various schemes. He has less than 20% of his time left for development work. Of course, this varies from district to district. In a smaller district where law and order problems are less he can devote more time to development. But even in these districts he cannot personally see all aspects of implementation. He has to motivate his team of development officers, design a system of effectively monitoring the programmes and selectively carry out physical checks. This is the only way he can ensure implementation of development projects.

In almost all districts of UP there is a CDO (Chief Development Officer). He is an IAS Officer or a senior PCS officer or promoted from BDO cadre. It is he who has to coordinate all programmes of rural development. The Collector has to operate through him and give him all support. The office of the CDO has the DDO (District Development Officer) and a Project Director, District Rural Development Agency. In addition, there are heads of departments of Agriculture, Horticulture, Animal Husbandry and Panchayat Raj etc. though the CDO is the head of the development wing he does not enjoy direct powers over these people and it is a difficult job for him to control them. He has to use the authority of the Collector to get work out of them. It would be useful to vest the post of CDO with more powers over other development officers.

Much of the work of development at the district level needs coordination with technical departments like PWD, irrigation, tubewells, jal nigam and others. They draw the maximum resources from the development pool, yet never give a detailed account of expenditure. The CDO is not even aware of their day-to-day progress. Yet the DM and CDO are responsible for the quality of the work. There is not direct authority over these departments. Yet a system of coordination committees has been set up to regulate their working. However, it is very difficult for the CDO to exercise any control without the active intervention and support of the DM. Since money goes to these departments from the district pool the power of not releasing money is used as an instrument of control.

The above discussion just goes to show that even though the post of the CDO is a vital one, he is, as yet, not strong enough. He has to derive his authority from the Collector. To a large extent this cannot be avoided. But the least what can be done is to give the CDO full powers over his development departments. It is ironical to see him battling with his own DDO and project director over establishment matters. We have to recognize the importance of the role of the CDO in the development hierarchy.

The pivot around which the entire development administration revolves is the BDO (Block Development Officer). When community development started in 1952 the blocks were created as units of development. A village was considered too small and a district too big. Normally, a block has a population of the one lakh and is in a position to serve as growth centre. The BDO is the heads of the block. He has several ADO's to assist him in the fields of agriculture, cooperatives, Panchayat, statistics and others. Finally, at the village level there is the VLO (Village Level Officer) and Panchayat Secretary.

Initially the BDOs were a tremendously motivated people who went about their job as a mission. They were mainly doing agriculture extension–their goal was rural transformation. Today, extension work is the least on their list of priorities. They are loaded with all kinds of works and the missionary zeal seems to have disappeared completely.

An enthusiastic Collector has a lot of novel ideas about development. He is bursting with enthusiasm. However, he is bound to come out of his meeting with BDOs not registering what is being talked to them. They are not inclined to accept new ideas. Their sole concern is with figures–achievement of targets. These they promise to meet and do so. In fact the joke is that the BDO has the capacity to come out with any figure of achievement in a moment. He simply wants to know what you want.

The BDO, today, is an overloaded person. Any programme that the government releases has the BDO as the focal point of its implementation. He is involved in distribution of seeds, implementation of IRDP, fulfilling the target of National Savings and also Family Planning., with the result that the BDO is often a muddled person who is not sure of what is expected of him. To make the block perform a clear-cut sense of direction with prioritization of objectives needs to be given by the Collector to the BDO. If this is not done then the BDO often responds to the plethora of schemes thrust upon him by just not performing.

Most of these schemes have to be implemented by the officers of specific departments but at the district level the BDO is held responsible. He does not enjoy direct authority and control over them. This inhibits the functioning of the BDO. It is not rare to find a BDO in his block not being able to get work out of his ADO cooperative or ADO Panchayat. His only recourse is to write to the departmental heads of the districts. His letters have little result as these officers have a tendency to support their subordinates. This often leaves the BDO a very frustrated man. To get meaningful results out of this structure the BDO shall have to be vested with more powers. Till such time, the Collector will have to give him a lot of support.

Insistence on targets has been the bane of the development process. The BDO is involved in distribution of seeds and fertilisers, implementation of MGNREGA, National Rural Livelihood Mission, selfhelp group, housing for poor, construction of toilets and several other rural development initiatives. Right from the government level, evaluation forms keep coming every month and the DM, CDO and the BDO are hard pressed to fulfill targets. The planning part, the project part and the physical verification aspects are ignored in the race to fulfill targets. The quality suffers. In fact, most of the meetings held of BDO's at district level are figure collection exercises. One by one, the BDOs stand up and give figures of their performance against targets. They are pulled up if their achievement percentage is less and asked to fulfill a certain figure by the end of the month. The BDO had learnt to say "It shall be done" and does it. Though, it is a matter of conjecture as to how it is done. This is another factor which blunts the zeal of the block level functionary.

Each scheme has a list of statements to be sent regularly and enormous amount of paper work. All the reports originate from the BDO. Reports on number of job cards prepared, mandays created, budget spent, self help groups created, toilets constructed, houses built etc. have to be periodically submitted by the BDO.

It is not uncommon to see a BDO spending almost all his time in compiling reports and statements. Whatever time is left he either prepares for an inspection or attends a meeting. A whole lot of officers inspect block and many call the BDO for meetings. The BDO hence, is left with no time to visit his area, oversee the implementation of schemes and think about rural development. He is in an unenviable position of being in no control of his time and effort. The District Officer has to insist upon allowing just one combined meeting of BDOs in a month and discourage needless inspection by officers. Asking for reports and data should also be cut down by strengthening the statistical wing at the district headquarters. In fact, even the state government has to rationalize its form and reports originating at the block level. This is possible only to an extent. The answer then is to have a full fledged statistical wing at the block level. It is necessary to free the BDO from paperwork to enable him to perform his field duties properly. The advent of computers has greatly changed the monitoring scene at the block and district level. Now for all schemes and projects a detailed computer based information system has been designed and reports are generated accordingly. The BDO and his staff have been trained in this work and also given the services of a computer operator. This computerized monitoring system has been greatly reducing leakages and making reliable data available for monitoring and policy formulation.

In one district I found that there were some BDOs who had enthusiasm for their jobs while there were others who reminded one of deadwood. A close scrutiny revealed that the former group consisted of freshly appointed BDO's while the latter consisted mainly of those who were in the last half of their career. Somewhere along the time these officers had lost their motivation and spirit. This point was brought more forcefully to me when I met a BDO almost eight years after he had worked with me. He was my best BDO–young, active, enthusiastic and with a sense of commitment to his work. He used to tour extensively and took pride in demonstrating his work. He just would not budge from his seat. He was arguing on every point and had developed a negative attitude.

I called him to my office and after putting him at ease posed the question to him. He shrugged, spread his hands and said, "What is the point, Sir, I started off as a BDO and shall remain a BDO when I am promoted at the fag end of my career, others who have not worked shall be promoted with me."

The above incident has forcefully brought out the point that the BDO cadre has no real motivation to do well. A definite promotion policy for them has to be evolved. They should be able to see the possibility of upward movement in the near future. Further, I feel an objective system of performance evaluation has to be built into this promotion policy. The BDO is the most vital link in the rural development hierarchy. We just can't afford a disgruntled and uninterested officer at this level.

Since a whole lot of funds are now routed through the blocks the office of the BDO has become the favorite halt of middlemen, contractors and touts. Bearing the badges of various political parties these people try to force the BDO to act according to their whims. The BDO is not in a position to resist them on his own accord. He has to be given a lot of support by the District Officer.

This interference becomes all the more pronounced if the block Pramukh also belongs to one of the above categories and has vested interest in everything. The block Pramukh is the head of the Kshetra Samiti (Block Development Committee) and also has the powers of putting his remarks on the annual confidential roll of the BDO. The system, per se is excellent. It ensures accountability of the BDO to the people. However, the problem comes when the Pramukh is not an upright person. The District Officer is bound to get inundated by complaints against the BDO in this case. If this does not succeed in dislodging the BDO then the Pramukh makes serious adverse remarks in the ACR of the officer. I have seen this happening in several cases. If the BDO is working honestly and diligently, he needs all the support in such cases. As a DM, I made sure that a very good report in favour of the BDO was entered in his ACR and all the points raised by the Pramukh were answered.

If the above aspects are kept in mind and the BDO kept in a strong position then he can exercise control over his Assistant Development Officers (ADOs) and Village Level Officer and Panchayat Secretary. The VLO is an important functionary. He has the power to select beneficiaries under various schemes and can get you a loan from a bank. It is important to ensure that this power is used in accordance with government policy and not as a system of patronage. A strong monitoring system at the block level and intensive touring by senior officers is essential to ensure this.

In recent years the Panchayati Raj department has become very powerful and almost a parallel power centre. In UP, I noticed an intense power struggle between the ADO Panchayat and the BDO. The former refused to consider himself under the BDO and would report directly to DPRO (District Panchayat Raj Officer). The genesis of this power struggle lay in the decentralization of development programmes and funds from Central and State finance commissions flowing directly to the village Panchayats. Substantial funds are now available with the village Panchayats. The Panchayat Raj department wants to monitor these funds at their own level without allowing the BDO or even the CDO to get into it. The DPRO has become a very powerful officer in the District. The conflicts even reached up to the State level where the Panchayati Raj Department was separated from the Rural Development department. Things became so bad that there was no synergy between the two departments which was greatly detrimental to the convergence required in development. Development schemes and programmes cannot work in silos. Convergence is the buzz word now and this demands a coordinating officer. The collector or the CDO fulfills this role at the district level but the basic unit of development is the block and the BDO has to play a leading role in coordinating various government scheme at the block level.

A major problem in UP has been the huge shortage of village development officers. To tackle this Panchayat Secretary is being used to do the work of VDO/VLO in several villages. Even then one employee is looking after more than half a dozen villages and is hardly able to devote much time to the selection of beneficiaries or spreading awareness about government schemes. Unfortunately, the Rural Development department is wary of filling up the vacancies as almost immediately there is a surfeit of allegations of corruption leading to enquiries which most officers want to avoid.

It is also true that everything about rural development comes down to the VDO–selection of beneficiary, selection of project, formation of self help groups and so on. He neither has the time nor the ability to do justice to his job and the result is unimaginative and poor quality of work. We need to train the VDOs better and fill up the vacancies so that he can do a satisfactory job.

District Rural Development Agency (DRDA)

In most states the District Board (Zila Parshad) is at the apex of rural development structure. This is not in Uttar Pradesh where the role of the Collector is still the most important. The crucial schemes like Prime Minister Awas Yojna (PMAY), Chief Minister Awas Yojna (CMAY), Sansad Nidhi and Vidhayak Nidhi (MP, LAD and MLA development funds) are monitored by a committee called DRDA (District Rural Development Agency). The Collector is the chairman of this agency which has all the MPs, MLAs and other officers as its members but it is normally the CDO who chairs these meetings. The DRDA used to be a very strong body some years ago when it controlled most of the schemes related with rural development but today this institution is in a decline but still remains an important forum for discussion with public representatives.

The meeting of the DRDA often witnesses a scene of heated arguments and controversy and requires very astute handling on the part of the DM. Actually the contentious issue is the division of funds which come for construction of roads, etc. Every MLA wants that the projects should be taken up. A method often adopted to get over this is to divide the funds equally between all the public representatives. This leads to satisfaction of all but does not always lead to optimum allocation of resources. A Collector has other ideas on how development should be controlled or directed. By just dividing the money it implies that the Collector has no control over the development process and is just performing the role of a bystander. The wisdom of the public representatives and their rights are not being questioned. But the MLA has his own priorities. He also has to respond to pressures. As such balanced development does not come about.

In district B, the Collector had to face this dilemma. He wanted those villages, which had no roads, to be connected with fair weather roads. Secondly, he wanted the *kucha* roads to be made *pucca* rather than come up with new mud roads. The MLAs were insistent upon the money being spent only on schemes being given by them. A cursory look at the proposals submitted by them showed that it was not conforming to the criteria he had in mind.

The Collector decided to take the MLAs into confidence. He called them separately and outlined the problem to them. They too, agreed that this should be the approach. The Collector then put forward the idea that the MLAs give their proposals accordingly. The MLAs protested but were convinced that they could always tell their people that this was the decision of a committee and that they could not help it. The MLAs saw the reason and also found a way of responding to the pressures on them. In the next meeting, all the proposals to DRDA came as per the criteria evolved.

The above example only goes to illustrate that if the Collector plans out this work properly and has good rapport with the public representatives to convince them, rational development can take place through bodies like DRDA. Rather than trying to impose one's will on the committee or going to the other extreme of giving up, the Collector has to guide the committee. He has to evolve a rational solution and make the public representatives come around to this on their own.

The DRDA is a useful body to monitor the quality of programmes and the pace of implementation. The officers of various departments have to respond to the public representatives who know the ground realities. The important task of the Collector is to manage these meetings well. Very often the public representatives start attacking the officers personally and even tend to use abusive language. This should be avoided at all cost. To be answerable does not mean that you can be subjected to abuse. If the DM does not protect his officers from indecent attacks in these meetings his development tam crumbles and he does not get results.

The Collector, however, has to guide and manage the DRDA meetings in such a manner that rational decisions as per government guidelines are taken. There are some Collectors who bemoan the presence of public representatives in these bodies and state that everything is done as per their will with the Collector having no hold.

A typical DRDA meet starts acrimoniously with the public representatives getting dominant over the Collector and his officers. They shout and argue with one other, they hurl accusations at officers, with the result that the Collector and his team get into the defensive and, in a move to placate them, give in to them. This leads to a situation where funds available with DRDA are not targeted correctly.

The general demand is for equitable distribution of resources among the constituencies. Whereas, this is generally acceptable but these are projects which require larger investment and are essential for the development of the district. For instance, there could be the proposal to set up a milk chilling plant. It would be opposed by all public representatives but the Collector will have to assert that this infrastructure is necessary for the development of the district, and push it through. Under no conditions should any decision be taken which goes against government guidelines.

The recent trend is that not only are particular schemes insisted upon by public representatives, they also quote the agency by which they want the work done. In fact, an unhealthy nexus develops between the unscrupulous officers, contractors and public representatives. Officers from various departments stoop to any level to get a larger chunk of DRDA funds. I recall the case of a Soil Conservation Officer whose project I did not agree with as I was not convinced of its usefulness. This officer would then appear in my office every second day trying to impress me with the project. When I finally told him that I would not do it he approached ministers and MLAs and made them ring me up. I still persisted. Consider my consternation when in the next DRDA I found that all my officers, MLAs and others vehemently supporting his project. I firmly put my foot down and did not allow their project to be taken up. The very same evening the officer came to me in tears and implored me to help him as he had a large family to look after. I felt so sick over the whole thing that I did not even shout at him.

This is not an isolated incident. It is a common sight to see officers of various departments doing this. This exposes them. The public representatives know that these officers are misusing public money. So the moment anything goes against their wishes they abuse the officers, talk roughly to them and the officers have no moral courage to talk to them. A Collector can control the DRDA meetings only if he has the moral strength which comes from right intentions and absolute integrity.

Even then, corruption is there in the system which needs constant vigilance to curb as complete eradication is not always possible. There was a young CDO of mine who told me that he was approached by his Project Director and hesitatingly informed that normally the share of CDO is one per cent but it could be negotiated. He tried to convince the CDO by saying that the commission would any way be drawn irrespective of the CDO accepting his share or not. The CDO declined but this exposed the working of the entire system to him.

The DRDA has to be made more efficient to curb this corruption and misuse of government money. The DRDA needs to be equipped with a fully fledged technical cell. The job of this cell would be to have a look at the projects when they are submitted to DRDA but it should not become a screening body. One has to rely on the technical skills of the department presenting the project. There is no point in adding another level but this cell is required to understand the projects that have been put up. The more important task for it is to carry out physical verifications of all works being done by DRDA funds and give regular reports. This technical monitoring is a must to prevent misuse of funds.

District Plan

The district plan provides funds at the disposal of the district to meet its developmental needs. The allocation is decided by a District Planning and Implementation Committee, consisting of officers and public representatives. It used to be headed by the DM till recently but now in most states the Chairman, Zila Parishad occupies the chair. In Uttar Pradesh the district planning committee is headed by a Minister of the State Government. Each district is put under the charge of a minister who chairs the meeting in which Chairman Zila Parishad and MLAs and MPs are members. The unfortunate fall out of this arrangement is that the Ministers do not convene the meeting or do it after a lot of delay leading to making the district plan exercise in fructuous. It would be better if this system is discontinued. The district planning exercise to have any relevance must be completed well in time so that this plan gets reflected in the Annual Budget. A disconnect between the district plan and the Budget makes the entire exercise meaningless.

After years of planning it was realized that it is difficult to fully ascertain local realities, their needs and problems from the state or central level. Decentralization was the obvious answer. The bottoms-up approach rather than top down was advocated. District Plan concept was an offspring of such an approach. Decentralization of financial powers and a division of the overall budget was the mechanism by which this was expected to be achieved.

The year 1981 was the first year when district planning was introduced. The enthusiasm was tremendous and district magistrates held various rounds of meetings on outlining priorities and allocating funds. Many officers wrote out the plan document themselves. The proposal prepared by the District Planning Committee were put up before the divisional committee under the Commissioner and then sent to state level. I recall, I was holding charge as DM of Chamoli (a hill district) when this concept of district planning was introduced. There was tremendous enthusiasm. At that time the elected Panchayat institutions were not functional and it was a district officer who was tasked to prepare a plan after consulting all officers. We really putting a lot of labour in this exercise and derived tremendous satisfaction from this work. In the initial year the plan prepared by the Districts were taken seriously by the State Government.

Over the years this freedom at the district level has been infringed upon. Every department at the state level lists out their schemes and sends it down. There is no flexibility to take up a new scheme at the district level. Worse, many of the earlier state funded schemes are pushed into the district plan. In fact, many state sector schemes being sent to the district plan every year. It is almost, as if, everything is decided at the state level and only formalities carried out by the District Planning Committee. I feel State Government should restrict itself to giving guidelines for the preparation of a District Plan and not go about earmarking regular departmental schemes to the District plan thereby greatly reducing the scope of local initiative.

Also at the state level the planning and the finance department must coordinate to make district plan as reality. Properly done District planning can have a profound and positive impact on the development of a district.

Almost all the officers at the district level felt that this tendency of the state to intervene and impose its schemes upon the district plan has been increasing over time and is going against the spirit of district planning.

Another point noticed is that more than 50% of the money allocated goes as payment of salaries. The result is that the visible impact of district planning is limited. But this cannot be done away with–somebody has to pay the employees.

Yet another tendency which must be done away with is to alter and amend the plan at the state level. This is resorted to by all members of the District Planning Committee and once again it implies that allocation of resources is not need-based.

The Collector has a major role to play in the formulation of the district plan. His approach has to be that of a leader. He has to resist pressures from two groups. Firstly, there are the public representatives. It is natural for the latter to support schemes of road building because this has the maximum visible impact. They tend to criticize important schemes of forestry, dairy development, nutrition, etc. it is here that the Collector has to intervene and maintain a sense of balance. He has to set the priorities in accordance with local needs and then convince the group of his views. The second pressure is that of various departments who want a large share of the 'cake'. They plead their case, invoke the help of Secretaries at state level and lobby actively with the public representatives. Once again, the Collector has to insist on rationality as the sole guiding factor.

The standard approach should never be adopted. In many districts the departments send their plans on set schemes they send proposals or, say, about 10% more than that of previous years. The District Statistic Officer tabulates these proposals and then arbitrarily slashes the excess amount. His main concern is to statistically balance the plan–the plan is something much more–it is one of the most important tools of development.

Every district has some basic problem–it may be drinking water, irrigation, health or schools. The Collector must assess this and a major portion of the allocation must go to these departments. This has to be a conscious decision. This alone shall lead to optimum allocation of resources. It is clear, thus, that to make the district plan work as a real tool for development a lot of planning and initiative on the part of the Collector is required.

Gaps in Implementation

The schemes for development are well-thought out and if implemented in proper spirit can bring about real development. But today there are a lot of gaps in the development process. The structural reasons I have already discussed. A proper analysis can only be done by taking up the case of a few specific schemes.

In the days when I handled districts we used to be monitoring the twenty point programme, integrated rural development programme and Jawahar Rojgar Yojna. These schemes do not exist anymore but the principles of development administration involved in implementation of these schemes remain the same. The most important of these schemes is the MGNREGA scheme.

Mahatma Gandhi National Rural Employment Guarantee Act (MGNREGA)

This very important rural development scheme was started in 2006 with the object of giving upto 100 days employment to an adult unemployed member of a family who demands employment. Job cards for the unemployed have to be prepared and the exercise is of great importance as it must be ensured that job cards of all eligible unemployed people wanting a job are prepared. A job card holder has to apply for work if he is desirous of employment and as per the act it is the duty of the government to provide him work within 15 days failing which it is eligible for unemployment allowance. In my experience, I have rarely seen anybody getting or demanding unemployment allowance. They used to be various allegations about proper wages not being paid. It has now become mandatory to transfer the wages by electronic transfers to the account of the beneficiary within 15 days to prevent such leakages. Even then there are complaints that the Pradhaan of the village often takes his share from the amount that is paid to the job card holder. The Collector must device a system whereby such malpractices are controlled. This can be done through frequent inspections and investigation if any complaint is received. It is of utmost importance that full amount of wage is paid to the job card holder. The act prescribes that up to 100 days employment in a year would be given to the job card holder. The wage rate is not very high but is linked to the minimum wage act and every year the wage rates for different states are announced by government of India. Last year the wage rate of state like UP was Rs 182 per day but this has been enhanced recently and especially after the Corona pandemic to about Rs 201. I must add on this point that MNREGA scheme has been a game changer. The UPA government is widely believed to have come back to power in 2009 on the back of the benefits of this scheme. The NDA government after coming to power in 2014 had some initial reservations about this scheme but soon realized its importance and not only continued it but increased the outlay every year. Recently when the Corona pandemic shocked the nation there was a continuous influx of migrant labour who returned from their place of work due to unemployment to take shelter in their own villages. They were faced with poverty and deprivation.

MGNREGA saved the situation as most states, especially UP and Bihar from where maximum migrant labour goes to other states, large scale employment was generated as all the Collectors were directed to have a special drive for preparing job cards and providing employment to this migrant labour. Needless to say, the suffering of the migrant labour was greatly obviated by the scheme and it showed how this can be a boon in times of economic emergency.

Employment related programmes existed earlier also and MGNREGA has been built upon the experience of these earlier schemes. There used to be a national rural employment scheme (NREP) and rural employment guarantee scheme (RLEGP). The MGNERGA is governed by an act of parliament and thus is far more comprehensive and potent than any of its earlier variants.

One major issue with MGNERGA has been that it focuses on generation of employment as this is its prime objective and does not concern itself with creation of productive assets. It is true that employment generation is the basic objective of the scheme but it is important that employment also leads to creation of rural assets. In recent years, the government of India has applied itself to this problem and now listed out a series of projects that should be taken up under MGNERGA. There are now about more than 250 types of work which are admissible under MGNERGA which can be divided into 4 broad categories. Category A relates to National Resource Management and includes work like construction of village ponds, repair and maintenance of water bodies, minor irrigation works, check dams etc. Category B relates to individual beneficiaries related works like construction of houses, land development, compost pit etc. Category C relates to worksheds for livelihood programmes while Category D talks of rural infrastructure like roads, toilets etc.

The labour budget for each village is prepared after identifying the needs of a village and classifying individual and community related programmes at the state level. Rural development commissioner is the person responsible for implementing the programme under the supervision of secretary rural development. He is assisted by a team which is headed by a senior officer working as additional commissioner MGNREGA. In UP the District Officer is the district programme coordinator and CDO assists him as the assistant district programme coordinator. This is the most important role of the District Officer in rural development schemes today. He has to ensure that job cards are prepared for eligible workers and that a shelf of projects of each village is available on which to deploy the labour. Payment of wages has to go directly to the bank accounts without any siphoning of the fund. It is important for DO to personally inspect these projects at the ground level and also have his team of officers carry out regular evaluation exercises to see that the scheme is running as per guidelines and the funds are being properly utilized. The evaluation of the scheme is generally done in terms of mandays created in relation to the labour budget and the percentage of funds utilized to indicate financial progress and also indicate when more funds should be sought. Very often there is a delay in funds being released by central and state governments and it creates an unhappy situation where the labour is not paid for long periods thereby considerably reducing the impact of the scheme.

The ingenuity of the district officer comes into play in bringing about convergence of MGNERGA with other development schemes. One of the classic examples of convergence was when as agriculture production commissioner of UP, I motivated the District Officer of Fatehpur UP to use MGNERGA in rejuvenating a river which had dried up for several years. She prevailed upon the farmers to remove the encroachments on the dry river bed and then used MGNREGA funds to employ labour to dig up the river bed for 36 km and carried out activities like afforestation around it. With the first burst of rain in monsoon the entire river sprang back to life. This unique river rejuvenation project received the Prime Minister's award for excellence in governance and is an example of the kind of benefits that an innovatively implemented MGNREGA scheme can bestow on the rural scenario.

As Chief Secretary UP, I was faced with a severe drought in Bundelkhand area of UP and one of the main measures we employed to deal with this situation was to implement MGNREGA on a massive scale in this area to provide employment to the existing labour force as well as the migrants returning from other states. Job cards were prepared on a priority basis for all and a major drive was launched for executing the projects. We exceeded the labour budget for these districts and it had a salutary effect on softening the impact of drought and saved the poor from the scourge of hunger. Huge amounts of funds are available under MGNREGA and the district officer can make a substantial impact by proper implementation of the scheme. It is to be noted that even though 100 days of employment are supposed to be provided to each job card holder on demand the actual figure is much less averaging anywhere between 40 to 60 days. This shows that there is a hidden potential of utilizing this scheme better. Government of India has prepared elaborate computer based monitoring formats which record each and every information to prevent leakages and ensure the fulfillment of the objective of the scheme.

Very often you will have the land holding farmers criticise the scheme on the grounds that now labour is not available for agriculture work and that the wage rates of landless labour have been pushed up by MGNREGA. This by itself is not a bad thing as payment of higher wage rates is for the betterment of the landless labour. However, the shortage of labour for agriculture work can be tackled by MGNREGA allowing labour working on the farms to be paid under the MGNREGA scheme. There may be issues in implementation but this remains one of the most important schemes of rural development and every year a massive budget is allotted to it.

National Rural Livelihood Mission (NRLM)

This mission focuses on providing livelihood opportunities to the poor living in the villages and is a successor to the earlier schemes of creating self help groups of women as viable economic units. NRLM is a major anti-poverty measure and calls for great imagination and leadership from the district officer and his team to implement it properly. Self help groups of women are formed through a process of awareness generation followed by selection and then these groups are given training in various skills and traits and then encouraged to take up income generating works with bank finance wherever necessary. If this scheme is left to village Development Officers or Panchayat secretaries to implement then this would languish into meaningless meeting of targets without making any dent on poverty. This requires immense communication skills to communicate with the women groups and motivate them into evolving and developing their own sources of livelihood. A Collector who is skilled in working with people can make a big difference to the quality of the implementation of this vital program. It must be understood that this implementation has to be done on a mission mode and at the state level there is a mission director coordinating all such efforts.

Pradhan Mantri Awas Yojna (PMAY)

The government of India has declared that housing for all will be provided by 2022. This is an extremely ambitious and important scheme and rural houses are being constructed on a massive scale. More than Rs 2 lakh are made available for each house which has being designed to have 1 room, 1 kitchen and 1 bathroom. This scheme has changed the entire landscape of rural India as the mud houses have been replaced by brick and mortar houses. Different states have been implementing their own version of this scheme. For instance, in UP we implemented the Lohia Awas Scheme whereby more than Rs 3 lakhs were made available to each house where there was a provision for 2 rooms, solar lighting and the floor was also finished and given. The District Officer and CDO play a major role in monitoring this scheme to ensure that the right beneficiaries are selected and the funds are released on time. The quality of the construction also has to be constantly reviewed. Some Collectors have used their ingenuity and created colonies of PMAY houses with all basic facilities of drinking water sanitation and lighting.

Pradhan Mantri Gram Sadak Yojna (PMGSY)

For several years linking habitation to main roads has been a thrust area with the governments. The current PMGSY scheme carries this further. Initially all habitations above the population of 1000 were saturated; then habitations having population between 500-1000 were taken up followed by villages between 250-500 population. Currently, it is the last segment which is being focused on as habitations above 500 populations have mostly been covered. This scheme is an important contributor to the development of villages as it allows their agriculture produce to reach the market and also access to help and educational facilities. Normally, a large number of agencies in a state are involved in construction of these roads and it is important for the Collector to have a regular review with all the agencies to ensure that there is no overlap or duplication and that the roads are constructed within the prescribed time schedule and are also of a good quality. The quality of implementation is of the utmost importance and this is where an efficient District Officer can make a huge difference.

Swatch Bharat Mission (SBM)

One of the greatest success stories of the recent past has been the declaration of India as Open Defecation Free (ODF) on 2nd October, 2019. This was the result of a tremendous political will behind this programme personally led by the Prime Minister of the country who announced his vision in the year 2014. From 2014-2019 Government of India launched a major initiative for construction of toilets, bringing about behavioural change to make people use toilets and create a general environment of clean sanitation. The District Officer was the key figure in this and it was through his rigorous monitoring that the targets were achieved and a transformation brought about. This success story only shows how strong leadership at the level of the district officer can create wonders. The second phase of this ODF movement is now in the process which aims to stabilise the gains of the first phase and make sure that people do not lapse back into the earlier habits. Sustainability of this behaviour change is very important and the Collector and his team have to play a major role in this.

Drinking Water

Rural drinking water projects have been implemented for quite some time but still the position cannot be called satisfactory both in terms of quantity and quality. As a Collector we would find that whenever you visit a village one major demand is for more hand-pumps to be installed which clearly shows how closely this availability of water is linked to the lives of the people. My experience has been that whenever I visit a village as a Collector I found that even though hand-pumps have been provided they are often located near the residence of the Pradhaan or other influential people in the village. This is nothing else but a reflection of the unequal power structure prevailing in the villages and if the Collector and his team are not alert the poorer section of the population would be deprived of drinking water near their place of stay. This becomes all the more urgent with the coming of summer when hand-pumps dry up or become defective and the demand for water goes up. Especially in times of drought this is a major concern. The Collector has to monitor the situation regarding each and every hand-pump and also provide water through tankers to remote villages where adequate amount of hand-pumps or piped water is not available. Ideally we should aim for providing piped water supply to villages. Numerous such schemes were taken up in UP but they did not succeed as the power supply in the rural areas was poor and erratic and also in mutli-village schemes the inter- village rivalry would lead to damaging of water pipes so that the water reached only a small percentage of the target villages. Recently, the Prime Minister of India has launched a drinking water mission with the objective of providing drinking water on taps to each and every household in the rural area. A similar high profile programme was implemented recently in Telengana. This initiative will require a lot of resources and mission mode implementation to make it a reality. The experience gained from the SBM programme would be very useful for the Collector and other officers and their role once again shall be vital to the proper implementation of this ambitious scheme.

An acute problem threatening the health of the common citizen is the presence of arsenic or fluoride or heavy metals in the drinking water available in the villages. The Collectors of districts where such problems are endemic have their hands full in identifying the problem areas and carrying out remedial measures to see that toxic water does not impact adversely the health of the citizens. Regular inspections, checking of quality and timely decisions would need the attention of the Collector. It cannot be just left to the discretion of the water supply agencies. In any case now that the will at the highest level of the Prime Minister is behind the Jal Jeevan Mission we can expect that by the target date of 2024 each rural household would be having tap water which will be a great blessing for the women of households who have to walk several miles to get water for the families.

Irrigation

Water for irrigation is another area of concern for the Collector. The farmers are very disturbed if they do not get adequate water at the right time to irrigate their crops. There are state tubewells in most districts but often many of them are out of order due to electrical or mechanical defects. The Collector has to regularly monitor and see that these tubewells do not remain out of order for long periods and rectification of defects takes place on priority. In UP, the private tubewells contribute the maximum to the irrigation potential available. The utility of this is greatly dependent upon the power supply which has shown definite signs of improvement over the years. In the absence of reliable power supply the farmers tend to use generators which increases the cost of production as such dispersible. Nowadays, the solar energy power water pumps are a viable alternative as they get huge subsidy from the government. This programme must attract the attention of the Collector.

There are states where sources of irrigation are less than 40% and agriculture is mostly rain fed. In UP also the Bundelkhand region is one such area. Watershed programmes and check dams to hold rain water and channelize it for irrigation acquire a lot of importance. Watershed development programmes are based on the principle of convergence and are complex in nature.

The Collector will have to lead from the front to make them successful otherwise funds would just go down the drain.

Even where canal irrigation is available there is an issue of water not reaching the actual field of the farmers. Every year there is a major exercise done to clean the canals to make sure that irrigation water reaches up to the tail end. The District Officer has to physically inspect the villages which lie in the tail and also make sure that nobody on the way is involved in cutting the canal to serve their own selfish interests. There is always a big gap between the irrigation potential created and utilized. Drains have to be constructed to connect the canal with the fields of the farmers. This is known as developing the command area of a canal system which is vital to improve the agriculture productivity of the area. The district officer has a major role to play in this. In the current scheme water use efficiency has become vital as the water sources are fast drying up. Each drop matters and there is a Government of India scheme which aims to utilize every drop of water. At the moment in most states they are not aware that water is a scarce resource and the farmers are growing water guzzling crops and are just flooding the fields with water even though much less water is required. The potential of drip irrigation and sprinkler irrigation has not been properly explored. Not only is water being wasted but fertility of the soil is also being eroded. The Collector as the leader can hold village level meeting to sensitize the farmer about conserving water and using it productively and economically. Another major problem regarding water is the fast depletion of the ground water in most states and more and more villages and blocks are being declared as over exploited or critical. Once again the Collector can use his leadership and convince the farmers about the situation and also converge funds from various schemes to carry out rain water harvesting and similar schemes.

Recently the Government of India has decided to launch a people's movement to "Catch the rain". The idea is to see that rain water which comes in abundance during monsoon is conserved to recharge the ground water and make water available for irrigation and drinking water purposes.

Agriculture

India is a pre-dominantly agricultural economy. UP has 25% of its gross state domestic product (GSDP) coming from this sector and with over 60% of the population subsisting on agriculture. Similar is the situation in most states. Removal of poverty is not possible without improving the productivity in agriculture and ensuring that the farmer gets a good price for his produce. The scenario in agriculture has changed over the years and the problem is less with input management and more about storage and marketing. In the days when I served as a Collector we used to be tasked with provision of seeds, fertilizer, water, credit and other inputs. There normally used to be a shortage of these inputs and especially in the case of fertilizers there was always the risk of black marketing and hoarding which the Collector and his team had to prevent by carrying out raids, inspections and developing systems to ensure proper distribution.

Regarding getting adequate price for the produce the farmer has to try and take the benefit of the government fixed minimum support price (MSP) for wheat, rice and about 20 other commodities. The major procurement operations take place for wheat and paddy especially in states like Punjab, Haryana, Western UP, MP, Telengana and some other states. In these states the successful operation of these procurement activities depends entirely on the leadership of the Collector. It is the Collector who decides the location and number of procurement centres to be opened in his district so that a farmer does not have to travel large distances to sell his produce. Then arrangement for staff and essential weighing and other equipments has to be made. The Collector has to ensure a regular supply of gunny bags and funds at the procurement centres. Further, storage has also to be taken care of. All this requires a very high level of field level monitoring to see that there is no corruption in the process and the actual gains reach the farmer rather than the middle men. It would not be an exaggeration to say that entire food security system depends upon how well Collectors handle the procurement operations. The district administration also supervises the working of the *mandis* where the farmers come to sell their produce. The *mandi* committees are expected to be elected but are often superseded and the charge is directly with the district administration. An innovative District Officer can really make the *mandi* a vibrant market place where sorting, grading and cleaning and value addition activities are carried out to give the farmer high return for his produce.

The income of the farmers can be further enhanced by supplementing normal agriculture activity by animal husbandry. Dairy is the biggest money earner for the farmer and the District Officer can once again play a major role in improving the breed of the animals in his district through artificial insemination and provision of adequate food and veterinary care for the animals. Then again the farmer has to get a proper price for his milk which has to be chilled, transported and value added. The Amul model is a classic example of this. A bright Collector can make the entire chain work leading to a subtle revolution in the incomes of the farmers. Same is true in sectors like poultry and fisheries where the Collector can coordinate with the banks to make loans available to farmers who have the entrepreneurial spirit and want to do something big.

Banks

Banks are an important source of development if they can provide finance to the right people at the right time. The kisan credit card (KCC) is the mechanism to see that the farmer gets credit in the right quantity and in a timely manner. The Collector has to coordinate with all the banks to ensure that KCC of all the farmers in his district are prepared. He also has to see that banks give loans to various beneficiaries of Government development schemes. There is a district level coordination committee where the District Officer and the lead manager from the side of the banks review bank finance to agriculture and rural development activities.

Many backward states have a very poor credit deposit ratio and the Collector must motivate the bank to lend more against the projects at the district level. He can also help in the preparation of viable and bankable projects. A couple of years ago the Prime Minister of India introduced the Jandhan Yojna with the objective of opening of banks accounts of maximum number of people. The idea has been to bring about financial inclusion which is a necessary ingredient of development. It has been seen that the response of bank depends largely on the dynamism of the Collector and his ability to coordinate and persuade. The Collector must cooperate with the banks by helping them realizing their bank dues through the revenue collection powers vested in the Collector.

Education

We can reap the demographic dividend that India can only if we can provide good quality of education to the youth. Unfortunately, in rural area the quality of government schools and colleges is generally very poor and churn out students who can merely join the army of educated unemployed and also give expression to their energies in crime, goondaism etc. Almost every village has a primary school. The government provides a lot of facilities but there are gaps in implementation. The Collector must visit the schools to understand the problems and also try and find solutions. A good Collector must develop a system to monitor the mid-day meal scheme and provision of free text books and uniforms. He must ensure that the school management committees function properly and that the village teachers are involved in teaching. Teacher absenteeism can be controlled by a vigilant Collector. These by itself give a big signal to the teaching community and the students. A Collector should inspect as many schools as possible to assess the learning outcome of the children. Inspections by the Collector and his team must focus on making the children read texts or solve problems in arithmetic. A very important duty of the Collector is to conduct the Board level examinations in such a manner that no cheating or malpractices take places. The Collector has to lead from the front to make this happen as he has to take up cudgels against the very organized and powerful education mafia. It is my opinion that education must definitely be one of the priority areas for a Collector.

Health

The delivery of health services to the people is another very important area of concern for the Collector. The Chief Medical Officer (CMO) is the head of the health administration in the district but a vast difference can be made if the Collector is involved with the functioning of the district hospital. Occasional inspections can improve the cleanliness, sanitation, hygiene and patient facilities. The government gives free medicines and treatment from its government hospital but certain doctors indulge in foul play and lure the patients into nursing homes where they have an interest and tell them that medicines are not available in the hospital pushing the patients to the chemist shops in the periphery of the hospital. Needless to say there is a monetary angle to all this. It is incumbent upon the Collector to see that these malpractices are curbed and free and adequate healthcare provided to the people.

There are numerous schemes of the health department especially those concerned with maternal and child care, eradication of T.B. and other diseases. The intervention of the Collector leads to better quality of implementation. An example of this has been the eradication of polio through pulse polio campaign which was spearheaded by the Collectors in the districts.

There is also this unique problem of doctor absenteeism especially in the primary health centres (PHC). The facility in the PHC's are poor and the situation is compounded by doctors just not turning up. The Collector and his team can inspect and monitor and bring about significant improvements in the health services provided to the poor. It was a district collector Indore in MP who took initiative in forming Rogi Kalian Samities (RKS) where he involved the citizens, the user of the hospital services, prominent people of the district along with the doctors to raise funds for the hospital and deploy the fund in improving the infrastructure provided. The district hospital was transformed and RKS entered the lexicon of Government of India policy on health. The national health mission which was initially called NRHM (National Rural Health Mission) is a major initiative of the government of India to revolutionize health care by communitising the services and managing things in a mission mode. The Collector has a major role to play as a chief coordinator of the project at the district level. The recruitment of doctors and other hospital staff is done on a contract basis by a committee chaired by the Collector. NRHM gives a tremendous opportunity to improve the quality of health services being provided. It has led to significant reduction in the infant and maternal mortality rates and also creating the important institution of ASHA–the community health worker.

Many backward or aspirational districts suffer from scourge of malnutrition. The Collector must lead from the front in implementing the nutrition mission and it must be his goal to eliminate or greatly reduce the incidence of nutrition deficiency in his district. To achieve this he has to use his ingenuity to converge the funds from the schemes of health, nutrition and sanitation departments.

Industry and Infrastructure

Industrial development is a subject generally in the domain of the State Secretariat but the Collector can make a dent by looking after the existing industry in the district and also identifying land and proposing new industry. He can contribute by making land available for industry and solving the problem of the business and industry people through a district level empowered committee working under him. The Collector must be concerned with the development of infrastructure in his district. He has to assess the condition of roads, new roads being constructed, new buildings being built and maintenance of roads and building infrastructure. He has to provide the right kind of leadership to the public works department (PWD) in this respect. He must not forget that roads are a visible indicator of the status of development and quality of administration in a district. I personally had the experience of constructing the Lucknow-Agra expressway (328 km.) in a record time of 22 months and this was made possible only because the Collectors rose to the occasion and acquired the land from the farmers through negotiations in the stipulated time period without any dispute. Land acquisition is a very important job of the Collector to enable fast implementation of industrial and infrastructure projects. The Collector plays a very important role in power supply also. The people in a district can get extremely agitated if there is a break down in power supply and it often leads to law and order disturbances. I recall my baptism by fire on joining as DM Agra and being kept awake the very first night as my residence was gheraoed by irate citizens in whose area the power supply had failed. The Collector has to take up power supply issues with the state government on behalf of the citizens. The situation has considerably improved nowadays with better power supply in rural and urban areas.

Urban Development

Urban development in big cities is in the domain of the municipal commissioner but in small town and semi-urban district headquarters the problems of the city are also the responsibility of the Collector. This is more pronounced when an elected body is suspended but remains relevant even if the elected local government is in place. The garbage cleaning and disposal, water supply, sewer system, drainage, city roads and lanes are issues that confront the collector. Taking concrete action to prevent air and water pollution is also assuming a major significance and the Collector cannot ignore it.

Social Welfare

There are a large number of social welfare schemes like old age pension, widow pension and disability pension as well as provision of scholarships to students which the Collector has to monitor at his level. He has to see that all eligible get the benefit of these schemes and that the money is transferred regularly to their accounts without there being any leakage. The schemes are for the poorest of the poor and maladministration in their implementation amounts to sacrilege. A vigilant District Officer can directly benefit the poor through the schemes.

The above list of development programmes is merely indicative and there are various schemes and projects that a Collector has to coordinate and implement through his leadership. The pressure on the Collector is huge and he will have to prioritize amongst the various schemes. To a large extent this prioritization will be decided by the nature and circumstances of the district. It is a tribute to the dynamism of the Collectors that despite being loaded with the responsibility of so many state level schemes they still find time and energy to innovate and come out with their own initiatives for the district.

Quality of Implementation

It is extremely important for the Collector to see that all schemes are implemented in a manner that the actual benefits reach the people. He should go in for third party evaluation of the schemes to ensure quality. I also feel there should be a system of concurrent evaluation operating throughout the year. It could even be done by an independent body like the State Planning Institute. It should be made clear that wherever major discrepancies are found the physical performance reported by the district should not be accepted. In fact, it should be treated as a negative point and district level officers held accountable. It is only when an officer realizes that his annual performance depends upon the quality of implementation that things shall improve.

There is no substitute for physical verification and stress on quality at the district level. The planning input has to be given by the Collector and his CDO. They must, then, guide the concerned officers and tell them clearly what is expected of them. It is this thinking part which is missing in the implementation of projects and schemes. The objective is lost sight of in the maze of targets.

Inspection by the Collector, CDO and other district level officers and SDM should be specific and purposeful. A study was done by Director of Mussoorie Academy and it was found that Collectors gave only 15% of their time to development work. One can imagine the almost negligible amount of quality checks being made by him. The same is true for CDO and even BDO. Everybody has become a staff officer; the line functions being exercised only by the village level officer. True development is only possible if these officers leave their desks and travel in the fields.

This culture of inspection has become almost negligible in the case of technical departments. It is rare to see a Jal Nigam Officer inspecting hand pumps or tubewell department person visiting the villages to oversee the functioning of tubewells. The main problem is that even the lower level officers like SDO or JE who are posted at tehsil and block headquarters do not stay there and are rarely available. The people cannot meet them with their grievances. This creates a situation of low quality of output and poor response to public aspirations. The answer is that the departmental heads must rigorously monitor the field work done by their subordinates. Random checks by superiors and action against defaulters can make a success of this.

The extent to which programmes can be properly monitored also depends upon the support that a Collector has in terms of trained and qualified staff. Many works can be properly verified by a technical person. It may not be a bad idea to attach an Executive Engineer rank officer with a technical team to the DRDA. This technical wing should work directly under the Collector and CDO. They should check estimates and also assist the Collector in physical verification.

The second important thing is to have outstanding officers of various departments come on deputation to DRDA. Better service conditions and higher pay, etc. can be offered as an incentive. This apart, we have to change the attitude of the concerned officers and equip them with proper tools. Officers like PD, DDO, BDO and others should be trained thoroughly in subjects like project appraisal. Their orientation has to be done to get them up to perform as agents of economic development.

We have seen that multifarious departments are involved in the development process. Most of them are not under the direct control of the Collector. The power that the Collector exercises is only because the funds are routed through him and, secondly, everyone has to depend upon the Collector for law and order and security support.

The amount of coordination that a Collector has with technical departments and the leadership he can provide to them is purely a question of man-management. There was one Collector who, while addressing a development meeting, found that an executive engineer of a department was missing. He was contacted and found sitting comfortably in his office. On being called he came but was extremely arrogant. The Collector lost his cool and asked him to behave or get out. The engineer walked out. The Collector fumed, dictated a strong letter to the Secretary. Nothing came out of it. Here the message is clear. The Collector is a lonely person. He is not likely to get any support from top. He has thus to get work done without getting into a situation like the above because ultimately he is the loser.

At the same time, certain Collectors start with the presumption that they are very honest and all the engineers are corrupt. I have seen a Collector literally poke his finger into the fat, protruding belly of a PWD engineer and telling him in front of all officers that he knew how he had filled his belly with ill-gotten money. Naturally there was a tremendous wave of resentment and the Collector lost the support of all the technical officers.

The Collector must behave in a mature manner. He should not personalize matters. At the same time he must insist on information about programmes from all these officers. He should also inspect their works and take them, along with him. He can always control these departments by getting information about them from the public. His daily visitors would give him sufficient knowledge which can be a powerful tool in his hands.

He has, thus, to control technical departments with knowledge, information, tact and using skills of man-management.

Still the above arrangement is not satisfactory. To get proper results some authority has to be given to the district officer over all the line departments. Least that can be done is to have the Collector give his annual remarks about all the officers concerned with development, and these remarks should be made a part of the officer's annual report.

Zila Parishad, Kshetra Samiti and Panchayati Raj

A structure for democratic control over the process of development exists, but in UP it is not very effective at the moment. Basically, there are three tiers–the village Panchayat, the Kshetra Samiti (block development committee) and the Zila Parishad.

The village Panchayat exists but it is in effect a one man show. It is dominated by the Pradhan. The current state of affairs is such that social disparities, inequalities and stratification dominate the village power structure. The Pradhan is the representative of this phenomenon. The other members of the Panchayat are silent and it is the Pradhan whose writ runs large at the village level. The role of the Pradhan and the village Panchayat has increased significantly over the last few decades. A lot of funds from various development schemes devolve directly to the village Panchayat. The central and state finance commission funds are also allocated to the village Panchayat. A lot of development at the village level can be done by the Pradhan and almost all the assets can be maintained by these funds. This has also created a situation where the post of the Pradhan is bitterly contested and there are a lot of cases of corruption at the level of the Pradhan. The Collector has to intervene by taking action against the Pradhan and also getting enquiries conducted. Despite this anomaly this is a welcome trend as the village Panchayat is in the best position to handle local development issues.

The Kshetra Samiti has the block Pramukh as chairman and all Pradhans and all departments as members. I felt that this samiti which meets once in a three months can be a very effective tool for control over the development process by the representatives of people. Though the meetings are held, their utility is almost negligible. Except for the BDO and some officers the other officers choose to stay away from these meetings. The crucial issues are that of power, irrigation, drinking water and roads. It is these departments which tend to avoid the BDC. The net result is that the Pradhans shout amongst themselves, some resolutions are passed and the matter ends. If the Collector can attend some meetings himself there would be a sea change. Departmental officers would follow. Even where the.Collector does not go he can have the attendance monitored and take up the issues strongly. I have experienced that this has an impact and officers attend BDCs. If only this much is achieved then accountability of officers results and they have to be more careful about their performance. This tier has become more irrelevant as no funds of any development scheme are devolved directly on them. Their role is merely supervisory.

But even if the BDC is well attended it loses its significance as its resolutions are rarely acted upon. These resolutions are sent to officers and the Zila Parishad. The Zila Parishad is not having any resources or powers to deal with these resolutions. They just fall. By the way, the interesting thing is that Pradhans come up with problems of their villages in BDCs and proposals are put forward. But these proposals find no favour in DRDA or district plan meetings where funds exist. The MLAs come for these meetings and it is their projects that have to be taken up. The MLA and the Pramukh or even a section of Pradhans do not see eye to eye–the resolutions of BDCs fail to become the basis of allocation of resources. As such the

BDC feels that it is a useless body and the officers also give less importance to it.

The Zila Parishad in UP has acquired a lot of financial and administrative powers after the amendments in the constitution. Currently the chairman of Zila Parishad has been made the chairman of the district planning committee and also plays a very important role in all rural development schemes.

What kind of a structure should there be for implementation of development? An alternative to the current approach is the vesting of power and authority in the Zila Parishad and make the three-tier structure a reality. This has been done in many states like Karnataka and Maharashtra. With the passing of the Panchayat Raj Amendment this pattern shall come into being everywhere. Actual delegation of financial powers and authority down to the village Panchayat level shall take place. Bureaucrats tend to be cynical of this. However decentralized model will give a more realistic insight into the problems of the people and give a better platform for coordination of the work of different departments and in essence give the Collector, the CDO and the BDO more powers and more control over the development process.

Development : An Alternative View

This alternative view subscribes to the idea that village should be made the unit for development. The second concept involved is that the impetus for development must come from the village itself. Rather than being dependent upon the government for everything, the village becomes self-reliant.

An experiment along this line was done by author. Some villages in a block were selected at random. Groups were formed from amongst people of the villages. These groups were given an orientation at the block level and then sent to these villages to prepare a plan for their development. After spending four days in the village each group came back and made a presentation. It was amazing how well the problems had been brought out and concrete solutions suggested. All that was required was devolution of funds to the village accordingly.

There is enough wisdom and awareness at the village level. They just need to be guided, to be involved and to be given some sense of control over their state of affairs. The government can act as the guide. Members of the village Panchayat can be trained at the block level and then asked to go back to the village and prepare a development plan of the village. Each village plan would have small things like minor repairs of school building, repairing of hand pumps, etc. for this the funds would be given directly to the Panchayat. There may be other needs which involve substantial money. These can be put forward before the Kshetra Samiti and after prioritization moved up to the Zila Parishad. At that level the allocation of funds under DRDA and District Plan can be made on those schemes. If this methodology is followed then development having an impact at the village level shall take place. Of course, certain amount of money can be left separately for things like inter-village roads or schemes covering more than one village.

Assets like roads, tubewells, schools and hand pumps should be erected and then handed over to the village community for operation and maintenance. A good example of this can be the state tubewells. There are persistent complaints about operators missing, tubewells out of order, etc. These can be avoided if the village community is made responsible for the running and maintenance. Same also with hand pumps even if there is one small problem the villagers have to wait for the Jal Nigam mechanic for weeks. Why can not the repairs be undertaken by the village Panchayat itself? Lots of mechanics have sprung up in remote areas. Further under various training programmes young people can be trained in the technique of hand pump maintenance. In fact, in district Banda, UP women hand pump mechanics have been trained and they are comfortably repairing their village hand pumps.

The same applies also to the village schools and roads. Funds are available with the village Panchayat and they should carry out regular and routine maintenance. A much better management of assets can be ensured this way.

Apart from maintenance, the village community should also look after its schools, child development centres and healthcare centres. A perennial problem in primary school is that teachers don't come. It is the responsibility of education officers to check but they cannot be present everywhere. In one district I found that the attendance was as low as 40%. A month long drive was launched involving SDMs, BDOs and other officers. Those found absent were severely punished. The attendance percentage went up to 90%. However, this continuous checking by everyone is difficult to sustain as there are so many other things to be done. If a committee of elders or the village education committee actively participates and checks not only attendance but the quality of teaching also then things are bound to improve. Of course, some authority would have to be given to these committees. For instance, if they complain against a teacher immediate action would be necessary. Similarly, the village should participate in the functioning of ICDS centres, stockman centres and health care centres.

This thought has been taken up, conceptualized and institutionalized by a programme known as community based convergence services which is in operation in selected districts. I feel that if the approach of this programme is taken up and adopted for all villages, a significant new direction shall be given to rural development.

The focal point of rural development is the poor in the village and no rural development can be said to be successful if it does not lead to social and economic development of the poor and under privileged class. But it is precisely these people who are not involved in thinking about their own development. They do not inculcate the culture of self-help but instead get the attitude of looking up to the government for alms. This state of affairs is most unsatisfactory and can never lead to the process of self-generating development.

It is in the above context that the proposed amendment in the Constitution regarding Panchayati Raj gains significance. It basically aims at constitutional guarantee for timely elections, reservation of scheduled castes/tribes and women and setting up of a finance commission in the states to ensure that Panchayati Raj Institutions have an assured command over adequate resources.

The bill provided for, among other things, a gram sabha in each village, constitution of Panchayats at village and direct, election to all seats in the Panchayat and Zila Parishad. It provides for reservation for SC/ST in proportion to their population and reservation of not less than one third of seats for women.

It also provides for conferring powers and authority, (including the power to levy, collect and appropriate taxes, duties, tolls and fees on local authorities) and holding elections within a period of six months in the event of supercession of any such authority.

These provisions and this reconstitution of Panchayati Raj shall make it a reality as opposed to the myth that it is today. A true representative body shall come up at the village level which shall be equipped with resources to solve their problems. Democratic decentralization shall truly filter down to the grass root level. Undoubtedly, this shall go a long way in ensuring people's participation in the poverty alleviation programmes. Strong institutions are essential for sustainable development. They require sound management, motivated people and an enabling environment of appropriate policies, legislation and incentives.

But all this shall come to naught if the village power structure does not change. A select few who are dominant socially and economically shall continue to dictate terms and corner all fruits of power. The District Officer has an important role to play here. He can act as an agent of social change and facilitate the functioning of Panchayati Raj in a manner to see that interests of all are represented.

However, the DM cannot achieve this goal by merely using his official team. He has to take the support of non-governmental organizations. The NGOs can certainly assist the Collector in improving the efficiency and expansion of service delivery. In any district there exist a number of voluntary agencies. Some are dedicated while others are not. However, many Collectors make the mistake of starting by considering them all as corrupt and taking action against them. He has to use his discretion and the moment he is convinced that a particular voluntary agency is good and sincere he should give it all his support. The role of NGOs should be acknowledged and strengthened. NGOs are able to experiment with innovative approaches. The government should make them partners. In particular the NGOs can do tremendous work in the spheres of education and public awareness.

The important thing is to make the people think for themselves. But years of deprivation have made them immobile. They have to be brought out of their shells. It is necessary to take people from the villages and train them. This training has to bring about a change in their attitude and behaviour. Voluntary agencies can do a great deal towards this provided they have the support of the collector.

In one district an NGO had tried an experiment in self-help which was really praiseworthy. They selected 20 villages, held meetings in these villages and formed a committee in each village for attending to their own problems. This committee consisted of able-bodied men and women in the village. Now these village groups adopted a policy that each individual shall deposit a fixed percentage of his earnings into a common pool. This being done it ensured that funds were available at village level. Then this group would meet and discuss how to spend this money. Small community problems were tackled by them in this manner. They did not have to look towards the government for everything. Whatever it achieved it made these people aware of their potential and instilled in them an attitude of self-help.

The Collector, by virtue of his position is a leader and it is not difficult for him to make people follow him. I recall the case of a village in district 'A' which had a very enlightened Pradhan. He wanted to construct roads and drains in his village. He approached me with this proposal. I told him that I did not have the funds for this but he promised to help. A few weeks later I was invited to the village. The villagers had got down to work and had cleared encroachments themselves and done the earth work on the roads. I promptly released funds for bricks, and this village became the first one in the district with every lane having a proper brick road. All this was achieved because the government and people worked together for their development.

A crucial issue in development is that of integration. A plethora of departments are implementing different schemes–as many as 18 field level officials visit the village for their departmental schemes. Many of these projects are inter-related. The ICDS scheme wants to give nutritious food to children. Should they thus be handled differently from health-care? This segmentation leads to confusion and a tendency for departmentalization. The requirement is cohesion and integration.

The need of the hour is integration. All related sources should preferably come together. However, the trend in government is just the opposite–departmentalism has come to the fore. Each scheme is now being looked after by a different director or secretary. At the district level the CDO has been divested of many of his powers. The BDO has nothing to do with programmes of education and healthcare.

The human being has to become the focus of development and all programmes designed to improve the human resources must be integrated. At the government level their policy planning can be done together taking into account the inter-relationships and linkages. The Collector will have to be given more authority over departments at district level to bring about proper integration. However, till the village committee, the block committee and the district board start functioning properly, real integration shall not take place. It is the users who sees the linkages best and will demand accordingly. Cohesion amongst government agencies shall be the result.

Corruption

Before one ends this discussion of development administration one will have to mention the biggest stumbling block–corruption. This is the bane of all development. There is no resource crunch but vested groups are siphoning off these funds. Development initially centered on extension. However, once that changed and sanctioning of schemes, giving of loans and subsidy started the whole system got involved in taking their share. The beneficiary, the government officer and the banker are all getting involved. Still, not everyone is corrupt but this phenomenon is spreading.

The best way out for the District Officer is to make everything open–to inform people about what money has come and how it is going to be spent. On each PMGSY road a board should be put up indicating funds allotted, name of agency, length and other details of the proposed road. This will encourage people to check for themselves and report if they find any discrepancies. The answer to corruption is to give maximum information to people.

Transparency and openness

There is no short-cut to inspection and rigorous checking by senior officers. This should be a mixture of planned and random checks. Wherever corruption comes to light exemplary punishment should be meted out. This should act as a deterrent.

Finally as people start becoming responsible and participants in the development process, corruption can also be checked. It is only when the power is in the hands of a few that corruption comes up in a big way.

Development administration is the most rewarding aspect of a Collector's job. He can plan, implement, inspect and see results for himself. This part of his job gives him the maximum job satisfaction. There is still enough scope for the Collector to assess the needs of his area and come out with schemes and projects. He can use his creativity. He should involve the people to the maximum extent. The people are the source of his information as well as knowledge. In the present set up it depends entirely upon the Collector to provide leadership and direction to development programmes.

Revenue Administration

The word Collector implies a person who is entrusted with the job of collecting money for the state. Land revenue, in earlier years, used to be one of the basic sources of state finance. A system of codification, recording, surveying and management of land was required to properly assess and collect land revenue. This formed the nucleus of revenue administration.

Today, land revenue had ceased to be of much significance. But the importance of revenue administration continues. To collect revenue, detailed record of rights was maintained. The revenue agencies represented by the Tehsildar, Naib Tehsildar, Supervisor, Qanungo and Lekhpal (Patwari) had to tour villages intensively to have information about each and every piece of land, its nature and the crop sown in it. This makes revenue agency the one group of people who have maximum contact with the people living in the village and since they manage land they have the maximum clout also. It is for this reason that the importance of revenue administration has not declined. This is why revenue agency is the most effective in conducting elections, census operations, collecting statistics of agriculture production, implementing land reforms and handling natural calamities.

This is one area of administration where the Collector has supreme powers–over the years, the Collector has been loaded with so much work that he requires a large number of additional

Collectors to help him discharge his duties. In a district, thus you would have Additional Collector (Executive), Additional Collector (Finance & Revenue) and so on. A big district like Agra or Allahabad has as many as nine Additional Collectors or ADM's assisting the Collector. The post of a Chief Revenue Officer has also been created for some districts which shoulders the Collector's burden of case work and looks after revenue establishment.

The next significant functionary is the Tehsildar. Interestingly, the word Tehsildar means the same as Collector. The tehsil is the basic unit of revenue administration. In UP the tehsil is coterminous with sub-division. With the insistence on sub-divisional magistrate (SDM) staying in tehsils the power of the Tehsildar has been greatly reduced. In fact, today SDO is working almost like the Tehsildar and people go to him for the slightest grievance. This may be a drawback but it is in accordance with the spirit of decentralization and the presence of SDM means that people have access to a significantly senior officer at the tehsil level. Naturally, staying in the tehsil reduces the glamour of the SDM (Deputy *sahib* as he is called). So many deputy Collectors lament that in the days gone by the SDO used to come to the tehsil for inspection and it used to be a major event with the tehsil putting in its best for him. But now the tehsil staff just takes the SDO easy. He is one of them and little importance is attached to the inspections and directions of the SDO. However, the truth of the matter is that this trend cannot be reversed and it must be admitted that despite weakening the Tehsildar the presence of SDO at the tehsil level is an important step in the decentralization of administration.

Revenue Court work

Disputes relating to title, possession and demarcation etc. of agricultural land come up before the revenue courts. This is one of the most demanding parts of a revenue officer's work and gives him tremendous power over the basic issue of sustenance of rural India–land.

I recall when I was a probationer and wanted to learn court work, an 'experienced' sub-divisional officer took me aside and told me that I should not bother about court work. It does not make news; it is dull and involves a lot of hard work but makes no impact on the people. He told me that as SDO or Collector I would be better off spending my time checking fair price shops and lodging reports against offenders. This would be flashed in newspapers and earn me a reputation whereas no newspaper shall ever cover the number of cases done by you.

One should not blame him for he was telling the truth. Many revenue officers subscribe to this doctrine. However, I feel that such officers are not able to view their assignment in its totality. Court work is certainly less glamorous but it is the real source of strength of a revenue officer. It is his basic job and brings him in close contact with his people. He also gets to know how land records are being maintained and his knowledge about revenue administration is constantly replenished. It is not the job of an officer to work for news in the press. He has to be anonymous, quiet but efficient. Court work, thus, is the most important part of the work of Tehsildar, SDO and even the Collector and should never be ignored.

The Tehsildar decides cases of mutation and encroachment on gaon sabha (village community land) the SDO decides title. The appeal from the court of SDO goes to the Commissioner and the final appellate authority is the board of revenue. Pendency of cases is monitored at all levels yet even a cursory look at the figures would show that the number of cases does not go down. In fact, the most disturbing thing is that cases are being kept pending for years for no reason. I recall a case which came before my court as Collector which had been pending for six years merely on a matter of substitution application which needed exactly two minutes for disposal.

The Collector does not have much time for court work and it is normally the Chief Revenue Officer or Additional Collector who handles his court work. Still most Collectors do have court for one or two days in a week. Cases of transfer from one court to another are moved before the Collector. The District Officer can show by example the importance that he attaches to court work. If he makes it a point to attend to his court then the signal goes down and his subordinate offices also attend their courts. This is the basic thing–if an officer gives time to court work then the number of disposals would automatically go up.

During inspection of subordinate courts a cursory perusal of any file would show that in majority of the court days it is written in the order sheet that the presiding officer is busy with administrative duties. This makes the control of the officer slack over his court and the person who suffers is the litigant. It is this state of affairs which has given rise to speculation about concept of having two revenue officers at sub-divisional level. One of them shall exclusively deal with court. However, this would create administrative problems and also lessen the authority of the sub-divisional officer. Still it cannot be argued that administrative work has increased and in a sub-division where there are large numbers of cases it is necessary to provide some support. Normally, there are a few deputy collectors available at the district headquarter. They can be made additional SDOs and a portion of case work transferred to them. Still there is no alternative to priority being given to court work by the SDO and Tehsildar. The court work of Tehsildar is, of course, shared by his Naib Tehsildars.

Every month in the Collector's staff meeting the case work of various courts is monitored. It is best to look at the following aspects:

(i) Disposal as a proportion of institution of cases–the former should be higher.

(ii) The ratio of cases of more than six months pendency to the total pendency–this ratio must go down.

(iii) Proportion of cases disposal on merit to total disposal.

(iv) A review of the oldest pending cases.

Jugglery of figures is resorted to by the courts to put up a bright picture. Many courts do not institute a case till it is ripe for decision. Many courts dismiss a large number of cases in default to boost up their figure. The only way out is rigorous inspection of courts by senior officers. Case files should be taken at random and perused. This gives a very good idea of what is happening in the court.

Various reasons are advanced by officers for long pendency of cases. The commonest reason is that lawyers do not cooperate; they always want adjournments and go on strike at the slightest opportunity–to a certain extent this is true but not entirely. It is a fact that there are frequent strikes. It is also true that adjournment is sought. However, they also see the attitude of the court. If the presiding officer chooses to absent himself from court at the slightest opportunity then he cannot expect to be tough on adjournment applications. If he is himself present on maximum court days and shows an inclination to decide cases early the advocates tend to adjust to his style.

I recall an incident when I was freshly posted as a Sub-Divisional Officer. The pendency of cases was very large. I made it a point to be at my court at 11:00 am and sit through till 2:00 pm All administrative work was taken up after this. Slowly the cases started moving but I found that a senior and respected advocate was the counsel in many of the cases. An adjournment application was always moved by his junior. I decided to be tough and started disallowing adjournments. After a few days the senior counsel appeared. He protested against my action. It transpired that he was an advocate of High Court and as such had little time for this court. I told him bluntly that the litigant in my court was as important as any other court. The senior counsel had a major complaint that the presiding officer never started court on time and rarely held court. As such the time of counsels was wasted. I told him that I would start court at 10.30 am and would take up his cases first and free him in an hour to go to the High Court. This arrangement worked efficiently. The result was that 100 revenue cases were decided on merit in one month.

The greatest satisfaction came when the same lawyer met me several years later at a social gathering. He came to me and congratulated me on the work I had done as Sub-Divisional Officer. He told everyone around that if the system worked in this manner the poor litigant would get timely justice.

The point to be emphasized is that the poor litigant is made to suffer as the cases drag on for years. He spends so much of money and time and the delay makes him lose faith in the judicial system. It is the duty of the presiding officer and lawyers both to ensure that justice is given on time. With this objective in mind the court should make a conscious effort to cut down delays in cases.

The best approach is never to allow an adjournment without an application. The application should be allowed on heavy cost unless it is a case of the counsel falling ill. A nearby date should be fixed and it should be recorded in the order sheet that no further dates shall be given. All this helps in focusing on delay and leads to pressure of the client on his lawyer and ultimately leads to speedy disposal of cases.

Old cases are complicated and there is a tendency for officers to attend to fresh cases and let the old once lie. This should be strictly monitored. Cases more than one year old should be rigorously followed up and the age old method followed is list the three oldest cases but this does not give the desired results. There is also a tendency to dismiss the oldest case in default and then restore it on current date. A better approach is to take year-wise backlog of cases and monitor accordingly.

The presiding officer must handle the case diary himself. He should peruse the cases of the day and underline in red the old cases. As soon as he sits in court he should have those cases called out. If an adjournment has to be granted then it must be a very short one. In this way the pressure is built up and old cases disposed off fast.

A very annoying delaying tactic is the transfer applications moved before the Collector. Any litigant who wants to delay a matter resorts to this. There are some genuine cases where there is an apprehension about the impartiality of the court but these are few. Such applications should not be allowed to pend and if the attitude of the Collector is tough the number of transfer applications tends to go down.

Corruption in the courts is a very serious malady and should be seriously looked into by the Collector and his team. It is interesting to note that people want to be posted as Peshkars and Ahalmads (Court clerks) in courts and lobby intensively for this. I confronted a peshkar in confidence and the candidly admitted that this post meant income above the 'normal salary'.

There are two levels of corruption that take place. One is that the peshkar takes money to have a case decided in someone's favour: sometimes a middleman or an advocate may also do this. The other is the system of 'baksheesh'–the litigant tips the peshkar and chaprassi just to keep them in good humour.

I recall a case when I was Sub-Divisional Officer of a much respected lawyer meeting me in the Dak Bungalow in the evening. After speaking on general issues he came to the topic of a case which had been argued in my court during the day. I told him that I had heard the case in court and did not want to talk about it. I also informed him that I had already dictated the judgement. He then asked me to just tell him in whose favour the judgement had been passed. He did not want it to be in his favour but just wanted to know. I refused point blank and requested him to go. On inquiring into the whole episode, I found that he had taken extra money from his client saying that he would meet the SDO later and have the case decided in his favour. If the judgement was in his favour he would tell the client that he had managed it. If not, he would say that the presiding officer had taken more money from the other side.

Peshkars in the court have been known to do this also. I recall that as a SDO reading case files and dictating judgements took a lot of my time. When this news reached my superior officers, the Collector, a venerable old man called me one evening. After general enquiries he asked me point blank whether it was true that I spent a lot of my time over judgements. When I confirmed this he patted me on the back and said, judgements are written by the peshkar. You just have to indicate in whose favour you want it. I was too stunned to react. However, over the years I found that this practice was quite prevalent. Especially with Collectors who were actually hard pressed for time. But I strongly feel that this should never be done–it opens up a Pandora's Box of corruption. The peshkar would make money and the officer would get defamed. Even otherwise, dictating a judgement should be a sacred duty because as a court one has to give justice. If the peshkar was competent to do that then there would be no need for a presiding officer.

Even if the above malpractice is not resorted to, the peshkar is a powerful person who harasses litigants and makes money. He has two powers–the power to give dates and to put up a particular case at a particular time before the presiding officer.

As a young SDO I decided to root out corruption by taking way these two powers from the peshkar. I made it a point to give the dates myself and also handle the case diary personally. I use to underline the oldest cases in red and call them out first. No adjournment was to be granted in my absence. If I could not attend court due to some work I would announce a general date and have it pasted on the notice board. I even made it a point to say in open court that no client/litigant need to oblige anyone and that if the has any query he should address it to me. It worked and a general reputation for honesty and integrity was built up. Even my peshkar–a man nearing his retirement came to me one day and complimented me saying that in his service career he had not seen such integrity. Imagine my shock, then, when one day I discovered that after 4 pm either the litigant or his lawyer used to come to the court and meet the peshkar. He knew the date for which his case had been fixed but he still enquired of the peshkar and then tipped him and the orderly. This shows that certain things are so institutionalized that it becomes difficult to break them completely. It also shows the working of the minds of our people who feel that howsoever honest a presiding officer is they must keep the peshkar on the right side.

What is narrated above is not to show that the system cannot be changed. It can be. In the incident narrated above blatant corruption was rooted out. I have seen ugly scenes in the court of an officer during my training where the orderly would take money from the litigant in the court room and put it in his pocket. The sound of coin falling upon coin gave ample evidence of what was going on. I had yet to recover from this shock when I found that lawyers moved towards the peshkar before leaving and I realized that money was being exchanged right under that table in the court. This kind of practice would happen if the presiding officer does not take any steps to curb corruption. With a vigilant presiding officer the corruption of the extortion type would be eliminated. This by itself would be a big achievement.

Judgements should be pronounced as far as possible on the date fixed. Delay leads to unnecessary speculation. Also the dictation to the steno should be given close to the judgement day. If it is given in advance then the steno can make money.

This does not mean that court work should be done in an atmosphere of total distrust. However, since the impression of the people has become so bad it becomes necessary to show that justice is being done and that the functioning of the court is above board.

In eastern parts of UP the court work is excessive. There is no court of Sub-Divisional Officers having less than 1500 cases. The reason is that the public is litigation-minded and the institution of cases is very heavy. The lawyers also abet this tendency by advising the client accordingly. Litigation is costly and time consuming and very often there is no definite solution for years. Of course, the way to tackle this is to control the institution of cases. Not automatically registering cases and having a careful look at the time of institution can itself lead to reduction of about 20% in cases. However an effort to settle the disputes out of court would really help in this matter.

In an eastern district of UP, I tried an experiment which worked, and I feel that it can work anywhere. The Lekhpal is a very powerful figure at the village level. His power can be used in this. I held a meeting of Lekhpals and gave them a list of cases in their *halqa* (jurisdiction). They were asked to meet the parties and affect a compromise. This was reviewed every month. Amazingly more than 50% of the cases got disposed off in this manner. The second stage was that the Lekhpal spread the word around that anybody having a problem should first approach him. As soon as someone did this the Lekhpal would advise the parties on settling the dispute out of court. This worked and the institution of cases came down significantly.

Simple cases of mutation should not take more than 45 days. In UP, from the state level it was mandated that no case of mutation would extend beyond this time limit. This led to a tremendous increase in the disposal of mutation cases and provided great relief to the people. However, there is still a huge pendency of cases because the presiding officer does not accord high priority to court work and general dates are given on some pretext or the other. Even as Chief Secretary I was amazed to find people approaching me to speak to the DM/SDM to dispose off their case which had been pending for several years. Some simple cases like those relating to demarcation or partition of land which could be disposed off in a couple of hearings are kept pending for years. This leads to litigants arriving at the courts on the appointed date and going back disappointed. It creates a very poor image about the district administration and also gives rise to the perception that the government is just not doing any work. The Collector must accord the highest priority to court work otherwise sooner than later these powers would also be taken away from them. In UP there is already a writ petition pending with the High Court to this effect.

Computerisation of court work has been a game changer giving a lot of transparency and providing a lot of control in the hands of the presiding officer. Monitoring of court work at all levels has become much simpler and open. The litigant has gained a lot from this modernization.

Collection of Revenue

This was the prime responsibility of the Collector in the British days. It has gone down in importance but still remains important as the state needs resources to run the government.

Two kinds of dues are collected–the main dues and miscellaneous dues. The main dues comprise land revenue and irrigation dues while miscellaneous dues consist of bank dues, electricity dues, sales tax arrears, etc. the machinery for collecting these dues is the Tehsil. The Tehsildar with the help of his Naib Tehsildar and collection Amins gets this job done. An efficient system of collection has been set up by the British and codified in the collection manual. To this day this system works to perfection.

Land revenue is no longer a major source of revenue. In fact it is a negligible amount. Questions have been raised about the necessity of having this revenue at all. It is true that the income earned is negligible but, on the other hand, this brings into being a system where revenue officials have to maintain an elaborate record of rights. Detailed village maps are prepared and there is complete knowledge of the owner of each piece of land, crops grown, source of irrigation, etc. This record keeping and the collection of revenue on this basis leads to revenue officials visiting villages. This creates a system of knowing about and supervision of all that is going on at the village level. Herein lies the importance of collecting land revenue and, therefore, I feel that this source of revenue should continue.

In addition, the same collection machinery collects dues of other departments like electricity which the department has failed to realize. This is a large amount and only the revenue agencies can collect this as they have powers to do so as arrears of land revenue. This is so because the latter procedure enables the collection agency to arrest the defaulter, attach his property and to auction it. This is the main source of power left with the revenue agencies and this gives them tremendous clout at the district level.

Even though the system of collection and procedure is well laid out, it is not followed. Supervisory officers do not perform their job well. If they take even the slightest interest, collection is bound to be very good. I recall that as a Collector in a particular district I found that huge arrears existed and were being accumulated for years. On being questioned the Tehsildar would respond by saying that a clique had been formed and nobody was coming forward to bid for the properties attached. I undertook a detailed inspection of tehsils. As I called for each file the truth came out that many files had not been prepared at all. Many others were lying without any noting or orders of a supervisory officer for years. Also, where property was put up for auction no publicity was made. It was clear that the tehsil staff was in collusion with big defaulters. Immediate review of each case was done and the SDO passed orders on the file regularly and wide publicity for auction was done in papers. The result was that collection doubled. Two types of malpractices crept into this also: auction at an absolutely low price and forcibly raking possession of properties that have not been attached. It calls for constant vigilance and strict monitoring at the level of Collectors.

Usually you find that small defaulters are arrested while the larger ones go scot free. It should be the opposite. A list of all defaulters of more than Rs 10,000 needs to be prepared and strict action taken against them. The Collector himself should review each case of a defaulter above Rs 50,000. The karguzari of amins, (field level revenue collectors) i.e., the amount they should collect every month is fixed. If rigorously monitored, it will always yield good results.

Good collection means a well-oiled revenue machinery which, in turn, means good administration. The Collector, hence, must devote sufficient time to this activity.

Revenue administration is also involved with land reforms. In UP the work of land ceiling is almost over. Some cases remanded from higher courts are lying pending and some surplus land still remains to be distributed. Repeated instructions came from the board to reassess ceiling in the light of increased irrigation facilities available. However, there is a general resistance on the part of lower level officials to do anything about this unless the Collector takes personal interest in the matter.

The main activity these days is allotment of land for house sites, agriculture and for planting trees. The last mentioned scheme has not fared well as most allottees have cultivated the land rather than use it for planting trees. There is very little village community land left now for distribution. As for house sites a close scrutiny would indicate that not more than 50%

of house sites has been used for construction of houses. One reason for this is that such sites are far away from the village. Secondly, it is not given to the right man. A third reason is that the poor allottee has not been able to get possession of his land.

Repeated drives are launched to given possession to the allottee of the land which has been given on Patta to them. However, the social structure of the villages is such that invariably the powerful land holders or dominant community tends to take the piece of land in its control. Visits by senior officers and police action are the remedies in case such incidents are repeated more than once. Thus giving of possession to allottees is an important part of land reforms, and should not be left to the whims and fancies of the Lekhpal. The Tehsildar/SDO and the Collector have to focus on this personally. In recent years, a tendency has come up of giving false information that kabza (possession) has been given. Sometimes this is encouraged by senior officers. As Sub-Divisional Officer, I had one such sad experience. The government launched a time-bound drive to give possession to the allottee. I took it as a sacred duty and went from village to village and found that the land was not in possession of the poor allottee. I had to take strong action including lodging of FIRs and arresting trespassers in order to restore possession in favour of the beneficiary. A meeting was held at the level of divisional Commissioner. It was found that in every sub-division possession had been given to 100% of the beneficiaries whereas my sub-division reported the figure of 75%. I was pulled up severely. I got up and agitatedly made my point. I insisted that no sub-division could show a better position if it really went about the job as social realities were the same everywhere. It did not work and I was severely admonished.

The same evening I met my Collector separately to explain the case. He listened for a while and then patted me on the back and said, "You are a sincere and hard-working officer but you have to learn to be practical." Practical meant doing as others do. I was shocked and felt beaten. I narrated this to my Tehsildar. The old man smiled in the "I told you" manner. He, however, joined me in condemning the system but a week after he sent me a report showing that all beneficiaries had been ensured possession of their lands. I signed the report–deciding to be practical. However, I carried on my drive to give possession.

The crux of the matter is that the SDO or Collector has to take this issue seriously. He must have a record for each village and have senior officers visiting the villages. A certificate from them should be taken and responsibility fixed accordingly.

Over the years the revenue agencies have got so involved in miscellaneous issues that the real work is forgotten. You find Lekhpals busy implementing family planning targets or national saving targets and ignoring their 'partaal and maintenance of land records.' A very important job is entering the name of the successor in khatauni. This is the record of rights showing the area and number of land along with the name of its owner. This forms the basis on which a person lays claim to title on a piece of land. On the death of the owner the name of his successor has to be entered. This is expected to be a regular exercise and the responsibility is that of the Lekhpal and supervisor qanungo. Unfortunately, these are never done properly unless senior officers go to villages and have the khatauni read aloud in the presence of villagers. In my inspections I came across some cases where a person has been dead for more than 20 years but the name of his successor had not been entered.

It is really amazing to see how everyone in the village seems to know everybody else. As you read out the khatauni in front of some village elders they are able to tell you everything– whether a person is dead or alive, the number of children he has and even the names of the children. I sometimes, feel that if this was to be tried in one colony of a city, one would find that not one person will be having complete knowledge of others.

There is a definite beauty about this oneness of the community at the village level.

Winter Tour

There is this unique concept of winter tour for the Collector and his team of revenue officers. This dates back to the glorious days of the Raj. Actually, the logic was that summers were very hot and during monsoon it was difficult to travel in the interior areas. The climate was right from 15th November onwards till March. The British chose this period for their village inspections.

It used to be a real romance. All household goods and tents were loaded onto bullock carts. A huge convoy of camp followers and officials moved along with the Collector and his wife. The latter would move on horseback or ride an elephant. Elaborate arrangements were made at the camping site—swiss cottages were set up having carpets and beds and mattresses. Pleasure was mixed with work, detailed inspections done during the day with time set aside for *shikaar*–the famous tiger hunts, etc.

The winter tour still remains but the scenario has changed a lot. Roads have been built and every part of the district can normally be reached in about two hours by car. The swiss cottages have rotted due to disuse and now there are hardly any available in any district. The officers stay for a day or so in a guest house and tour the nearby area. There is no question of things like tiger shoots.

There are detailed instructions issued about winter tour by the Board of Revenue. The essence is that the inspecting officer has to check almost everything in a village–whether the hand pumps are functioning, whether the school is running properly, whether the villagers are getting kerosene oil, etc. the Collector is expected to tour for 45 days and the SDO for 60 days. However, these days the pressure of work at headquarters is so much with repeated meetings, etc. that at least the Collector finds it impossible to complete his touring. His ADMs share his touring. So many times I have decided to camp at a particular place for three to four days. Inevitably, on the second day itself a message comes and one has to rush back to the district headquarter.

In the current set up it seems advisable to have touring all the year round than only during winters. One day in a week can be easily set aside for touring. This can be increased in the winter months. With the coming of the development programmes it becomes essential to visit the village throughout the year to maintain quality.

What about night halt? Does it have any relevance today? An officer can reach back after a full day's work. The people see him throughout the day. Camping for the night does not really make much of a difference. I have seen that very few visitors come after dusk. On the other hand, the tehsil staff gets burdened by the arrangements for stay and food. However, there is a psychological impact of the Collector going and staying in a rural area. Also, insistence on night-halt ensures a minimum degree of touring which the officers would otherwise avoid.

The records of the Lekhpal—khasra and khatauni–are checked during winter tour. Implementation of land reforms is verified on spot. Beneficiaries of various development programmes are called and physical verification done. Village roads, schools, tubewells and canals, etc. are checked.

Inspection of block, tehsil and thana are done. Statements are prepared and kept by the staff and many officers tend to do a routine inspection. It is best to go behind these statements. Files and registers should be called for. These actually show the level of working. Personally I feel less time should be given at the office and more on actually seeing things at the spot. This is especially true for development programmes. The figure in the statement might show that 100 houses for the weaker sections have been built. Physical verification might show that 40% are lying incomplete.

Moreover, this is one opportunity of meeting as many people as possible and listening to their problems. If the concerned officers of other departments are also present then a decision can be taken on the spot. It is best to spread out the map of a tehsil and select villages which are really interior. I recall as a SDO of going to a really interior village, to reach which one had to walk over a log over a stream. There was total shock in the village over my arrival. They gave me a cot and sat down around me. It transpired that not even the Lekhpal had even visited that village. The simple village folk did not know what problems to address to me. One young man came up and told me that his wife had run away. He wanted me to help him get his wife back–first he wanted advice whether he should get her back at all. They thought that 'Sahib' had all the answers. I did manage to say something though I am not sure I satisfied him.

If one really visits the interior areas and stays there, strange but interesting experiences take place. On one of the tours I found an old woman crying and saying something incoherently. My orderly and the police Sub-inspector were pushing her about. She was lamenting that everyone thought her to be mad and would not listen to her. I told my staff to leave her alone and asked her about her problem. She produced a photograph of a young girl who, she claimed, was her daughter and said that a group of snake charmers had forcibly carried away her daughter. She knew about the village where they were keeping her. She had spoken to the local SO who had declined to intervene saying that the girl must have gone willingly. This is what he expressed to me also when I summoned him and also told me that this old woman had lost control over her senses.

I dispatched the SO and Tehsildar to the village. They were to interview the girl alone. If she was not willing to stay then they would bring her back. Imagine my surprise when the party came back with the girl a few hours later. She had been found tied to a cot in an inner room. Arrests had been made. The old lady was really thrilled. I gave them some money and put them on the next train to Bihar as they belonged to that state. Few things have given me more satisfaction than this incident.

The point is that camping out brings one into contact with many problems that would never come to the Collector at the district headquarter. It makes you understand your people better; you get to know how your officers are working and get intelligence which would not be easy to come by otherwise.

However, there is one very tricky aspect of such camping. It turns out to be a burden on the tehsil staff. They tend to make elaborate arrangements for food, etc. and end up spending a lot of money or taking undue favours from the local Zamindars. This practice has to be consciously controlled. In my earlier years I used to move with my ration and my cook would prepare my food at the camp. This is a cumbersome method and impractical at times. In one such camp I reached the night halt site at 11.00 pm Since I had specially instructed the tehsil staff not to make any arrangements they had done precisely nothing. As I came out of my room after half an hour I found my old peon gathering twigs to light a fire. This, the old man told me, is the fate of all those who try such innovative measures.

It is best to instruct the tehsil staff to cook very simple food. The Collector's staff has also to be told to abstain from making any demands. It is always best to pay for the food. If you ask for the bill it would not be produced. If you insist a bill of a ridiculous sum would be produced. The best is to make a rough calculation for you and your staff and pay a lump sum figure. This payment should always be done in public or else the concerned person would pocket it. These are small things but they send signals that are large. And administration at the district is a question of sending the right signals.

Collector's Staff Meeting

My first exposure to this monthly review of the Collector of his ADMs, SDMs and Tehsildars was as a probationer. Voluminous statements had been prepared but the discussion tended to be centered on the general. The Collector would point to a particular tehsil and say that their collection was not up to the mark. The SDO Tehsildar would get up and give some explanation and promise that it shall all be made up this month. So at the end of a daylong meeting I got the impression that nothing worthwhile had been achieved.

The Collector's staff meeting is an institution which must be made effective. Leave aside the review of law and order and of prosecution it is the one opportunity to study the working of the revenue system. The first step to make the meeting effective is to update the proformas and to simplify and rationalize them. Enormous amount of information is collected and put up, in a loose, disjointed form which does not lead to identification of problems or setting of targets or coming out with a specific action plan. In fact, the same information is being put into different proformas. It is best to standardize one format so that a lot of paper work can be reduced. Fewer formats but pointedly showing the crucial indicators of performance and comparing them with the relevant period of last three years gives the best feedback. In the crucial matters like collection and court work specific month-wise targets can be kept. These can be done in consultation with the concerned SDM/Tehsildar. A rigorous monitoring against these targets can yield tangible results.

The office of the Collector functions under various office-in-charges. Each of them should be made to spell out a detailed objective plan for themselves and this should be time bound.

They have to be monitored in such a way that it gives them a proper sense of direction.

The style of the meeting is also important. It should be pointed and specific rather than vague and general. Problems and issues than personalities should be monitored. Minutes of the meeting must be recorded properly. Normally, the proceedings are drawn up in a very general manner and the same is repeated every month. The Collector must ensure that decision points have been recorded and each meeting must start with a review of the action taken against these.

The crux of the matter is that the Collector will have to take personal initiative if he wants to make his monthly review relevant and effective.

Collectorate

This is the Collector's office. Normally lodged in a historical building, there is an aura of power and importance all around it. The clerks of the collectorate are aware of their roles and do feel that they are the centre around which the entire working of the government revolves.

The revenue assistant, judicial assistant, revenue record keeper, chief revenue accountant and nazir are some of the key posts. This team is headed by an office superintendent who has now been upgraded as senior administrative officer. As compared to other departments these clerks of the Collectorate know their job well and their notings and drafting are of a really high order. Another significant thing about them is that they don't cheat their Collector. They would not misrepresent facts in their notings always clearly state the relevant Government orders. The draft letters they put up are so well written that normally you don't need to change anything. In fact, they can be overheard saying, 'I put up a draft letter and the Collector did not even add a comma to it'. They are aware of their competence and knowledge and full of sense of importance of their role. The story goes about of a Collector who was sitting in his office and clearing files and discussing matters with some visitors at the same time. He would just half open the file and sign without reading. One of the visitors could not restrain himself and questioned the Collector on signing without reading. The Collector explained that these notings have been put up by RA and JA of the collectorate. There is nothing else you can do about it but sign.

Such has been the standard of the collectorate. Only recently I went to the farewell of a nazir who had retired. He was a short, old man but I discovered that he had been so conscious of his work that he came to his office at 8.00 am and did not go home till even one paper was there on his desk. He had come to the farewell after clearing his last paper.

There is no doubt that these standards are going down. Also complaints of corruption are increasing. It is also a fact that these clerks get so mired down in rules and procedures that they become insensitive. It is here that the Collector has to provide leadership to them and effect an attitudinal change.

The revenue department is the oldest department and one cannot help but marvel at the systems and procedures that have been laid down by the British. The revenue manual, collection manual and land record manual list out each and every detail. It is as relevant today as it was when these manuals were written. In fact, if inspection of offices is done as per the guidelines given in the revenue manual then every aspect of office functioning can be seen and real improvement in office working brought about.

Modernisation

The old systems are good. They have given good results but the workload has increased. The pressure of population has made everything so unmanageable. It is in this light, that, it becomes necessary to modernize revenue administration. This can be done by evolving a proper system of grievance redressal, microfilming of records, computerization of land records, arms and collection documents at the collectorate level.

Computerization of land records is the most necessary item. In the manual system it is all in the hands of the Lekhpal. This functionary is the most important person for the simple village folk. Whereas the efficiency of the Lekhpal is not denied, the very fact that so much power is centered on him makes him liable to misuse of power. It is a common sight to see people running from pillar to post to get a copy of their extract of khatauni (details about their land ownership). Incidents are on the increase where, through fraudulent entries, the Lekhpal has obliged people and often written away large tracts of government land.

A major transformation has been brought about by the computerization of land records. Before this it was an uphill task to get a copy of record of your rights. This is now become online in most states and copy of khatauni is generated through computers. It has been a major tool of empowerment of the common man and reduction in corruption and harassment. The Collector has to see that this system works efficiently.

In the first instance, the khatauni–record of right should be computerized. Software for this has been developed. Data entry can be done on a job basis. Suitable amendments in law can be made to make an extract issued by the computer a legal document. Initial data feeding might take one-and-a-half to two years. But after that the results would be tremendous for the administration. This programme can only be pushed through by the Collector. Everybody else in the system resents it and tries not to cooperate. In UP and in most of the states this work has now been completed.

The people visit the revenue offices to get copies of their income, caste and other similar certificates which the revenue officers are authorized to issue. This was another area of corruption and the poor applicant had to run from pillar to post. Now most states have a public service delivery act which stipulates making these certificates available within a fixed time period and through computerization which mean the applicant does not have to run around revenue offices.

Computerization of court work has been another great contribution of modernization. This work has been completed in UP and most other states. It has greatly helped in demystifying the court processes for the ordinary citizen and enables the presiding officer to be in command over his court. He need not depend upon cronies like Peshkar and petty clerks to put up case files and applications before him. The information is now fully available to him and the litigant and the lawyers.

Computerization of the village map is another significant transformation where each bit of land, ponds, public lands, trees are plotted and can be seen by just pressing a button on your laptop. This greatly helps in planning for development and monitoring schemes for the rural poor and treating the village as a unit of development.

Land Acquisition

Development requires land which has to be acquired as public land is not available in sufficient quantity. The Collector has a major role to play in this. All the national highways and major infrastructure projects relating to roads, dams, power stations etc. require land and it is the job of the Collector to make this land available at the earliest. The Collector has to decide the compensation to be awarded to the land-holder and for this purpose he decides upon a rate and declares an award accordingly. This exercise has to be carried out in a time bound manner. However, often the land owners dispute the compensation award and there are a plethora of court cases causing abnormal delay in infrastructure projects. As Chief Secretary I, along with my team built a Lucknow–Agra expressway (328 km.) in a record time of 23 months. It was possible to do this because the land acquisition from the farmers was done in a seamless manner through negotiations by a committee headed by the Collector who was empowered by the Government for this purpose. Land from more than 30,000 farmers was acquired within six months and there was not a single dispute. Not even a single farmer went to the court and the project was completed on time.

Things have been made much easier after the new land acquisition act has come into force. This allows payment of compensation at twice the circle rate in urban areas and four times the circle rate in rural areas. This is a substantial amount of compensation. For projects where people have to be displaced a humane relief and rehabilitation package has to be prepared. Innovative ideas like land pooling and giving a share of the developed land to the displaced land owners have also contributed to making land acquisition a win-win situation for all.

However, the Collectors must be very careful in carrying out this exercise of land acquisition as charges of corruption are often leveled against the officers and they should be able to justify the rate at which they have awarded compensation.

Revenue administration is still the basis of district administration. It is the focal activity of the Collector. Over the years, the Collectors have been ignoring this very important work. However, any Collector who does this runs the risk of not coming to grips with his district at all. This work should be given primary importance. Every other aspect of administration can be built on this.

Relationship with Politicians and the Press

Politicians

In a democracy there are the elected members of the Assembly or the Parliament who represent the will of the people and sit in the legislature to make laws for the benefit of the people and to keep a check on the working of the executive. From amongst these elected representatives members of the ruling party become ministers and chief minister or prime minister. The system is designed in such a manner as to make the representatives of the people superior to the civil servants and this is how it should be in a government of the people and by the people. The Collector must give due deference to these elected people and act fairly on any grievance or problem raised by them.

The district Collector has to deal primarily with the members of Parliament (MP) and members of Legislative Assembly and Council (MLA and MLC). Political leaders of various parties also keep approaching the Collector even though they may not have been elected. A significant portion of the Collector's time is spent with politicians. They come to him alone as well as leading large delegations. They put forward problems and very often have certain requests or demands. It is a necessary skill of the Collector today to keep them satisfied without doing anything wrong to appease them.

The Collector has to follow the rule of the law and work according to the Constitution.

Experiences

My first district, in the backwaters of eastern UP, was a hotbed of politics. In fact, politics was a way of life with more than one-third of the population. I had approached my job as a Collector here with much trepidation because of this. Sure enough, just a few days after I joined, a local MLA at the head of a huge delegation came to me. They were shouting slogans. It seemed the local Station Officer (SO) of police had beaten up and locked up a pradhan. The SP had already informed me that the concerned pradhan was a criminal. I called the MLA and some people in for talks. Immediately, the whole lot rushed in brushing my chaprassi aside and started shouting that they would not go till the station officer was suspended and the pradhan released. I turned towards the MLA requesting him to restore order. This particular MLA had met me earlier and had been all smiles. He had, in fact, promised me all support. Consider my surprise, then, when the MLA told me that I could not shut the voice of the people, and he himself started talking loudly. He announced that he and his supporters would sit on a dharna in front of my office till I suspended the SO. I offered an enquiry into the whole matter by the local SDM and also informed him that the SP had told me that the pradhan was a criminal. The MLA passed bitter comments against the entire police administration. He even threatened to speak to the Chief Minister about the SP. He said an enquiry could be conducted fairly only if the SO was transferred.

Heated exchanges took place. None of us deviated from our stand. This went on for an hour. Finally, it was agreed that SDM would complete his enquiry within a week and also if the SDM felt that the SO was hindering his enquiry he would be transferred. The crowd went away shouting angry slogans. I heard the MLA saying outside that he would approach the CM about the matter.

I felt a little upset about the whole episode and it took me some time to get back into a proper frame of mind to work. Late in the evening I was informed that the same MLA wanted to speak me over the phone. I thought this would be another round of exchanges. With some irritation I said 'Hello' over the phone. To my utter surprise the MLA was speaking softly and in hushed tones. He told me that the concerned SO had been a good and tough officer and that I should carry out my enquiry fairly and not bring the SO to any harm needlessly. I could not help asking him about the reason for this volte-face. He was candid enough to tell me that the concerned pradhan had been very helpful to him during the elections and thus, he had no option but to lead a delegation of the pradhan's supporters and come to me. He also knew that the pradhan was not a straight-forward person and felt that the SO had been right in reacting in the manner that he did. The MLA further complimented me on my handling of the situation. I asked him what would have happened if I had relented. "I knew you would not", was his reply.

The lesson I learnt was clear. The public representative cannot be blunt and say no to his voters. He has no choice but to go along with them. He is responsible to them and depends upon them. At the same time, most of them realize what is right and what is wrong, and would not insist on anything or make it a prestige issue if he is convinced that you are just and reasonable.

There was another case of a district where a political leader (MLA) known for his roughness along with a few of his supporters met me just a few days after my taking charge. He sat down, crossed his legs, lighted a cigarette for effect and pushed an application towards me. He also directed me as to the order I should pass on it. Maintaining as much of coolness as possible I told him that I could not pass that order till I had examined the file. The MLA shouted and told me that in this district things had always been done like this and I should follow suit if I wanted to survive. I told him that irrespective of any district this is how I functioned and would not change my style for survival. The MLA stormed out but I was surprised to find him a changed man on his next visit. He was cordial, courteous and called me *barre bhai* (elder brother).

Incidents like the above are common at the time of taking fresh charge of a district. The attempt is there to browbeat you just to understand how much you will bend. Once they know your nature and style of working they will adjust themselves to it. In essence, how a political leader behaves with you depends upon how much dignity you carry yourself with.

Right from the days in the training academy, I found officers obsessed with dealing with politicians. Almost everybody seemed to talk of not bending to politicians, about not allowing them to interfere with one's job. I felt then as I do now that rigidity and inflexibility of mind is the root cause of conflicts between officers and politicians. The society is made up of all kinds of people. This is true for officers as well as politicians–there are reasonable and unreasonable people but nothing should be generalized. One should approach one's relations with the public representative with an open mind and deal with each situation and each individual on its or his merit.

Any civil servant has to appreciate the fact that he is functioning in a democratic state where elected representatives of the people are in power. The service has to advise and assist them. Despite any fault this system may have, this is the best possible system and one should mentally accept it.

Political Interference

Everywhere you hear the cry about political interference. In fact, when a couple of officers sit down together the stories of valour that they recount are those where they are portrayed as heroes and the politician as the villain. They narrate how they fought with so and so and came out victorious. I, for one, feel that this business of political interference has been stretched a bit too far. I am not saying that it is a complete bogey but more often than not it is used as an excuse for lack of commitment or effectiveness.

We must appreciate that in our system the public representative has to 'interfere'. The word 'interferer' should not be taken in its negative connotation. We could well call it intervention on behalf of the people. We are accountable to the people and the MLA or MP represents them. They, thus have a right to question the administration, suggest measures, put forward proposals, or even oppose decisions of the officers. This is how the system is expected to move and we should not view it with hostility.

The public representatives or politicians have to depend upon the votes of the people. He has to meet them, listen to them and try to keep them happy. He is accountable to them and his entire career depends upon whether he is able to carry them with him. Daily hordes of people approach him and forward a list of demands. He avoids some but the rest he takes up and puts before the officer. He will always plead the case of his people. This does not mean that he wants the officer to do all his work. I have seen that many politicians do not press most things. Only on some issues they take a special interest. Very often they move applications and request you to hold an enquiry. I think, if an officer can appreciate the kind of situation in which a politician functions the relationship can be very smooth.

Take the case of a district. Politicians will meet the district officer regularly. They will come with their supporters and a bag full of applications. There would be requests for hand pumps, village roads, tubewells, schools or arms license or granting employment to someone. There would be complaints against certain officers or about implementation of some programmes. There is no harm if the district officer gives them a patient hearing and does what is possible under rules. Most of the issues put forward are genuine grievances of the people and it is the job of the officer to have them resolved.

There are two rules which are important. One is that basic courtesy must be extended to the representative of the people. After all our scheme of government has given him that status. The officer can always welcome the MLA, MP, shake hands with him, offer him a chair, and attentively listen to him. Even if there is something which cannot be done there is no point in being arrogant abbot it and saying that I shall not do it. You can politely tell him the legal position and assure him that you would still look into the matter. On a later date you can always politely explain to him why the work cannot be done. Most of them accept it.

The other rule is never to insult an MLA or MP. If you refuse to meet him or tell him bluntly in front of his supporters that he is talking nonsense then he is bound to react. It is agreed that often some of them come to meet you at odd hours. It is advisable not to refuse but politely tell him to give a ring before coming. Most of them do that. If there is a lot of disagreement on some point then one can always talk to the MLA, MP alone and convince him. They are also human beings and they understand.

However, the crucial issue is impartiality and fairness. Small gestures matter. If you offer tea to one MLA then you must do so to others. Nowhere, should there be a perception that you are giving more importance to some. Ruling party MLA, MPs do tend to get some precedence but opposition MLA, MPs should never be neglected. In fact, the success of a district officer very often depends on how the members of the opposition party regard him.

Much of this talk of political interference is actually a facade. Most public representatives want details of development programmes–list of roads being constructed, tubewells out of order, etc. Why this should not be given to them? After all everything is being done with public money and the public has a right to know how that money is being spent. Officers tend to resent this. I feel that a District Officer gains by disseminating maximum information to them. It helps him in controlling the various departments. No District Officers can possibly check the implementation of all the schemes. Nor does the official feedback tell him everything. It is these representatives of the people who give a lot of valuable information to the DM. I recall various DRDA meetings where MLAs informed that certain roads were being claimed to have been constructed by PWD as well as rural engineering services. The MLA/MP knows his constituency. He has traversed it on foot and has his voters all over. His feedback can be a tremendous asset to the DM.

There was this case of an important link road being built to link two villages to the main road. The project was sanctioned and work started. One day the local MLA and his supporters went and stopped the work. The PWD engineer came to me and requested for police assistance. Almost immediately afterwards the MLA came. I requested him not to stop the construction of the road. "I am not against the road but the alignment is wrong. With the same money four villages can be linked," he replied, and on a sheet of paper drew a rough sketch. I called the PWD engineer later on and showed him the alignment suggested by the MLA but the engineer immediately scoffed at it and pronounced it as impossible. The next day I went to the spot with the MLA and the engineers. To my surprise I found that the MLA was right and the engineer had no idea of the local situation. The alignment was changed and four villages got linked instead of two.

The point I want to make is that even though the MLA is not professionally qualified most of them have strong common sense. They live in the villages and understand the ground realities much better than officers who have come on postings from outside. His interventions, thus, should not be resented but looked into. Greater public good might result if his suggestions are taken seriously.

Things always become difficult for the district Collector and his team when a new government comes to power. It is particularly so if the elected representatives are new. They tend to be extra sensitive and are not well conversant with rules and procedures. If you tell them that a particular action is not possible as per government orders they are apt to feel that you are deliberately not doing their work. There is also a tendency to call officers in front of a lot of people from the public and expose them to all kinds of allegations and loose talks. The District Officer has to carry himself with dignity. There is no need to allow oneself to be subjected to humiliation. A little bit of tough attitude on the part of the DM makes the other person realise and they change their style. I have found that most of the ministers talk to DM alone. They never encourage their supporters to talk directly or insult the DM. Some new ministers sometimes fall in the trap of arranging a question-answer session. However, if politely requested they understand. New legislators also adjust and understand very fast and normally everything becomes stable often within two to three months.

The point to understand is that the politician and the administrator are not adversaries. They are actually supposed to work together for the development of their area and maintaining the rule of law. However, there exists a tendency amongst the officers to be resentful of anything that a politician says. Actually he very often highlights the weakness of the administration which is mortally resented by them. Talking of interference I have found that senior officers and colleagues also intervene in administration–there have been countless requests like not to suspend a particular Lekhpal, stay the transfer of a Tehsildar or even to look into a particular case pending in court. We do not say anything to that but react the moment a politician says something.

I think the explanation lies in the difference in background –the administrator has put in more years in college and dresses up in a coat and tie and hence feels superior to the person who has studied less and wears pyjama-kurta. The second reason is, of course, the feeling amongst officers that they have a right to rule like kings and nobody should ask any questions. Frequent is the lament about the good old days of the Raj.

This is not to say that the fault lies only on the side of officers. It takes all kinds to make this world and the same applies to officers as well as politicians. There are politicians who regard officers as obstructions and believe that everything should be done as per their desire. There are those who misbehave and are rough–one has to deal with each accordingly. In fact, a major part of an officer's work today is to reconcile the various aspects of the political process. It can be regarded as a headache by many whereas others might feel that this political management is an essential part of the job of a district officer. I believe that the best way to manage the political environment is by playing straight whereby all possible courtesy should be extended and anything put forward by the MLA/MP should be given serious and sincere consideration. It is, however, never obligatory on the officer to do something which is against rules or which could demoralize his administration.

I always use the analogy of cricket for the above situation. For the District Officer it is like batting on a turning wicket with uneven turn and bounce. The best thing for a batsman is to play straight and technically correct cricket. This is the only way to get runs–using cross-bat method or trying to be too adventurous can lead to an early dismissal. A very disgusting phenomenon that is increasing every day is the use of politicians by the officers for postings and transfers. If an officer does that then he cannot be immune from political interference of the negative kind. The worrying part is that IAS officers are resorting to this. So many times a district magistrate manipulates his posting or chooses to stall his transfer by hanging on to a political father figure. Under such circumstances it is not possible for the officer to be fair and impartial. He is also viewed by politicians other than his mentor as being less than fair. This makes his functioning doubly difficult and for such an officer running a district becomes an endless stream of adjustments and compromises.

To sum up, the district level officer and the district level public representatives have to work together. This is how the system can deliver the best results. Their partnership has to be for the good of the people and the district, and fairness, impartiality should be the governing principles. The officers have to realize that their oath is to the Constitution and rule of law and should never compromise this for petty gains. The Collector, however, should never have this unctuous feeling that only he is correct and political people are all talking nonsense. He must shed this ego and appreciate the significance of rule of people. Both wheels of the district vehicle have to move together to ensure best results.

The Press

Nobody can deny the paramount importance of press in our society. It acts as a watchdog for democracy and ensures accountability to the people. Press can mould social opinion, highlight public grievances and pinpoint the weaknesses in the administration. A large part of the success of the DM depends upon how he can tackle the press.

The government has a small information office at the district level headed by a district information officer. This officer maintains liaison with the press. However, I have found that if the press is left only to him then proper understanding with the press can never be developed. This is one area where the District Magistrate will have to lead from the front.

One might be doing a lot of good work in the district but if it is not brought in the press then nobody comes to know about it. There are so many government schemes in operation about which the general public knows nothing. If informed they can participate in its implementation and point out problems also. There are two concepts–propaganda and publicity. Propaganda is not for the administration but publicity should not be shunned. Propaganda implies that you actually do nothing substantial but cultivate the press and ensure that a lot of news about you is published. This must be avoided however; publicity implies that any good work being done must be brought to the notice of the people. Facts must be reported. This is not bad and, in fact, adds to the strength of a district administrator.

Many officers religiously cultivate the press for personal fame. They will go around inaugurating schemes and buildings and give speeches at functions and then expect it to be published in the papers. They speak personally to the press to ensure good coverage. There are others who oblige pressmen even if it means bending the rules. There are great believers in throwing lavish parties for the press. Their sole objective is appeasement of the press for personal gain.

The above tendency is dangerous. I have noticed officers who follow the above method becoming personally very vulnerable. The press praises them but is also quick to criticize at a personal level if things go wrong or if they get offended in some way. Actually, the press also identifies an officer hankering for name and fame very easily. They begin to play with him.

They use him and the moment he does not oblige they tend to dump him like a piece of hot coal.

The moment a new officer takes over at a district, the press wants to meet him. It is advisable to call a press conference. However, an effort should be made to keep the conference at a low key. There are two pitfalls to be avoided–one should never criticize one's predecessor and secondly one should not make tall claims which indicate as if nothing has been done in the past and promise the moon in your tenure. It might get you a good review initially but the same promises tend to boomerang on you and the catchy phrases used by you are used against you by the press.

Normally, a press conference should be held every three months. This is the best way of communicating to the people the problems and achievement of the administration. The press has a lot of queries and complaints which can be heard also. The only problem is that these conferences involve calling a large number of journalists. Some of them, like in any other profession, are not the serious type. They have personal grievances and tend to divert the press conference on these issues. This sometimes leads to acrimonious press conferences and it is one reason why many officers do not call press conferences regularly. However, despite this, it is necessary to keep the communication channels open with the press and as such press meets should be convened.

Very often in a district the press comes out with stories which can be very damaging to the district administration. The news is reported on the briefing of people who have a grievance against the administration. The facts are also not fully given. The DM then issues a contradiction which is published in a manner that nobody notices it and the damage is done. The best way to tackle this is to request the member of the press to take your views in the matter before publishing. They normally tend to ring you up and ask and thereby give a balanced view. This does not mean that they will always ask, as there is a desire in the press to sensationalize issues to make their story interesting.

In one of my districts there was a very healthy tradition of all the major newspapers ringing up the DM at night and exchanging news and views. I found that the reporting in this district was most balanced. The only problem was that one had to spend quite some time talking on the phone daily and it could become irritating at times.

In any case a culture of trust and openness has to be created. The press should feel free to give a ring and take your views and you should also not ignore their calls. Calls made by members of the press should be responded to at the earliest. If a press reporter comes to meet you then it is always preferable to give him time. If these small aspects of courtesy are ignored then you are bound to face a hostile press.

In the event of a major riot or law and order problem the district administration always has a grudge against the press. They feel that matters are sensationalized, inflammatory news published which only succeeds in further complicating issues and adding fuel to the fire. This is true but unavoidable to a large extent. Apart from the official view, a whole lot of people approach the press with news and the press cannot ignore everything and carry only the official version. The best way to tackle this is to hold regular briefings of the press everyday during such days of crises. The great advantage is that at such briefings the press comes out with all that has been reported to them. The response of the administration is taken and a reasonably balanced account follows in the press. It gives an opportunity to scotch rumors which would otherwise hog the headlines. The essence of relationship with the press is to keep as close a line of communication as possible.

Inevitably in a district there are a couple of 'yellow' journalists. They are actually not professionals but have just taken out a one page monthly or weekly with the sole objective of gaining status and making money. One should be able to identify such people and avoid them. If they print anything false the best things to do is to ignore them. Getting into defamation suits or taking recourse to retaliatory measures like arrest or closure of press are never very advisable.

If any newspaper prints anything which, according to you, is blatantly false then the best thing is to speak to the editor personally. One can write to the editor also. Rarely does one have to go beyond that, though, of course, the option to go to the press council is there.

Daily there are several news items about the administration and not all of them are complementary. There is no need to get unduly upset. In fact, very often such reports are a source of valuable information to the administrator. The cuttings of such reports are put up daily before the DM. He should send them to the concerned officers and get a time-bound reply. In some cases a reply can be sent to the newspaper concerned also.

Individuals can be good, bad or indifferent but a jaundiced view of the entire institution of press should never be taken. The press is a useful tool of information, communication and there is no doubt that it makes you accountable for your actions. Managing press relations is a necessary attribute for a district administrator.

Redressal of Public Grievances

One of the major tasks of the district Collector is to meet people and attend to their grievances. In UP these people are called mulaquatis and the best part of the day of a modern period Collector is spent in meeting them and listening to their grievances, taking their petitions, passing orders on them and seeing that their job is done or that they feel satisfied that they have been heard.

Even in the days of the British Raj the mulaquati existed but things have changed considerably now. Today it is the MLAs, MPs, small time politicians, journalists, pramukh, pradhans and citizens who all together comprise the mulaquatis. The District Magistrate is expected to have an answer to everything. He cannot shrug his shoulders to any petition and say that this does not concern him. He has to listen, be sympathetic and pass suitable orders on application put up before him.

A typical scene in the office of a Collector is that the room is full of people and outside the orderly is having a tough time restraining many others wanting to rush in. Any effort to keep a register succeeds only for sometime as the number of the visitors is so large that it is quicker and better to keep calling them in together and disposing them. Applications are being put up one by one before the Collector and the latter listens and then marks it to the concerned officer with suitable directions.

Applicant 'A' wants an arms license. The Collector asks the SSP for a report about his character. Applicant 'B' has a complaint against the fair price shop in his village. It is sent to the District Supply Officer for enquiry and action. Applicant 'C' has a complaint against the Pradhan of his village who he alleges has embezzled the MGNREGA funds. This is sent to the Chief Development Officer for enquiry and report. Applicant 'D' has a complaint against the Station Officer of this thana who is not lodging his FIR. This is sent to the SO to lodge an FIR. Applicant 'E' has got a wrong electricity bill and wants it to be corrected. Applicant 'F' says that there are government dues against him and he wants some time to pay them. Applicant 'G' wants a road in his village. Applicant 'E' has a complaint against the tubewell operator while applicant 'H' does not like the face of the village headmaster of his village school.

So and so forth it goes on. On any day on an average more than a hundred such applications are moved. Apart from individuals, there are delegations. They could be protesting against a government policy or demanding action against a particular officer or taking sides on an issue which has got politicized. One of the most interesting delegations I had was of students who refused to come and see me in my chamber and asked me to come out and hear them, I did so. They were protesting against the policies of the US administration and warned me that students would not allow the US President to interfere in our internal affairs. I took their memorandum. They were not satisfied. They wanted to know what I would do with it. I assured them that I shall forward their memorandum to the government. "No, we are not satisfied," they said. It then transpired that they wanted me to speak to Mr. Bill Clinton over the phone and convey their feelings. I was amazed that they could even imagine that their DM could get directly on the line to the US President. In any case, I assured them that I would do so.

The people still have faith in the institution of the DM. They are confident that action on their grievances shall be taken. Even the most violent of crowds are satisfied if the DM gives them proper assurance of action. The DM acts as a shock absorber, arbitrator, judge, mediator and the problem solver. There would be total anarchy if this institution does not deliver. Grievances would then spill onto the roads and violence shall erupt. It is thus very important for the DM to be accessible and available. He has to give a patient hearing to people and satisfy them that action on their grievances shall be taken. But the faith of the people would be completely shaken if nothing happens even after representing to the DM and increasingly this is what is happening. More than a hundred applications would come to the DM daily and the workload increases. He passes some orders on them and sends them to the concerned officer who in turn passes it to his subordinate. Very often on revenue matters the application travels to the Lekhpal and in police matters to the beat constable. These lower level functionaries are the ones who have often created the problem and the petitioners might have complained against them in their application. The chances of getting any justice from this level become negligible. Very often the applications are not responded to. Sometimes, a report comes after six months. There is no doubt that sensitivity to public grievances at the lower level has certainly gone down. This has increased the pressure on the DM and also the expectations of him are heightened. If the DM cannot evolve a system whereby the grievances can be attended to then his administration shall certainly collapse.

The orders passed by the DM on these applications should be specific. There is no point in marking them for necessary action. The DM must indicate the action required. If there is a complaint against a particular officer then it should be mentioned that at least one level above him must enquire into the matter. It is best to ask for a report and that also should be time bound. The time given should take into account the nature of the complaint. Very often a routine endorsement like "please enquire and report within a week" is made. This has no impact, it gets treated as a routine, and a report, if it comes at all, may take several weeks to reach the desk of the Collector.

Computerisation

A system I devised as a Collector gave good results. These grievances had been computerized. The software is very simple and is available. One can design it also depending on one's needs. Accordingly, the applications were divided into priority, urgent and ordinary and the Collector personally marked the applications as priority, urgent and ordinary. In the priority items the report was expected within 7 days, in urgent within 15 days and in ordinary within 25 days. The lower level functionaries might not understand, so I persisted in giving the expected date of the report in my endorsement, e.g. please enquire and report by 15.3.94. All such applications were entered daily into the computer. Every Monday the computer would print out the applications on which a report is due but has not come. The list would be sent for my scrutiny and reminder issued automatically by the computer. If a report did not come after the third reminder then I call the officer concerned to appear before me with his explanation. The list was taken up for discussion in the staff meeting also. The results were very good as constant and regular monitoring of all grievances began to take place. When I inspected the tehsils later on I found that they had opened separate registers for priority, urgent and ordinary and were monitoring it accordingly.

Still there were cases where the reports were delayed. I would check the dates at the time of reading the report. An unusual delay would lead to a letter to the concerned officer for fixing responsibility and taking action. This ensured that everyone became serious towards attending to public grievances. Once this culture is developed and officials at all levels become conscious of the importance of being attentive to grievance redressal the results start coming.

The next important part of grievance redressal is to see what exactly has been done with the complaint. Very often a cursory report is prepared by the lowest level functionary and is duly forwarded by all. It must be insisted that the senior officer apply his mind and give his clear views. Any application on which a senior officer has not applied his mind should be sent back to him. Then it should be seen whether an attempt has been made to solve a problem or just a routine bureaucratic report has been submitted. Reports which throw the responsibility on other departments are often put up. This is not redressal. The officer concerned must coordinate with the other department and try to find a solution. Very often in complaint cases a lower level functionary might just write that the complainant is a habitual complainer and nothing needs to be done. An enquiry in such matters by a person higher in hierarchy has to be insisted upon.

In fact, the complainant must be contacted and findings communicated to him verbally. If that is not possible then a written reply can be sent. These days almost everyone has a mobile and every applicant can be asked to indicate his mobile number along with his name. It becomes easy to contact the person on his mobile and find out whether he is satisfied with the way in which his complaint has been handled. The crux of the matter is that a person who approaches the Collector and gives an application must realize that his grievance has been seriously attended to.

Redressal of grievances can reach a new level through use of computerization and information technology and also the mobiles. A young collector of Sitapur in Uttar Pradesh became the pioneer for such a redressal system by starting a "Lokvani" system where all complaints were registered on the computer, sent to the concerned departments and responded to within the stipulated time. This system became a trend-setter and thereafter many similar IT based redressal systems have been evolved by Collectors to provide satisfaction to the people that their grievances are being attended to. However, no technology can succeed if the intention to genuinely address the grievances is not there and regular monitoring is not done by the collector himself and each officer held accountable for disposal of grievance within the desired time period.

Mulaqatis

Accessibility to the people is important but the Collector would have to manage the time at his disposal. The tendency in UP is for mulaquatis to come on any day at any time. If a Collector keeps sitting in his office with an open door he can do nothing else but meet people throughout the day. There is nothing wrong in meeting people who have a grievance at any time of the day but the fact is that maximum time is taken away by touts and small time politicians. This is why it becomes necessary to manage one's time spent with visitors. In fact, if a close scrutiny of visitors is done it is found that there are about a dozen or so people who keep coming regularly to the Collector. They collect applications from people and have orders passed by the Collector. Many of them start making money in this manner. The worst is that these people can defame the Collector also. They will show that they are close to the DM and then demand money on his behalf. This is particularly true in the case of issues like arms licenses. This practice is very much prevalent in the eastern part of Uttar Pradesh.

More often than not you would find that the visitor would come and sit and not come to the main point for a long time. He would enter, smile, shake hands and sit down. The Collector would ask him for his work. The man would say that he had no work but had just come for 'darshan'. To this the busy Collector might smile weakly and try to look at his files. But mulaquati would not allow this. He would launch into a long speech praising the Collector. "Never before has such an officer come." He would say. He would also try to criticize the officer's predecessor. If the officer falls for the bait then the visitor's job is done. In this manner more than five minutes would go by. The Collector would have to be a little rude and say, 'O.K. and try to dismiss him at this point the visitor would search his pockets and come out with bits of paper on which some work would be written and start putting it before the officer.

The above is not true for every mulaquati. In fact, the poor man who comes hardly takes any time. But this is true of the countless middlemen. If the Collector does not resist and allows such people to take his time then the message goes to the general public that it is better to approach through middlemen. The poor man now does not come himself but approaches through one such tout. This is extremely damaging. The Collector would lose touch with the problems of his people and remain surrounded by sycophants who tell him what he likes to hear and keep him involved in quotas, licenses and granting of small time favors. Several are the cases where these people exploit the poor public by posing that they are close to the Collector and they prove this by spending maximum time with him. They then go on and make money in this manner.

It is not easy for the Collector to refuse meeting them but it is best to meet them in the office in the Collectorate during regular meeting hours. There is a huge crowd at such moments and one can dispose them off faster. These middlemen are not satisfied. They would request you for time alone at your residence. This should be refused. Sometimes, they try and impress by taking names of senior officers and ministers. It is best to rebuff them when they try this.

The best guarantee is to be available as much as possible to the ordinary, poor people. Listen to them and solve their grievances and then gain confidence. Resort to the middlemen automatically comes down.

Another very distressing trend that has started and is more prevalent in some districts than others is lawyers meeting the Collector with applications on behalf of the people. The lawyers obviously charges fees and this implies that there is a heavy cost attached to meeting the Collector. Actually with the tremendous increase in advocates they do not have many cases to handle and are forced to adopt this measure. Officers who refuse to meet them find themselves facing an ugly situation and a lawyers' strike follows. A better method is to ask for the client when the lawyer produces an application and talk only to him. Also, priority can be given to those who have come without any lawyer. A notice can be put up encouraging people to come without a lawyer or middlemen. This would reduce the problem. However, the best solution is that when the ordinary citizen develops faith in the Collector and his grievance redressal system, he automatically shuns the middle people and approaches himself.

At least three days a week can be set aside for meeting the people in your office from 10.00 am to 2.00 pm The crowd is always largest on Mondays so this should be one of the three days. One day in a week for court work and two days for touring is the ideal combination. Anyone who comes must be met and given a patient hearing. The system should be first come first serve. This ensures impartiality and sends the right message.

An institution of great interest is the ubiquitous orderly to the Collector. He is the person having power to influence as to whom the Collector shall meet and whose telephone call must be attended to. In my first district I found that the orderly would come silently in at all hours and tell me that Mr. so and so had come to see me. When I would refuse saying that he should come in the office, the orderly would whisper that he was a very powerful and important man. Much to his chagrin I would refuse still. Even in the office I had got a register opened and would meet everybody according to that. My chaprasi did not appreciate my style. He strongly felt that it was his prerogative to determine as to who should meet me and what should be the order of preference.

Things came to a crux when one day my wife confronted me with the comment that the general opinion was that I was not conducting myself with dignity. She seemed to be quite upset. It took some time for me to realize that my chaprasi having found me heedless had done the next best thing. He poured out his grievances to my wife. He told her that I was meeting every riff raff and the impression had gone around that "Saheb did not behave like a Collector." He told her that I was too soft and far too polite and in this manner the administration could not be run. "Saheb is too simple. This district has seen Collectors like Mr. X and Mr. Y. Nobody could dare enter the office of the Collector." Fortunately, my wife understood my point of view and the poor chaprasi was left wallowing in self pity.

The chaprasi at the telephone has no parallel. He chooses who should be put through to the Collector and who should be avoided. To my horror I found that I was not even being informed of the calls made to me. It so happened during the President's rule in the state, and the advisor to the Governor rang me up. The chaprasi promptly told him that the Collector was busy and he could not speak to him. Later on during the day he casually told me that some "advisor saheb" had rung up. I promptly rang back and was not surprised to find a very cold voice at the other end of the receiver.

Even more so, I once had a terrible throat and could not speak at all. I put an officer to attend to my phones and take messages for me. Evidently, the Chief Minister rang up to speak to me. The chaprasi coolly informed him that "Saheb has a bad throat and so would not be able to speak." Despite the insistence from the other side the chaprasi refused to give in and did not even elaborate that Saheb could not speak and some other officer was on duty to take messages. Imagine my consternation when the CM, on his next visit, told me that he had wanted to get through to me but evidently I had a sore throat!

The chaprasi is undoubtedly important and has a role to play. He is the symbol of authority and his intervention is necessary. But he should not be allowed to use his discretion. Clear instructions must be given to him and it should be ensured that he follows them. If the Collector does not exert then these chaprasis build a wall round the Collector and insulate him from public opinion. There have been cases where they take money also in allowing people to go in. The Collector has to give the message that he is accessible and available and not dependent upon his steno or orderly. Accessibility is more than 50% of grievance redressal.

Janta Adalat

As a young collector I started the system of holding Janta Adalats (Public hearings) where I used to go personally along with all departmental heads and assemble at one place which had been previously announced to listen to the problems of the people who turned up and provide a solution on the spot. This worked like a dream and there was tremendous satisfaction amongst the citizens and even the media was fulsome in its praise for this administrative innovation of taking administration to the door of the common man. I remember presenting this idea in a meeting of Collectors at the state headquarters and this was a major contributor to the evolution of the concept of "Tehsil Divas" in UP which is now regularly held every month in every district of the state.

An analysis of the visitors show that important people, public representatives and delegations led by the political leaders get to meet the Collector. People from district headquarters or nearby also manage to approach. However, the poor villagers from a village which is far away from the district headquarter rarely gets a chance to meet the DM. To administer the district effectively, it is imperative to solve the problems of these people. Different methods have been adopted by Collectors for this purpose–some call it 'administration on wheels' while some others call it 'public complaint camp' etc. the name that I had coined was Janta Adalat.

The concept is to take the administration to the people, solve their grievances at their doorstep without delay and also to eliminate the middlemen and corruption. So many times one has seen people coming from a long distance to meet, say, Executive Engineer, UPSEB (UP State Electricity Board) but find that he has gone on tour. Their whole day and money is wasted and they return feeling that it is very difficult to get a hearing at the highest level and fall back into the clutches of local officials. They end up by paying bribes to get their work done.

Janta Adalat symbolized taking the entire administration to a remote corner of the district.

Normally, a block headquarter can be chosen for this. The Collector, SSP and all departmental heads go to a block on a particular day. This adalat is given wide publicity so that maximum people come forward to air their grievances. In a big hall or in a ground. Counters for each department are set up, i.e., Jal Nigam, UPSEB, Tubewells, Education, Revenue, Police etc. There is an enquiry counter also. The period from 10.00 am to 1.00 pm is fixed for individuals to approach the Collector and various heads of departments with their applications. Some problems are such that can be solved immediately. In fact, the emphasis is on solving maximum grievances on the spot. There are some issues like sanctioning of a road or building of a school which would take time to be processed. All of them are assured that replies would be given within 15 days. Thereafter, about one hour can be kept for the local MLA, pramukhs and pradhans to come out with community issues. The respective departmental heads and the Collector then respond to these issues.

To make the system really effective a master register is kept in which all the grievances are entered. The local SDM then monitors to ensure that all of them are attended to within 15 days. As Collector I would put it on my computer and monitor the progress. Also, in every case a reply was sent to the applicant. It is true that in many cases the limit of 15 days got exceeded but all the complaints got attended to. A tremendous impact can be perceived in the area where a Janta Adalat is held. It is a really potent tool of grievance redressal. It makes senior officers available to people and also accountable to them. It is different from just touring as you have all the officers together and the emphasis is on problem-solving at the spot. Call it by any name but this method of grievance redressal should be adopted. No proper redressal of grievances can take place without tackling the crucial bottleneck–corruption. In fact, if you ask an ordinary citizen his view of the bureaucracy is that it is slothful and corrupt. It moves when the palms of petty officers are greased. The DM to be successful has to create an administrative ethos where the people perceive that work can be done without bribing anyone. His response and action should denote this to the people. It is a fact that subordinate officers and employees also mend their ways if they realize that the man at the top is scrupulously honest.

Even then corruption cannot be wished away. It has got ingrained into our system and the worst is that people accept it. An elderly and respectable subordinate of mine gleefully told me that he had found an excellent match for his daughter. Excellent, when paraphrased meant the prospective son-in-law has a really high income from sources other than salary. The reasons for corruption are social, economic, political, cultural and individual. An analysis of these would be a thesis by itself.

The administrator during his stay of one or two years cannot root out corruption by attacking its origins. The disease is already there and he has to treat the symptoms.

Openness of administrative style and accessibility are the best insurances against corruption. If a person can approach the DM with his grievance and be confident of its redressal he would not have to meet the concerned employees who would not move the case without getting something.

It is also important for the DM to clearly project that anybody found guilty of corruption shall not be spared. Allegations of corruption should be immediately enquired into and if prima facie evidence is found then strictest possible action should be taken. Personal incorruptibility of the DM gives him tremendous moral courage and strength to enforce his authority and control corruption.

However, corruption is so endemic and rampant that if a DM takes on corruption headlong with the intention of rooting it out it will be left with little time to do anything else. There was this case of an outstanding District Magistrate who took on corruption. He would park his vehicle away from the sub-registrar office and go on foot to approach and nab officials personally. He would make the sub-registrar and the peshkars and chaprasi empty their pockets and ask them to account for the cash. He would inspect engineering works and if things were not up to the mark order suspensions.

The result was electrifying. Corruption was brought under control but it led to strikes, protests and direct confrontation between the DM and his employees and other departments. This left very little time for the DM to apply his brain to planning and doing something really constructive for the district. Also things returned to square one once he was transferred.

A better method which is much more lasting is to build systems and procedures which would eliminate corruption. The DM should himself formulate these systems and monitor their implementation. For instance, let us take the case of issue of domicile certificate, income certificate and caste certificate at tehsil. The applicant has to approach various people and pay up everywhere. We formulated a system where the applications were received at a counter and the applicant told to come back within 15 days. During this time the Tehsildar got all the reports taken and had the certificate ready.

In a similar manner I recall when I was SDM, permits for cement were issued by the SDM. Lot of complaints of corruption was there against the supply clerks. On checking, I found that there was indeed a great degree of arbitrariness which would certainly give rise to corruption. We made a system where applications received were kept on a 'first come first served basis.' As soon as the allotment for cement came I personally sat down with the supply staff, scrutinized the applications and signed permits. We then sent these permits by post to the people. There was tremendous appreciation for this measure.

In a similar vein there are a lot of complaints about Lekhpals charging money for giving extracts of khataunis and people being harassed for getting copies of judgements and extracts from the record room. In fact, the central theme in the famous novel *Raag Darbari* is of a lame person unable to get a copy of his document from the tehsil. Till the very end he could not obtain it.

In a particular district I started a campaign of issuing extracts of khatauni free of cost to all the land holders. It was resented by the subordinate staff initially but systematic monitoring ensured its success. Similarly, 'first come first served' method should be strictly applied in most matters and rigorously enforced. Discretion, if any, is to be used at the level of the Collector. It should not be left to the discretion at the clerk level. In fact, contact between public and dealing assistants should be kept at a minimum. Members of the public should meet senior officers for their work.

The job of the DM is to build systems and then monitor their implementation. I feel this can effectively control corruption. At the same time, things like random checks, inspections and exemplary action against corrupt employees also help. The main thing is the atmosphere. Lead has to be provided from the top. However, one point must be borne in mind. It is important for the Collector to be honest and to be seen as such but this does not give him the right to be rude or arrogant. This is the mistake that most honest officers commit–they treat everyone else as dishonest and believe that this gives them the right to proclaim their honesty from rooftops and insult others. This leads to losing support from his team and people, and makes it very difficult for him to carry out his job properly.

It is unfortunate that more and more Collectors are now being perceived by the people as being dishonest. There was a time when nobody could lift a figure against the young Collector and he was considered a paragon of virtue. It is indeed disturbing that an increasing number of young officers are falling to the lure of the lucre. Officers and others in the district try and find out if the Collector is amenable and then they exploit the situation to the full. Any IAS officer, including the Collector, should be conscious of the fact that allurements in plenty shall be offered to him and it would be really a test of his moral fiber to resist them. A Collector must realize that even the smallest aspect of his character or personality is the talking point in the district and people are only too willing to believe the worst about him. It is important for him to have a spotless reputation of integrity which nobody can tarnish. I remember when I was DM of a western UP district there was this annual excise auction. Every year the same contractor, a politically and economically powerful man used to get the contract as he made sure that nobody else had the courage to bid against him. Stories of his having bought over Collectors were the talk of the town. I realized that the district had immense potential for increase in excise revenue and along with my team of officers took all measures to make it a free and transparent auction and invite bidders from other districts guaranteeing their security. The perturbed excise contractor sent me a proposal through the district excise inspector. The government had set a target of 10% increase in revenue he offered to bid 12% higher thereby ensuring that the Collector exceeded his target and the government was also happy. Of course, the Collector and his team would be adequately compensated. According to him, it was a win-win situation. I declined and made my intentions clear. One evening before the auction this contractor came to my camp office to meet me. I called him in and was shocked to find that he offered a bag full of jewellery as nazar (paying respects). I told him bluntly that I was not interested. He folded his hands and said that he was not expecting any favour but that it was a tradition to offer "nazar" to the Collector. I emphasized that I did not agree with this tradition and ended the meeting. Next day we ensured a fair auction where income of the district went up by as much as 100%! It was a different matter that the same contractor won the auction as he would not allow anyone else to enter his territory and kept bidding higher and higher to ward off the bids of his competitors. This excise auction really established my reputation for integrity in the district and earned me a lot of respect.

These days a disgusting system has started of Collectors asking for commission while sanctioning development funds. Nothing could be more degrading than this. The money in the schemes is meant for the poor and taking commission is nothing short of day light robbery. Rest assured that if a Collector allows his integrity to be breached in this manner then he would lose all respect in the eyes of his officers as well as the common man in the district. His image would be irretrievably damaged.

Though I have emphasized the use of systems to control corruptions but there has to be a display of zero tolerance also.

If a case of corruption comes to light the Collector should make an example of it and take the strongest possible action. Just a few such cases will build an atmosphere and corruption in the district would be controlled.

Integrity regarding money has been discussed but equally important is intellectual integrity. One should have certain principles of administration and abide by them irrespective of pressure from any corner. No decision should be taken on the basis of caste, community or even personal prejudice. Commitment has to be objective and one should not derail from that. A good example of this is officers giving adverse entries to subordinates if the wife of the subordinate has not behaved properly with the boss's wife. I feel, if the subordinate is a good officer then his performance should be assessed as such. Extraneous considerations and personal issues should not be allowed to interfere with one's judgement. This, I feel, is the true definition of integrity which is a much wider term than just being honest in matters of money.

The above ensures that the administration is projected as neutral, impartial and responsive and it gains the faith of the people. This by itself leads to an effective atmosphere of grievance redressal. This is the ultimate litmus test of the success of a District Officer.

Management of Elections

When there is a discussion about the inefficiency of the government, I point to the conduct of election as one shining example–a mammoth, herculean task which is performed with pin-point accuracy by the government. It is indeed one of the most challenging tasks that confront a district officer and with the frequency of elections in recent years most Collectors have to conduct an election.

Before the notification of elections the work of checking of polling stations from the point of view of suitability and checking of electoral rolls is done. Quite a large number of polling stations are temporary in nature and the idea is to shift them to a government building which has come up nearby. Normally this work is done by the Lekhpals and a report sent by Tehsildar/SDM. These proposals have to be discussed with members of political parties and then a final proposal sent to election commission for approval.

Actually, the location of a polling station or booth can have an impact on the impartiality of election. Very often if the polling booth is made at a place around which members of dominant community stay then there is always the risk that members of minority or backward communities shall not dare to come out for voting. This can also happen if the route to the polling booth is through an area surrounded by houses of a particular community. It is for this reason that political parties always press for change of certain polling booths. Very often their aim is to benefit their own party. The election commission is very strict about allowing any change. It is reasonably assumed that since a polling booth stood the test of time in previous elections it should be ordinarily not interfered with. Thus, apart from shifting extra booths where populations of votes have increased no other change is recommended.

To the district administrations, however, there is another point on which change becomes necessary–experience of past elections. A booth might be badly located leading to booth-capturing or violence in previous elections. It is advisable to change this. However, invariably at the time of sending recommendations to the election commission these aspects are not brought out. Most often, the checking is done by lower level functionaries like the Lekhpal and their suggestions agreed to by all. After notification of election the SDMs and Tehsildars and other officers suddenly inspect the polling booths and come up with suggestions for change. However, it is too late and normally the election commission does not accept the recommendations. The only way out is to insist on checking of booths by senior officers and their report taken during the time schedule mentioned.

Electoral Rolls

The procedure regarding finalization of electoral rolls is elaborate and well-defined. The problem comes only when once the election is declared, individual and collective lists of commission and omissions start flowing in. There are complaints and allegations. Change, however, is possible till the date of filling the nomination and accordingly instructions have to be issued to SDM/Tehsildars. I feel that despite all the procedures and checks quite a few mistakes still remain. It is not deliberate but it can cause law and order problems. I recall an experience where a complete mohalla belonging to a minority community was missing from the electoral rolls and this was detected only on the day of the election. A huge crowd gathered and there was pelting of stones. It was only lathi-charge by police that controlled the situation. People were silenced but not convinced and their resentment found expression at the time of declaring results. As the district officer, the RO got up to declare the results he was surrounded by a slogan-shouting mob who hurled personal allegations and abuses against him–the point to emphasis is that the mistake inadvertently occurred at the level of a Lekhpal but in the public mind it was as deliberate act of omission on the part of the Collector.

The only way to check the above situation is by having a thorough verification of rolls by senior officers. A prescribed percentage of checking exists and the District Officer has to insist on having it complied with.

The scenario in a district changes the moment the elections are declared. Elections have to be conducted under the directions of the Elections Commission. The duty of the District Officer is to conduct free and fair polls and for this he has to gear up the entire machinery at his command and provide personal leadership.

Administrative Structure

The Collector has a district deputy election officer as his immediate deputy to look after the elections and he is usually of the rank of an additional Collector. There is an election office which has an assistant election officer and his staff who are well versed in election law and procedure. However, this set-up acts merely as a secretariat with the actual implementation to be done by a team of officers. There are a few clearly identifiable tasks to be done: selection and posting of polling personnel, arrangement of small and heavy vehicles for transportation and procurement of stationery, printing of ballot papers and organizing movement of vehicles on polling day with the parties. The best thing to do is to appoint officers as incharges of these sections. One can have a team of three officers to look after each task. However, the selection of this team and in particular the officer-in-charge is an important exercise. If the right man is chosen then half the job is done. For instance, the officer looking after transport has to be tough, active and aggressive. He has to deal with transporters, truck drivers, and government departments refusing to send their vehicles. He has to perform unpleasant tasks like sending the police and forcibly requisitioning vehicles. It has been my experience that this job is done best by a magistrate who is local, aggressive and has a reputation for wielding the baton.

Similarly, the officer in-charge of polling personnel has to be a hard working, meticulous type of an officer who is rule-bound and known for his integrity and ability to say no to pressure. The reason why I am emphasizing this point is that normally the proposal for these postings of officers/in-charges comes up in routine but the District Officer must apply his own personal discretion in the matter.

Polling Personnel

The posting of polling personnel is a huge task. A presiding officer and three to four polling officers have to be posted for each polling station. If this work is not done fairly then the impartiality of the election process can be affected. It is usual to find requests from various groups asking that a particular person may be posted in a specific polling station or that member of a community to be posted in a constituency. The other kind of pressure is from people who want to be exempted from election duty. It is, therefore, best to impersonalize the whole process. First some basic criteria should be evolved. This could be as follows:

(i) A mix of state and central government employees at each booth.

(ii) Employees of same department not to be posted at the same booth.

(iii) Caste configuration to be kept in mind.

(iv) Women employees to be posted in city areas or nearby.

Once the above has been done then the posting of personnel can be prepared by the use of computer. A very simple software is required for this and not only the posting but posting orders can also come out as computer printouts. The use of computers make a huge task look simple. One can imagine the dimension of the work if it was to be done manually. In a district like Allahabad, posting of 16,000 polling personnel had to be done. One week was required for feeding the data and thereafter immediate printouts were obtained. To do this task manually it would take well over a month and the results would not be consistent with the criteria used.

To maintain secrecy it is best to make postings on the basis of a code number and the place of posting disclosed only on the last day. I had implemented this system in Allahabad in 1994 but today the election commission has designed a software for this purpose and it is mandatory for all Collectors to use it.

Many employees want to evade duty. The moment they get their orders applications start moving in for exemption from duty. One has to be tough and uncompromising in this. There may be some genuine medical reasons which can be allowed but most employees tend to come up with fabricated excuses. Some are defiant by nature and just do not turn up for duty. The District Officer must use his powers in making them comply. An FIR under the peoples representation act against a few normally ensures results. Of course, exemption of employees connected with essential services should be done and the pay scale of employees should be guiding factor in determining his posting.

Transport

Organizing vehicles for transport is a big, unpleasant task. You require heavy as well as light vehicles. Normally the requirement is worked out assuming that each vehicle shall carry seven to eight polling parties. Vehicles have to be requisitioned well in advance. The problem comes more in smaller districts where heavy vehicles are not available and they have to get them from other districts. The larger districts having important trade or business and normally do not face such a problem.

The light vehicles have to be requisitioned from government departments. Most of them are unwilling to part with their jeeps and the majority of them are in a terrible condition. A lot of force and threatening postures have to be adopted not only to get the vehicles but to have them in proper working order.

One aspect must always be kept in mind–the demand for vehicles is always over-projected. This is specially the case with police and home-guards. Keeping in mind the requirement of economy and the shortage of vehicles this exercise must be done very thoroughly.

The crucial aspect about transportation is the movement of vehicles on the day prior to polling. If this is not properly organized then it can lead to excessive delay and lot of confusion. Normally a large field is selected from where polling parties are put into tracks/buses and moved. Very often the vehicles stand in a haphazard manner and the polling parties take hours to recognize their vehicles. Then if the vehicles are parked according to the will of the drivers then there is the inevitable traffic jam. I always insisted upon preparing a layout plan where vehicles would be parked serially. The exact place of their parking would be outlined by chalk. Sufficient space is left between two rows to ensure free movement and a proper exit route prepared. This requires not only a lot of planning but personal physical exertion on the part of officer-in-charge of transport.

Training

Training of poll personnel is an important function which is often ignored. Often the training resembles a large mela where over 3,000 to 5,000 people gather and senior officers come to the stage and give speeches which no one hears. It is best to plan out the training programme in detail and identify the points one wants to highlight. Practical demonstrations are best and as many mock polling booths as possible should be made and people asked to go through a mock poll exercise. Another effective method is the use of video cassettes but the only drawback is that a large number of TV screens are required. A good idea would be to make a film and screen it–an expensive measure if taken up for one district but manageable if done at state level. In any case an effort must be made to make training a two-way process.

Law and Order

Every arrangement comes to naught if the law and order is not maintained. This leads to violence and booth capturing. The first step in this regard is identification of sensitive polling stations. There is a tendency to blindly repeat the polling stations considered sensitive in previous elections. This exercise must be taken up afresh and handled at a senior level. The job is best entrusted to the sub-divisional magistrate and circle officer of police. They should jointly visit each police station in their area and identify and categorize the polling stations on the basis of their sensitivity. There are various reasons for which polling stations can be considered as sensitive–there could be a history of booth capturing or poll violence, communal or caste tension may be prevalent in the area; a major dispute between two parties may exist or simply polling station is in the village of an influential candidate. I have always found that the initial reaction of the officers is to declare as many stations as possible as sensitive. The problem with this approach is that there is never sufficient police force to cater to this sensitivity. It is for this reason that the sub-divisional police and revenue officers have to be personally involved and properly briefed.

Once the identification has been done all such villages or mohallas have to be visited jointly by the Magistrate of the area along with police officers. They have to hold meetings of residents and convince them of police protection and strong action against those creating trouble. The very presence of senior officials creates a psychology of fear and instills a feeling of security in the law-abiding citizens and depressed sections of society.

The emphasis, however, has to be on reduction or elimination of this sensitivity. Prevention is always better than cure. Issues like land disputes can easily be resolved. In areas where there is tension between two groups on caste or communal lines, Section 107/116 of CRPC is very effective. However, the effectiveness can be ensured only if the parties are bound down under Section 116(3) for maintaining peace with heavy sureties. Close coordination between SDM, CO and SHO is required for this. They should jointly scrutinize the lists and wherever convinced use of Section 116(3) should be done.

There exists a level above that of SDM and CO–normally the ADM and additional SP. They must thoroughly visit each category 'A' sensitive polling stations and the DM and SSP have to visit the most critical places. In fact, constant pressure of visits, meetings and preventive actions have to be taken during the last one month building up for the elections.

The deployment of police force depends upon availability. However, it is done on a scaled basis. A certain minimum force is posted in 'ordinary' polling booths.

Additions to this are made on the basis of whether a polling station is in category 'C', 'B' or 'A' sensitivity. Normally category

'B' and 'A' polling stations should have a sub-inspector in-charge along with half a section of armed constabulary. In addition there is the force with the Section and Zonal Magistrates, reserve at police outposts and force on certain mobiles strategically located in sensitive areas.

Things have changed a lot over the years. Initially several polling stations were manned by a home-guard and a village chowkidar and this was considered sufficient protection. But with the increasing cult of violence and planned attempts at booth capturing by many contestants this deployment has to be scaled upwards. It is a pity that our society is at a stage where free exercise of franchise is not possible without heavy policing. One can only hope that with education and maturity things would change. However, I may like to point out that things are different in different states. The situation in states like UP and Bihar is very problematic and the likelihood of poll violence or booth capturing is significantly higher in these states than in others. I recall being posted as election commission observer in Maharashtra for the state elections in 2004. I called a meeting of the DM and SP and asked them about booth capturing incidents in the past. They looked at me with surprise and informed me that there had been no case of booth capturing in any election in that district. The whole idea of categorizing districts into A, B or C according to sensitivity was found to be unnecessary in the peaceful environment that prevailed in the district.

Very often it is found that police personnel on duty also abet booth capturing by a particular candidate. This happens particularly in the case of those candidates who have been powerful enough to post police officers of their choice in their area. Thus, this deployment of police personnel exercise has to be done with a lot of discretion on the part of the police chief. A general shuffling of the police personnel is required and secrecy maintained.

Normally the constituencies are divided into sectors. One constituency can have anywhere from 10 to 15 sectors. This is done on the basis of geography and sensitivity. The unit to be formed as a sector should be manageable. Each sector is then put in-charge of Sector Magistrate who is provided a counterpart police officer at least of the rank of a Sub-inspector and given police force. The Sector Magistrate constantly tours the polling stations in his charge to ensure free and fair poll. The selection of Sector Magistrate is an important job and though pay scales and seniority are guiding factors the personality of the officer is very crucial. This exercise has thus to be taken up by the District Officer personally in consultation with an experienced ADM or other officers. The Sector Magistrate does not only ensure law and order; he has to see that the polling stations have been properly constructed, that they are accessible, he has to ensure that all his polling parties take their stationery on time; he has to see that the parties move on time and reach their destination safely. After poll he has to personally see that the polling parties leave the centres on time and deposit the ballot boxes at the appointed place in the district headquarters.

With possibilities of poll violence ever on the increase it has become customary to appoint zonal magistrates above the Sector Magistrates. Some have one per constituency, some deploy two. Officers experienced in law and order are appointed and they have with them force and a wireless set. The Sector Magistrates are numerous and as such it is not possible to give all of them wireless sets. The first information of a problem is flashed to the zonal magistrate who rushes to the spot.

The basic point to be kept in mind is that there is never sufficient force available to police the polls. This inadequacy has to be made up by as many mobiles as possible. It gives the impression of a lot of force and it also ensures that during polling each polling centre is visited every 20-30 minutes by a mobile.

The objective is to prevent booth capturing and poll violence. It is a psychological game that has to be played between the administration and the anti-social elements. The administration has to be constantly on the move from at least one month before the polls. Selective but qualitative preventive action has to be taken–goondas have to be rounded up. Criminals out on bail have to be roped in under other sections. Paroles have to be given in a selective way. Barriers and check-posts have to be set up for constant checking.

Above all, one has to talk tough and use the print media, radio, TV and social media to impress upon people that their safety shall be ensured and to instill a sense of fear amongst the anti-social elements.

The impression that the administration shall shoot without asking questions has to go through. I recall the classic case of a district where distances were large and police force available nominally. The district had a history of booth capturing in remote areas.

The DM and the SSP decided to move together for one week before the elections with at least a dozen vehicles with them. This included an open jeep with LMG mounted on it and several vehicles with stengun wielding policemen. The carcade would stop at strategic points and just walk around and talk to people. The reaction was electrifying. People would collect and watch anxiously and then quickly disappear indoors. Throughout the district the message spread. The press contacted the district administration about this and were told that the administration would not hesitate to use guns and if a "post mortem was to be done it should be of a body killed by a police bullet." The results were tremendous–the district had violence-free poll.

A major dimension to law and order recently added has been that of terrorism or outside agencies trying to disrupt the polls. These agencies tend to use bombs and also target important VIPs visiting during the elections. VIP security during this period becomes very important and should be looked into in detail by the DM and the SSP. No compromise with security instructions should be made under any condition.

Intelligence collection is vital. Along with the police and local intelligence unit the district magistrate must develop his own intelligence network. Members of the public, revenue officials can provide a lot of information. The eyes and ears have to be kept wide open and no information regarded as insignificant.

The Poll Day

Despite all the preparations, there can be any number of situations that can arise on the poll day and one day before which have to be tackled with firmness and great presence of mind.

In a district where there were a large number of polling personnel to be deployed, meticulous planning had been done and orders served on everyone. They had appeared for training also. But on the day the polling parties were being dispatched, a large number of parties were incomplete and the vehicles could not move. Repeatedly the names were called out over the public address system but there was no result. Reserve was available but if one started taking from the reserve then it would be an incentive for more people to disappear. Hence, substitution was resisted and officials and Sector Magistrate deployed to search out the missing members. The repeated threats over the public address system had its effect and more than 50% turned up but still this was not enough and the day had advanced and the parties were getting late. It was at this moment that after weighing the pros and cons the Collector ordered for substitution from the reserve.

The people called on reserve duty were sitting under a *shamiana* and feeling quite comfortable. They were taken by surprise when the district deputy election officer reached for the mike and announced that he would call officials by name and they should come forward to receive their orders. In an instant pandemonium broke loose and everybody got up and ran towards the exit. Fortunately, this tendency was known so the Collector had taken due precaution by posting large number of police at the entrance. However, when the people from the reserve ran the police was too shocked to act. It was a moment of crisis which called for rough measures and the deputy DEO responded accordingly. He rushed physically and caught hold of a couple of fleeing personnel and pulled them in and also shouted instructions to the police. The police swung into action. Very little force had to be used but the situation was soon brought under control and reserve personnel–a chastened lot—were brought back into the fold.

But the problems were not over–as soon as the name of substitute was called out total silence would prevail. The person, obviously in the crowd would try to avoid. If one skipped over his name then others would adopt the same subterfuge. Being in a hurry the deputy DEO moved over some names till he came to someone he could identify. But now sections of the people were up in arms. They claimed that those who are avoiding are getting away with it while the straightforward are being caught. Instantly a group was formed which threatened to boycott poll duty. It took the addition of a couple of seasoned officers to calm down the situation and then a method of picking people randomly from the crowd evolved. This worked and finally the parties were reconstituted and dispatched on time.

The above tendencies are increasing and one reason is that action for non-compliance of instructions is not taken. If cases are registered under the people's representation act and followed up then this shall act as a deterrent for the future. Cases are registered also but forgotten as soon as the elections are over. In a district, the Collector had personally directed the officer in-charge, polling personnel, to lodge an FIR. After the elections the Collector was transferred. Some months later the officer met him and informed that he was in deep trouble because of this. It seems that the new Collector had called him and asked him to withdraw the case as this was leading to a lot of bitterness. If this attitude persists then employees shall realize that no action will be taken against them and violate duty instructions with impunity.

On the polling day the crucial task is to see that polling process goes on smoothly and that there is no booth-capturing or poll-violence. An analysis of booth-capturing shows that people come in vehicles. They rush to a booth, enter it and capture it and then move away from the site within minutes. Most often they are armed, and as such people at the booth do not speak anything against them.

I found in a district where I was conducting elections that in every previous poll there had been a history of violence and as many as 40-60 booths were regularly captured. The modus operandi was that they would approach the booth in motor-cycles or jeeps, explode some small bombs which would make people run and then capture the booth. We did two things which ensured that not a single incident of booth-capturing took place. We rigorously imposed ban on movement of vehicles. Barriers were set up on all major road junctions and they were sufficiently policed to check each and every vehicle. One vehicle for a candidate, one for his agent was allowed but we restricted the number of people who could sit in this to four. Same restriction was applied to motor-cycles also. No convoy was allowed to move and no one was given permission to carry arms. We also deployed police mobiles on each route which constantly checked all vehicles to ensure compliance.

This ensured that anti-social elements could not reach the booth in a convoy and the police presence at strategic points was so significant that nobody dared also.

The Collector and his SP must start together on the day of the poll and visit the sensitive polling areas. There is no point sitting in the control room as the car has a wireless and one can monitor the reports from the entire district there. If the polling starts at 7.00 am then it is best to move at least half an hour before that. This ensures that all Magistrates and police officers are on duty on time and that the polling commences on time.

Reports of booth-capturing would keep coming over the telephone but most of them are fabricated for political objectives. However, immediately senior officers must rush to the spot to verify. Not a single bit of information should be left unattended to. But such false information can unnecessarily waste the time of the administration. In an election when we found that too many such incidents were taking place we insisted on taking the name, telephone and address of the caller or if he came in person then note down all particulars about him. They were told that if the information was false then a case would be lodged against them. As soon as this message went around the false complaints were controlled.

While on their round the DM and SP would come across cases of impersonation, intimidation at the booth, etc. Exemplary action should be taken in such cases. I recall, in an election we were visiting a sensitive area when we were told that in a particular booth the ruling party was intimidating or unduly influencing voters at the booth. We arrived at the site. It was a crowded booth and things looked a bit disorganized. We went around but could not discover anything. We organized the process and were coming out when we saw a lady literally pushing lady voters around and also telling them that they should not forget that they have to vote for a particular candidate. We sent a lady constable to tell her not to canvass for votes at the polling booth. The lady turned around and slapped the constable saying that they should know who she was. We swung into action immediately. The lady and her supporters were arrested. Immediately, a mob started gathering from all sides shouting for her release. We called for extra force which came and we announced that a lathi-charge would be ordered in minutes if they did not disperse. Seeing our threatening posture the crowd melted away and we achieved our goal. The impact was so electrifying that for the rest of the day we had no further incident.

Exemplary action is essential but one should not get provoked to the extent that an ugly situation is created. In an election the SP and I were on tour right from early morning. At several booths we found cases of impersonation. The people caught were made to hold their ears and do sit ups in front of everyone. There were mainly local toughs who lost face in this manner and the effect was tremendous. We then received reports of impersonation from the village of one of the candidates who happened be having links with criminals. We found that the polling booth was quite in the interior of the village and we saw a couple of people coming out on scooters. The SSP advised them not to move on scooters and that there was restriction on movement. However, their attitude was tough and after parking their scooters they began to argue in an arrogant manner. They were roughed up and their scooters taken away. We then approached the booth. The staff on duty informed us that everything was going on smoothly. We stayed around for some time and the SSP got around checking. He found a young boy impersonating. The SSP pulled him out of the queue and asked him to hold his ears and apologies. The lad, however, was defiant. He refused to admit his guilt and started arguing. Naturally the SSP lost his cool and picking up a lathi he gave a couple of strong blows to the boy. All of a sudden the pradhan and several people emerged and started shouting and arguing. We arrested the boy and asked him to be taken to a police jeep. It transpired that the boy was the son of the village pradhan. The pradhan started collecting people and the boy also began to resist. He was thus badly beaten up. In no time people had accumulated from all lanes and stood on their rooftops shouting anti-police slogans and approaching us. In no time brick-batting would have started and since we had a meager police force with us we would have been left with little option but to open fire. The SSP however, responded brilliantly. He took all the police force available and carried out a quick and effective lathi-charge. This was so sudden that the crowd fled. The pradhan and several others approached me. Their objection was to the beating up of the boy. After quite some time I was able to calm them down, the boy and the pradhan apologized and we released the boy.

The above is the kind of incident that can take place in case of booths in remote areas. One should not, I feel, resort to violence in front of a crowd. It is best to arrest. The action taken should not be construed as brutal and should be in proportion to the misdeed.

Total vigilance on the day of the poll and constant patrolling by senior officers is the finest way of ensuring a free and fair poll.

Counting

In district 'B' the Collector had a strange desire; he wanted to finish counting first in his district. He called a meeting of all his returning officers and others concerned and put the proposition before them. It was the general consensus that counting would take 24 hours and very little could be done to reduce this time. But the Collector was adamant and with this in mind he decided to adopt the principles of time and motion study he had picked up at a training course. One after another the group came out with various activities involved in counting. Even the smallest activity was put down in the form of a chart. The time taken for each activity was considered. It soon became evident to most that due to faulty planning many activities did not start on time and that there was a lag between two activities.

Elementary things were considered. Counting was supposed to start at 8.00 am. The general experience was that it normally started anywhere from 8.45 to 9.30 am. This time the Collector and his team had the training for counting personnel in the training pandal itself. Each person was made to sit on the seat where he would sit the next day during counting. They were then called at 7.30 am next morning. Since they all knew their seats they went in and sat down well in time. Normally, they would have taken quite some time to locate their seats. Then complaints like broken chairs and table had been attended to in advance.

Sufficient number of chaprassis were posted for each constituency and there was division of labour amongst them. Two were taking out the ballot boxes and handing them over to two others who in turn gave them to others. There were 15 tables and a chaprassi posted for three tables. The arrangement worked so well that by 8.10 am a ballot box was on each table.

Whichever table finished counting its first round the fastest immediately got its second ballot box. There was no time lag between this. In some earlier elections they had waited for all the tables to complete their first round before sending in the second round of boxes. This meant that the slowest table was leading the others, and there was no incentive to count faster.

All this would have come to naught if proper arrangement for tea and food was not made. In fact, the principle adopted was that the food should be of a very good quality and plentiful. It was ensured that it would be served on time–between 1.00 pm and 2 pm, tea and snacks were served every two hours while water was being constantly distributed. For each group of five tables an officer of the rank of supply inspector or Naib Tehsildar was made responsible to see that there was no problem regarding food.

Despite all this planning there was a time when arrangements were about to break down. The food for police people was organized separately but did not come on time. The policemen forcible took away the lunch packets meant for counting personnel. The Collector and his team rushed to the spot. More food was prepared and distributed. A senior officer went around the tables and apologized for the delay.

Above all, to instill a spirit or competition cash prizes were announced for the first three tables in each pandal. This made the whole exercise very interesting. As a consequence the results started coming by 8.00 pm and were over by 12.00 pm. It was a pleasure to hear over the television that the first results had come from district 'B' and the Collector and his team achieved their objective.

The above case study illustrates how careful planning and attention to detail can make things go faster and better. Speed in counting is not all–there should be very good training imparted to ensure that there are no mistakes. The RO should be clear about what makes a vote invalid and his decision should be prompt and confident. Counting moves much better if the presiding officer had been trained well and his ballot paper account is proper. The RO should attach competent people with him to tabulate the results of each round and to tally the accounts. Generally, amins and bank employees do this job very well.

The above experience that I have recounted belongs to a period when ballot papers were used. Today the electronic voting machine (EVM) is used all over the country. The entire process of counting of votes becomes much simpler and faster because of this and now almost within 5-6 hours of the beginning of the counting process the results are available. Still, a lot of meticulous planning is required to see that the entire counting process is done in a fair and transparent manner.

Applications for recounting are moved in a routine manner. They must be treated on merit and a speaking order passed in writing.

The result should be declared immediately and not held up. The latter situation creates a doubt in the minds of the parties. However, instructions of Election Commission in this respect have to be adhered to. The role of the election observers also becomes very important and they also give their opinion on whether counting has been done properly and results can be announced.

Generally, innovations in election are not encouraged. The premium is on conducting the elections peacefully and the smallest failure can disrupt the entire process. Still, one feels that innovative concepts can be tried at the district level. One idea is to send the ballot papers on the morning of the polls with the Sector Magistrates and not send it with the polling parties a day before the poll. Actually, several cases have come to light where the ballot papers are stamped in the night itself. Losing of ballot papers can also take place. Hence, this is a plausible method–let the presiding officer count the ballot papers, then put in a cover and seal it. The papers can be kept in the sub-treasuries at the tehsil. The Sector Magistrates pick up the ballot papers in the morning and take them to the polling stations.

Another innovation that comes to mind is decentralization of the activities of dispatch of polling parties and counting. At the moment it is done centrally at district headquarters. This could be done at different tehsils. It will certainly make things easier and much more manageable–only problem could be to ensure security at several places instead of one.

The conduct of election is a major feather in the cap for the district Collector and the entire team of officers in the districts and the state level. It is a huge task which is conducted smoothly and shows the kind of leadership that Collectors are capable of if they are allowed to carry out their responsibilities without any undue interference from the political level. Conduct of elections is something that the government should be proud of and the district Collectors should always perform this task with utmost devotion and a sense of responsibility. The Collector should not only be impartial but be perceived by all the political parties as being so.

Election Commission Observers

Over the years the election commission has appointed more and more observers to supervise the fair and impartial conduct of elections and also do keep a check on election funding. These observers now spend almost two months in the district and almost every aspect of the election has to be approved by them. The Collector must brief the observers on all issues and if any complaint is referred to him by an observer it should be attended to immediately. It is important for the Collector to maintain a very close and open communication with the election observers.

The Election Commission has initiated several reforms like issuing identity cards to voters. Electronic voting machines have been introduced and there are various other electoral reforms on the anvil. However, for the District Officer the challenge always remains to provide personal leadership and lead his team in a manner that free and fair elections are ensured. On this depends the success of the democratic set up of our country. The administration must keep the magnitude of the task and its repercussions in mind through the election process. An election conducted well and fairly is a significant contribution to the democratic life of our country.

Management of Natural Calamities

Natural calamities like floods or earthquakes or famines have to be managed by the Collector using all the resources at his command. Famines do not take place now but a drought situation does arise. The moment the initial shock of a natural calamity is over; politicization of the situation takes place which puts the forbearance, patience, determination and management skills of a Collector to its severest test. Only recently there was this case of a district struck by a massive earthquake. One Collector was moved out because it was felt he was too liberal with the government aid and was frittering away scarce resources. His successor tightened the purse strings only to have an agitation against him on the grounds that the government assistance was getting unduly delayed. The extent of politicization and involvement of vested interests was such that the district saw three Collectors in a year's time.

Floods

My first exposure to floods was as a sub-divisional officer. Incessant rains for over a fortnight created a situation where all the rivers were swollen. The cry that floods are coming went around the tehsil and I, accompanied by my Tehsildar, went to a bridge above the river to find the water just a few feet below the bridge level. The portents were alarming and immediately an alert was sounded. Within the night itself the staff was rushed to its duties at flood outposts and warning issued to villages which were likely to be submerged. Regular monitoring of weather reports and water level was being done.

The floods came in full fury within the next 24 hours. The road leading to the District Headquarters was cut off and more than a dozen villages were flooded with water.

We moved from village to village. Much of the distance had to be travelled by boat. But the very fact that we would reach a village gave the people a lot of relief. Gram, salt and match boxes were distributed along with packed food which we had taken from voluntary agencies. The sick were attended to and medicines given. With great persuasion the marooned villagers were evacuated to flood relief shelters where they were looked after.

Imagine my consternation then when after a couple of days a local political leader along with his henchmen approached me and motioned my vehicle to a stop. They started complaining that hundreds were dying and the administration was not doing anything. A verbal exchange followed and I told them about the work that had been done. They named a couple of other affected villages. I assured them that on my return from a place where evacuation was taking place I would visit these villages. I returned only by evening and went to the village which was that of the leader, Mr. Pandey. It was not much affected but there was another village 2 km down where the water had entered. We went there on foot and had to wade through knee-deep water at times. We reached the village, did our job of providing relief and returned by midnight. Mr. Pandey was totally taken aback at the way and the zeal with which the administration was working. He apologized for his behaviour and became one of our strongest supporters.

Mr. Pandey had a change of heart but many others do not. They want to exploit the situation and so create an ugly scene.

The Collector has to be firm and not allow such interference in his working.

Handling of floods requires a detailed flood plan to be prepared well in advance. This is prescribed and detailed instructions are issued but somehow this tends to get ignored at the district level and very often a loosely drafted skeleton plan is prepared. I feel it is important to sit down and prepare a proper plan. Once this is done, then it can be regularly updated every year. After a proper survey it should be ascertained as to how many villages shall be affected at what water levels, the likelihood of reaching a particular water level and the past history of floods. One has to select sites for flood shelters, have them properly inspected beforehand and a clear plan made out as to which village shall be shifted to which flood shelter and the names of staff on duty at each shelter. The essential commodities required should be ascertained and kept at focal points for movement to shelters. Stock of medicines for men as well as animals along with roster of duties for doctors should be prepared. Number of boats available has to be physically ascertained and their rates finalized in advance. If a plan comprising of these and other similar aspects is properly made and everyone is aware of it then more than half the job is done.

In districts prone to floods the rainfall and water level of the rivers is taken daily. A close watch on them needs to be kept. As soon as there is a rising trend in the water level and if it crosses the low flood level mark, general alert must be declared in the entire district. It is good to do this a little in advance and even if the water level recedes after that this exercise acts as a rehearsal.

Saving life and property is manageable. All it requires is the presence of senior officers at the site. The most difficult part is handling the distribution of relief. Normally this is done at such a large scale that there is every chance of the wrong person getting relief and also much of it finding its way into the pockets of lower level functionaries. I have found to my surprise that some of the really well-off people stand in queue for aid when they are not eligible for it. When they are not given aid they create a scene and they are the people who start a maligning campaign against the administration. There is no other way to control this but intensive touring and checking by the Collector and his senior officers. If any case of official bungling or corruption is detected strongest possible action should be taken.

The real conflict arises in the preparation of list of beneficiaries. The officials entrusted with this job collude with local vested groups and include the names of non-eligible people in the lists. As such the list prepared has to be verified by a group of senior officers and there is nothing better than if the Collector can spare time to visit a couple of villages randomly and do some sample checking. This ensures that a proper list is made. The second problem is that at the time of distribution of relief full amount is not given and various functionaries and vested interest groups share some part of the relief.

In a district which was flood ravaged there were serious complaints coming from a distribution centre which was in the interior. It was not approachable by jeep. We then decided to go on bicycles. The moment we reached the centre everyone was taken by surprise. They never expected the Collector to reach there. A quick enquiry revealed that out of Rs 100/- to be distributed, only Rs 80/- was being given to the beneficiaries and the balance taken away. The entire staff was suspended. This had an exemplary effect in the entire district. Hence, it can always be expected that there would be some bungling in distribution of relief, it is necessary to check personally and take exemplary action.

There are also cases where excessive rains or hailstorm take place which damages the standing crops and also the houses of the poor. In such cases the Collector must conduct an immediate on the spot enquiry. It would be preferable if he himself visits some of the affected areas to assess the extent of the damage for himself. The guidelines for providing relief are clear and the collector must begin providing this relief at the earliest. If required he may request the state government to send more funds to the district. In such cases, proper implementation of the crop insurance schemes also become important and the Collector must ensure that the insurance claims made by the farmers are honoured by the insurance companies. The leadership of the Collector again assumes a lot of importance because the insurance companies tend to evade granting claims.

Drought

The moment the rainfall fails there is a cry of drought. There is tremendous pressure on the Collector to declare a drought. Daily there are processions led by various political parties handing over memorandum to the Collector to get a drought declared. It must, however, be borne in mind that there is no such thing as declaring drought. If there is persistent scanty rainfall and more than 50% of crops are damaged then the district is said to be affected by drought. Suspension of land revenue, a deliberate go-slow in recovery of other dues is the immediate relief that can be offered. If the situation becomes serious then test works have to be opened up to give employment to people and availability of food grain and essential commodities ensured.

With the substantial increase in irrigation coverage the specter of a major famine has receded. At times of scanty rainfall if the resources available are closely monitored then the dry spell can be managed.

The first thing to attend to is the tubewells and canals. The water in the canal system goes down. A revised roaster has to be prepared to ensure that proper distribution of water takes place. Various vested groups intervene and try to take maximum water for their villages. In one particular district a group of farmers led by a powerful person sat on a fast in front of the head of a canal protesting against diversion of water to other areas. When it was explained to them that the scarce resource would have to be equitably managed they resented it and made an attempt at self-immolation. They were forcefully prevented from doing so. In a sudden rush of anger they rushed to the canal and started attacking it and damaging it. lathi-charge had to be used to disperse them.

Such situations are bound to arise but have to be tackled firmly. Instances of canal cutting increase. Vigorous patrolling by the police and lodging of cases against those involved helps.

The functioning of state tubewells has to be constantly monitored. Even though their contribution to the overall irrigation coverage is not high they create a tremendous psychological impact. There are constant reports in the press about majority of tubewells being out of order. During a drought situation more tubewells are likely to get out of order.

Regular monitoring of this process and prompt repairs is essential. One should try and keep the percentage of tubewells out of order to less than 10%. There is always a dispute about this figure. The tubewell department underplays this figure whereas people and politicians and the press exaggerate it. The best method out is to have joint inspections undertaken by tubewell and revenue authorities. This ensures a correct picture. This should be made the base of monitoring.

Electricity availability has to be monitored. If this supply goes down then it affects the running by the canals, tubewells and also private tubewells. It is perhaps one of the crucial aspects of fighting droughts. Overall shortage cannot be countered at the district level but breakdown at the local level can be controlled by rigorous monitoring. A weekly feeder-wise report of supply should be taken from electricity department and cross-checked with reports given by the Sub-Divisional

Magistrates. Transformers burnt are to be promptly attended to and immediately replaced–carefully planned and directed roistering can also help.

Drinking water is a major issue. Most of the rural areas are served by hand pumps. These get out of order and an excessively long time is taken for their repairs causing problems. In fact, there are so many hand pumps installed that Jal Nigam (the agency responsible for maintenance) does not get to know how many pumps are not functioning till a complaint is lodged. This can be in the form of a postcard, or an application to the senior officers or complaint can be noted in the registers opened up at Tehsil and block headquarters for this purpose. Even then Jal Nigam has limited teams of mechanics and the repair process is slow leading to a lot of hue and cry. In a drought situation this becomes all the more pressing because the water level persistently goes down rendering hand pumps useless.

Rigorous monitoring of repairs is the only way to speed up the process but a change of approach is also necessary. In various schemes one can get people at the village level trained in repair of hand pumps. Ideally almost every second village should have a trained hand pump mechanic and the pradhan of the village should call him and get the hand pump repaired and pay him out of the funds allotted to him under various schemes. I tried this in one of the districts and the results were most rewarding.

Typically, the government sanctions more hand pumps to be installed every year but the funds normally reach after the onset of summer and the hand pumps are installed in monsoon months. In a drought year when the public clamours for relief the government responds by sanctioning more hand pumps. The dispute then comes about site selection. It once again tends to get politicized with lists being prepared and given by the public representatives and others. One should respect the lists given by MLA/MPs but prioritization needs to be done on the basis of actual need. I found that this very important task must be entrusted to the SDMs who should satisfy themselves personally as far as possible. Not only must the village be selected but also the site, for very often the pradhan or influential members of village would install the hand pump in front of his house.

The installation of hand pumps then has to be carefully monitored to ensure that work is completed early and the quality of work is good. The latter tends to suffer in these situations as because of drought there is more emphasis on speed of construction. Constant physical verification by a team of officers is the best way to ensure results.

There are, in addition, the drinking water schemes which meet the water needs of several villages through piped water supply. Normally the maintenance level of these schemes is low.

During drought there are frequent cases of motor burning and low availability of water due to reduction in water level. Adequate spare parts have to be procured and kept and constant vigilance maintained. Since electric supply also becomes erratic and gets reduced during a drought it becomes essential to install generators. The generators can be taken on rent but money for its running will have to be provided.

Then there is always the danger of an epidemic spreading during a drought. Dehydration cases are on the increase. This area deserves the most attention as even a single death becomes an issue and leads to discrediting the district administration. Adequate supply of medicines at primary health centres, frequent visits of health workers, cleaning and testing of waste sources, vaccination and inoculation are some of the ways in controlling this situation. The main thing has to be a very alert feedback system from the village where the first sign of an illness or epidemic should be communicated to the authorities. Nobody can do this better than the Lekhpal and it is his job to move from village to village during this period.

Diseases tend to spread amongst animals also and there is also shortage of *chara* (fodder) for animals. Adequate stock of *chara* has to be made available at reasonable rates for farmers and their cattle inoculated against diseases. The veterinary doctors and hospitals have also to be on constant alert and regular touring of villages should be done.

If the situation becomes particularly bad then test works for giving employment can be opened up. Normally, funds are available under district plan, and other schemes at the district. These can immediately be deployed and more funds called for. Work should be selected in a manner that they are spread out over most of the affected villages and the poor, landless people given work. One has to be careful otherwise again the unscrupulous contractor would try to move in and deny the benefits to the poor.

But giving of wages is not enough. Foodgrains have to be made available at controlled rates. The public distribution system comes under severe stress during this period. If necessary, temporary fair price shops must be opened and all shops adequately stocked with foodgrains. Distribution has also to be monitored in a manner that benefit reaches the poor. Regular monitoring of lifting and distribution of grains and working of public distribution system has to be done. Additional quantities of grain can be requisitioned and the government does increase the allotment of a district affected by drought.

Two points are important in managing a drought condition– regular inflow of information and coordinated action. A review used for this which proved very effective was weekly meetings at the tehsil level under the chairmanship of SDM. This was attended by officers of all departments. The Lekhpals would bring information about each village on all relevant points, e.g. number of hand pumps out of order, hours of electricity supply, spread of diseases, etc. This information is discussed and remedial measures planned. The next week the implementation of these measures and any fresh information is discussed and remedial measures planned. A day in the week was fixed for these meetings. Two days after this day a weekly meeting was held by the Collector in which the SDMs and district level officers of all departments met and reviewed all aspects. This method ensured that the drought situation was handled by a tehsil level and district level task force and that there was constant flow of information all around.

Nevertheless, these days a severe drought can be tackled effectively. It is true that despite the availability of irrigation coverage, if rainfall is scanty then the water level goes down, the tubewells fail, the canals dry up. Yet if an alternative cropping pattern is adopted then disaster can be averted. One can easily switch to a crop like toria, which require less water. The job of the administration is to make seeds of such crops available at subsidized rates. Above all, the administration has to constantly inform and educate the farmers about the alternative crops available.

When I was Chief Secretary of UP, the Bundelkhand region faced a severe drought for three consecutive years and the situation became very difficult for the poor people in the third year. I recall having a detailed meeting with the Collectors and through them implementing several measures to counter this problem. Job cards under the rural employment guarantee scheme MGNREGA were prepared on priority and anybody who wanted work was given employment in the village itself. Electricity supply to the villages was ensured for at least 12 hours a day and irrigation water made available wherever possible. Bundelkhand had a system of meeting their irrigation and drinking water needs through tanks which had all got silted overtime. I directed the Collectors to use MGNREGA and desilt all the ponds so that the moment some rain comes these ponds fill up and meet the water needs of the people. Essential commodities like food grains, oil, salt, ghee and sugar were packaged by the Collectors and delivered to the homes of the affected people. Ration at subsidized rates was made available from fair price shops.

Immediate cash relief as per guidelines was also distributed. The Collectors rose to the occasion to carry out these relief measures on priority and we could alleviate the suffering of the people to a great extent.

Fire and Hailstorms

There are chances of fire and hailstorms every year in a district. The moment a hailstorm hits an area there is a cry for relief and suspension of collection of revenue. Much of it is not warranted as the loss may be minimal. The Collector has to be firm and get a thorough enquiry conducted as to the extent of loss. Senior officers must verify the reports of lower level functionaries. If actually a serious damage has taken place then, of course, relief has to be provided immediately.

Fire takes place after harvesting when the crops are stocked up in the village stock yard. They can be deliberate as well as due to chance. Fire tenders have to be dispatched on first information and thereafter loss assessed and relief provided. The crucial principle to be borne in mind is that to provide relief speedily, is the duty of the state but the Collector must ensure that it goes to the genuine person and that there is no wastage involved.

Disasters and Accidents

Apart from the above the Collector is called upon to tackle situations of serious accidents and disasters. Major fires break out in the cities. The Collector will have to monitor the position on wireless. Fire brigades are sent. Police force is dispatched. If the fire does not come under control then the Collector has to liaison with Defence, Railways, etc. to get their fire brigades and try and control the effects of the disaster.

Major accidents can take place–rail accidents or road mishap. Here again the Collector has to visit the sport, assess damage, ensure medical help to the injured and coordinate all activities. In all such matters the Collector shall have to lead from the front. He has to reach the spot and use his presence of mind.

He has also to take measures to see that such incidents do not recur. I recall in a district there was threat of bomb explosion by terrorists. One day a bomb exploded in a bus, killing a couple of people. The Collector then had to devise a plan for checking, verifying and warning people to see that no such incident occurred in future. Our vigilance and efforts paid off. A vigilant policeman discovered a bomb at the railway station and another one near the telephone exchange. Thus proper planning and alertness can avoid a major disaster.

A major tragedy that took place in one of the districts where I was Collector related to almost a dozen deaths due to mixing of a lethal insecticide with water. It so happened that this insecticide got mixed with water at the supply tank. It never became clear as to how this happened. One plausible theory was that this insecticide looked like bleaching powder and was added to the water by mistake by water corporation employees. Anyway, all of a sudden by mid-day on that fateful morning people living in a particular area started developing strange symptoms. They had nausea, dizziness and within minutes they collapsed. The medical college was just adjacent and within a matter of an hour hordes of cases were being brought to the emergency section of the medical college. The news spread like wild fire that a mysterious illness had gripped most people of a locality. As Collector I rushed to the spot with my other officers and I rang up the principal of the medical college and Chief Medical Officer to rush with their teams.

The sight at the hospital was truly alarming in front of me. I could see patients coming and collapsing before they could enter the hospital. The doctors told me that these were cases of poisoning. A possible source could be water as a large number of cases were coming. We had to act fast. We disconnected the water supply of the entire city. Then we fitted loudspeakers on auto rickshaws and made them go around every locality warning people not to drink the water collected since morning and to throw it away. We recruited volunteers who went from door to door to spread this message.

At the hospital there were no beds left. Patients were lying all over the floor. The relatives of the patients were full of panic and this turned to anger when they were told by a doctor that the drug required to tackle such poisoning cases was not available in the hospital. The agitated mob started shouting. They forcibly entered the hospital rooms and threatened to lynch the doctors if proper attention was not being given. A couple of small time leaders used this opportunity to make allegations of corruption against the doctors and demanded blood. Suddenly a cry went around. They had caught hold of a couple of doctors and were trying to beat them up and someone was shouting that houses of doctors should be set on fire.

I had to move in personally to placate the mob. The agitated mob would not calm down. Some of them even pushed me around. The police had to use the baton on them. I tried to raise my voice and speak to them. Slowly they calmed down, "save our children Collector Saab they shouted," I told them that I would do so but they should also cooperate.

After calming them we opened up rooms in nursing homes and other hospitals and shifted patients so that everybody got a bed. Private doctors were called up for help and for every two/three affected people we had one doctor. Medicines were purchased from all the chemists and given free of cost. The shortage was made up by ordering drugs from adjacent districts and even Delhi which came within a couple of hours. By late evening the position had been controlled. There was no fresh case. All the cases had been attended to and after initial deaths there was no further casualty.

The cause was then analyzed. Water supply to rest of the city resumed after chemical testing. The test reports of water from the reservoir showed presence of an insecticide. The tank had to be emptied and thoroughly cleaned up. A high level enquiry was ordered and senior officers of Water Corporation placed under suspension.

The above is just to illustrate the type of disaster/calamity that can take place. The Collector then has to be a leader. He has to gather all possible resources around him and act. There is no time to bother about rules and procedure. The Collector must maintain his cool, his presence of mind and personally supervise all the operations. Handling of calamities and disasters is one of the major tasks of a Collector.

Handling a Pandemic

The country has been struck by the Covid-19 pandemic. As per the act to deal with a pandemic the entire powers are vested with the District Magistrates. The power to impose a lockdown, declare containment zones with restrictions on movement, social-distancing practices to be followed, not allowing gathering of people for any function without permission, maintaining law and order are the responsibilities of the District Magistrates. They have to ensure that even at the time of a lockdown essential commodities are made available to the citizens so that they do not suffer. Large number of people lost employment and so employment schemes like MGNREGA have to be increased several times to provide money to the impoverished people. Testing for disease has to be done at a very high level and on the basis of this tracking, tracing and treatment has to be done on a war footing. Covid-wards have to be declared in the hospitals and doctors and healthcare staff put on regular duty and provided with essential protection kits. All essential medicines have to be made available and monitoring of each case of an infected person ensured. Monitoring of the deaths has to be done to find out the reasons to ensure that preventive measures are taken in future. Vaccination of all according to government guidelines is another task which has to be managed by the Collectors so that the vaccine is kept at the right temperature, transported to the sight of vaccination which should have adequate number of trained vaccinators who would ensure that all eligible persons get vaccinated without any hardship. The recent pandemic has been a one in a lifetime event and has tested the calibre of the Collectors to the maximum. It is heartening to note that a lot of Collectors have done an outstanding job once again proving the point that the institution of the District Magistrates and collector is capable of responding to any situation. It is the leadership of the Collector which will determine how the entire pandemic is managed and crucial lives saved.

The government as well as the people look towards the Collector in the time of any emergency. They accept him to handle the situation and have faith in the institution to deliver. I recall in UP there was a traumatic earthquake in Uttar Kashi (now in Uttaranchal) and it was handled by the Collector in an exemplary manner. The first Collector had to be transferred as the situation got the better of him and he himself got so emotionally affected by the disaster that his sense of balance and equanimity was affected. The second Collector used his leadership skills to bring the situation under control, provide relief and go about reconstruction. The Collector is under great stress in such situation and he has to have the quality of remaining calm and stress free to be able to act with common sense and a sense of perspective. The Gujarat earthquake was another example of this kind of a situation where the Collector played a huge role and many officers got awarded for their brilliant performance in reconstruction and rehabilitation.

Handling VIP/VVIP Visits

A significant part of the time of a Collector at the district is taken by handling VIP/VVIP visits. These are important because mishandling brings bad name to the district administration and the Collector in particular. The issues are always so sensitive that even the slightest slip can cause embarrassment. This is one area where one should never make the mistake of being even a trifle complacent. It should never be taken as a matter of routine and it is always advisable for the Collector to review the arrangements personally and also check on the spot.

As a young probationer I had occasion to observe an old and experienced ADM at the job. The Chief Minister along with his cabinet was coming and halting at the airport for about an hour and then going ahead. My Collector called me and told me to go with the ADM and get trained on VIP duty. This ADM had been promoted from Tehsildar but was known to be an expert at handling VIP visits. I saw him going around checking everything personally: the cleanliness, the toilets, the sofas, the air-conditioners and also the elaborate security arrangements. I also found that he had water boiling for tea, cold drinks, fruit juice and even butter-milk in ready condition. I asked him the reason for having so many alternatives available. He smiled and then told me that the crux of VIP duty is "tarkari (vegetable dish) is more important than sarkari (official work)."

I think these were really gems of wisdom and should be kept in mind while organizing a VIP visit. He did not mean only the eating part but he was referring to all arrangements. No matter how good your official performance is, if the VIP is upset over some arrangement then he is bound to carry a very poor impression about you. The essence of VIP duty is an eye for detail and a personal touch. In the incident I am talking of, when the VIPs landed they were offered tea or cold drinks or juice. Sure enough they opted for *mattha*–a drink made of curd. The ADM had anticipated well and the *mattha* was on the table within minutes.

The point was driven home to me later on while handling the visit of a VIP who was fond of tea. As soon as he set down for the meeting the tea came. The VIP took one sip and pushed it away as it was cold. There was a flutter and the tea came again. This time the water had not been boiled properly. A third time the VIP found that it was cold again and also commented on the quality of the tea used. He was a nice person and said that he did not want more tea and would rather do with a glass of water. I got a real dressing down from my boss after the VIP left. My boss was understandably livid. I tried to explain that I could not possibly see everything. My boss however had a point–when it was known that the VIP was fond of tea, better arrangements could have been made. He also emphasized that doing a job well meant that one has to strive for excellence in the smallest item.

But VIP visits are not all matters of food habits and comforts. They require a lot of management. Detailed planning has to be done beforehand and the Collector must hold a couple of review meetings.

Whenever a VIP is due to visit they first ask for a minute-to-minute programme. This should be made carefully in consultation with organizers and keeping the time element strictly in mind.

If the VIP is coming by helicopter then the site has to be carefully chosen. It is always advisable for the DM and SP to see the site personally. Then the helipad must be constructed as per rules and barricading and security arrangements done accordingly. The fleet of cars must be as per instructions and a regular dress rehearsal done one day before the visit of the VIP.

Visit of Chief Minister/Prime Minister

In the visit of CM/PM the first problem comes in is the number of people to be allowed at the airport/helipad. The political party people resent this as they want to turn out in large numbers but for security reasons not many people can be allowed in. It is best to have a dialogue with the party president and make a list of people and vehicles which would be allowed. It is preferable to issue passes to them. The pass, however, becomes a status symbol and everybody starts hankering for it. One should keep a 10% margin as some people cannot be denied and shall have to be given a pass at the last moment.

The garlands that these people bring have to be thoroughly checked. They should then all be made to stand in a line and ensured that they do not rush towards the plane. Once the CM comes out then it becomes difficult to contact them and they surround the VIP shouting slogans and garlanding him. A security ring (manual) should be made around the VIP to ensure that he doesn't get pushed or hurt. The best strategy is to keep his car nearby and let the VIP enter the car early and leave.

Very often a dispute starts on who would sit with the VIP. The tussle between the political people on this was that each one wants to show that he is close to the VIP. They start pushing open the door of the car and I have been witness to events where there has been a regular scuffle which causes no end of embarrassment. Police intervention at this stage can cause problems as a particular person could get hurt and also view police action as being partial. This is indeed a ticklish issue but most VIPs themselves find a way out by asking the Commissioner or Collector to sit with them.

In every political party there are clashes of ego and differences amongst personalities. This often leads to ugly situations. In one of the VIP visits the names of people allowed at the airport had been finalized in consultation with party president but several people opposed to him had been left out. As soon as the carcade of the CM moved out of the airport they found that a large number of party people were sitting on the main-road shouting slogans against the administration. As the police ran to disperse they refused to budge. The situation warranted use of lathi-charge but they all belonged to the ruling party. The CM, however, solved the problem adroitly by getting down from his car and meeting them. He agreed to listen to their grievances at the circuit house and take appropriate action. The matter was resolved.

The next point is the circuit house. Most VIPs want to meet the public. The DM collects list of delegations which are coming but in the event of a visit this list is endless. They are given passes to enter the circuit house. In one VIP visit these delegations were all waiting at the lawns. As soon as the VIP carcade came they jumped, pushed the policemen aside and surrounded the VIP shouting slogans. It was with great difficulty that the VIP could be taken to his room. The huge crowd at the veranda broke the metal detector, posts, glass panes and started shouting and banging at the door–a mild lathi-charge had to be used which become an issue by itself. As soon as the door would be opened for the delegation several others would try and push their way in. And when stopped they would get restless and shout slogans.

A better way to manage this situation which I subsequently used has been to have a *shamiana* in the lawn with chairs for people to sit. There should be a stage for the VIP. Heavy barricading and deployment of police force should be done to ensure that people do not cross the lawns to the circuit house. As soon as the VIP comes, meeting these people should be kept as the first point on the agenda. The VIP stands on the dais and takes memorandums which at times can run into a thousand. Thereafter, the VIP speaks to them over the mike assuring them of prompt action on their grievances. The VIP then goes to the circuit house and these people are escorted out of the premises. This way the pressure is eased.

A few select and important delegations can then meet the VIP inside. Here also one thing must be kept in mind. People have an annoying habit of not getting up even after they have said whatever they had to say. They try to take as much time as possible and would begin to consume time by talking of as many extraneous issues as possible. One method of combating this is to have two to three interconnected rooms set aside for meeting of delegations. One delegation meets the VIP in room 'A' while another delegation waits in room 'B' and yet another in room 'C'. The VIP then moves. As soon as he is over with one delegation he gets up and moves to room 'B' and so on. Meanwhile room 'A' is vacated and a fresh delegation comes in there. In this way least time is lost and meeting with people managed.

The Route

The route duty and fleet should be properly managed. Not a single extra car should be allowed in the fleet irrespective of the status of the person concerned. There is also an order in which the cars in a fleet are kept. This should be strictly followed. In fact, the DM and the SP should keep themselves just behind the VIP car. The cars of Commissioner and DIG should preferably be behind that of the DM and the SP. The policemen on route duty should be alert. Very often they start watching the VIP carcade. They should, instead, concentrate on their surroundings. In one VIP visit a couple of people opposing the VIP visit rushed out from a side lane and came very close to the VIP car. The car swerved and there could well have been an accident. The policemen on duty at the lane were looking towards the road and were unmindful of the people rushing in from the behind.

Public Meetings

In the event of a public meeting being held, elaborate security arrangements have to be made. The first thing is the podium. It has to be made as per rules and personally checked for strength.

Once again, there is a resistance that this stage should be made bigger than prescribed as there is a huge list of people who want to be on the stage. No quarter should be given in this discussion with party president and MLAs should come out with the number and names of people allowed on the dais. This has to be strictly followed and there is always a magistrate and police officer on duty at the steps of the dais. No extra person should be allowed on the dais.

There are detailed instructions available for the barricading the minimum distance to be kept from the dais. These instructions are not to be compromised with under any conditions. Elaborate magisterial and police duties have to be deployed. The issue of parking, lights and sanitation has also to be carefully seen. One sensitive issue is traffic diversion. The principle to be followed is minimum inconvenience to the public otherwise it brings a bad name to the VIP and also to the administration.

The sound system should be thoroughly checked. In one meeting the mike failed for a several minutes. The DM was held responsible and got a dressing down from the VVIP, in another the electricity went off for a few minutes for which the executive engineer UPSEB had to answer. All these small details have to be checked and cross-checked. Nothing should be left to chance.

In certain districts you have the occasion of the visit of heads of states. One such district was Agra. Almost every other day a very important foreign dignitary would come. Elaborate protocol arrangements have to be followed in consultation with the ministry of external affairs. Normally an advance party comes to check all arrangements. The DM has to be personally present to receive and see off, and in certain cases accompany the VVIP. The golden rule here also is to check everything to the minutest detail. Nothing can be overlooked.

VIP/VVIP duty can be extremely taxing for the magistrates and police officers on duty–an important point for the DM and SP is to brief them properly together.

There have been instances of lack of coordination between the magistrate and police officers leading to trouble. They would be explained everything in detail and instructions should be clear and specific and not ambiguous. However, these officers have still to exercise their discretion. An unexpected VIP can come along and if you refuse entry to him hell will follow. At the same time, if they make an exception then it should be really unavoidable, otherwise a difficult situation arises. In one case no cars were to be allowed into the circuit house. All cars were being stopped and guided to the parking place. One MLA who was a particularly strong person came and was stopped. He made a scene and the magistrate and police officer on duty allowed him in, just behind him was the car of the editor of a newspaper. He was stopped. He gave the example of the earlier car allowed in but the magistrate on duty refused to relent. An ugly situation was created which forced the DM and the SSP to come to the gate and intervene. Here the MLA should have been stopped. If exceptions were being made, then the editor should surely have been allowed to take his car inside.

This apart, there are always those who are unhappy with the administration over the arrangements which do not give due importance to them. There could also be hot exchanges between officers on duty and members of the public. The DM and the SSP should always support all bonafide actions of their subordinates specially those undertaken at the specific instructions of the DM and the SSP. This goes a long way in building the morale of the team and they do no grudge the long hours spent in VIP duty.

Handling the media during a VIP visit is quite an issue. The media cannot be stopped yet they cannot be allowed everywhere. The Collector can handle this situation by using his personal rapport with the media and also utilizing the services of the district information officer. A separate enclosure for the media should be kept at all public meetings. The media people should be given a pass to avoid incidents of lower level police constables or officers getting into a clash with them which can become very embarrassing for the administration.

There was this incident in district Agra during governor rule when the governor came on a visit to Agra. I was the District Magistrate and was sitting in the car with the governor on the way to the airport. All of a sudden, a young political leader of the same political dispensation as the governor broke the security cordon and ran towards the carcade trying to open the door of the car with the intention of getting in.

The SP (city) physically caught hold of him and dragged him away and also administered a tight slap to him. The leader was incensed and made a political issue of it and the entire political party began to back him. I got instructions from the office of the principal secretary to the governor to send a report against the SP (city) so that he could be suspended. I refused. The officer had done his job–it had been a major security breach. The officer in my view needed to be rewarded and I sent a report accordingly. I am told that His Excellency (HE) was annoyed with my report but now suspension of the officer was not possible. The Principal Secretary to the governor rang me up saying that the HE desired that at least the officer should be transferred. I reluctantly agreed and asked the officer for his choice. He opted for another posting in Agra itself and the state government accordingly transferred him to the provincial armed police at Agra. I was also assured by the state government that this officer would be adjusted in a district after a few months and this, in fact, happened. The point I want to emphasize is that the Collector must support his officers if they have taken bonafide action. These kind of risks are always present in VIP duties and the Collector has to handle the political parties with a lot of tact and firmness. He cannot be rigid and at the same time cannot allow the security of the VIP to be compromised in any manner.

Politicians and ministers apart, the visit of senior officers have also to be taken seriously and due courtesies and protocol extended. In UP, there is a tradition of inspection by the Chairman Board of Revenue who is often the senior most IAS officer in the state. These Chairmen have been known to have their idiosyncrasies. One Chairman loved his game of tennis and the Collector had to provide him a good game but also make sure that the Chairman won! Another had quirky food habits and started his day with pomegranate juice, papaya and dry fruits. Still other Chairmen could be unhappy with the colour of the curtains or notice specks of dust somewhere in the room. The Collector needs all his tact, patience and sense of humor to handle the different behaviour patterns. Calling the Chairman over for a drink and dinner at his house would often help the Collector in soothing the ruffles, if any.

The Collector must be extremely cautious about the visits of the Honorable Judges. One colleague of mine faced a contempt of Court case for not being able to allot the best suite in the circuit house to an honorable Judge of High Court. Even I got into trouble once when I was DM Allahabad. An Honorable Supreme Court judge had come on a visit and we had made all proper arrangements for him. Unfortunately, it happened to be the last week of March (closing of financial year) and the executive engineer of power department in his zeal to meet his targets cut of the power supply to the Circuit house at 2.00 am in the night as the electricity dues of the Circuit house had not been paid. We made arrangements to immediately shift the Honorable Judge to a hotel and got the power supply restored and took action against the concerned officer. Next morning I personally went to the hotel to request the Honorable Judge to return to the Circuit house. He was in a terrible mood. He made me wait for half an hour and then emerged looking very grim and cold. I apologized but he gave me a piece of his mind. I kept apologizing and soon the Honorable Judge calmed down and returned to the Circuit house.

The way you handle a VIP duty can make or break you. All your good work can come to naught if you fumble in a VIP visit. The Collector must not depend on his team but handle everything at his level.

The Expenditure

The question of expenditure is also important. Limited funds are made available by the government. One must keep the expenses within that level. There is no reason to put up banners, posters and to do stage decoration for a public meeting. This has to be done by the political party concerned. Also collecting money from the lower staff to finance expenditure should never be done. Careful planning and strictness can ensure this.

VIP visits take time and effort but it is one area where despite delegation the Collector must check things for himself. The overall image of the administration depends upon handling of VIP visits.

The Collector as a Leader

The institution of the Collector is such that he gets automatic support from the people in any programme or endeavour that he takes up. He is perceived by the people and officers as number one and everything revolves around his personality. There are a huge number of government programmes and schemes that the Collector has to implement. Now, every Collector has his area of interest and whichever scheme he takes interest in really succeeds. In fact, if any programme is not doing well the Secretary of the department writes to the Collector to review personally. The moment the Collector does so the results are immediate.

There is a tremendous creative aspect to the job of a Collector. He can assess the needs of a district and identify areas that require concentrated attention. He can then formulates projects, get government approval and implement them. This is one of the greatest satisfactions that the Collector can get from his job. The role of the Collector is all the more important in programmes where public opinion has to be mobilized and people made to participate actively in the implementation of a programme. The Collector by virtue of his post is a natural leader and the people tend to follow the lead given by him.

Case Study

In this connection I would like to narrate my experience in implementation of total literacy project in the district of Agra. The level of illiteracy was as high as 61% and as Collector I strongly felt that making people literate was the first step in taking them on the path to development. Immediately on my taking over I formed a core group of officers and asked them to prepare a project. We got the literacy projects of other districts and studied the guidelines issued by National Literacy Mission and on this basis a project was prepared. We decided to take the entire district at one go. A total number of 5,50,000 illiterates were to be made literate.

Survey

The first stage was the survey itself. We took the help of primary school teachers and Lekhpals and Panchayat secretaries to carry out the initial work of survey. Villages were distributed amongst them and it was so ensured that each functionary had about two villages to cover. A format was designed–the objective of which was to give us the name and other details of all illiterates and literates in a village.

One method of doing this work could have been to carry out a census type of operation. But this would not be worthwhile. No programme like this which seeks total voluntary action on the part of the people can be achieved without proper environment building. We decided to use the survey itself as a tool of environment building. At first all the surveyors were trained. They were made to understand the meaning of the literacy programme. Their doubts were cleared and then they were sent to the village. The idea was that not only would they talk to the people, they would motivate them to become literate. They would also influence the literate into becoming volunteers.

The survey was done within time. However, this environment building part was done well only in some areas. The rest went about it in a routine manner. In any case the survey figures were available on the basis of which a project was formulated. To make 5,55,000 people literate 5,500 volunteers were required. The volunteers would have to be from the same village or locality. For every 40 volunteers we would have a master trainer who could be a school teacher or a block official and above that we had resource persons taken from various departments. The project was prepared and presented by the Collector before the National Literacy Mission and approval granted. Initial sanction of funds also came through.

Training

Training of people involved was the most important step. We got the resource persons and core group of officers trained at the state resource centre at Lucknow. They were there for more than a week. On their return, training for master trainers was organized at block headquarters by resource persons. The Collector and his core group personally visited these training centres to ensure that these sessions were taken seriously. In the next round the master trainers gave training at the village level to volunteers. Here again senior officers visited the villages to check. The training was to be done in three phases at various stages of the literacy movement and we planned to give about nine days of training in all.

All the officers of the district, the block pramukhs and pradhans were called and given a one day orientation about the programme. It was realized that the campaign cannot succeed if everyone does not get involved and for that everyone would have to be oriented towards the programme.

Environment Building

This is easily the most crucial part of the campaign. We formed a separate committee to plan and implement this aspect of the campaign. We started by holding a large rally at Agra city which culminated into a function where the Collector, Mayor and other important people gave their views on literacy.

This rally kicked off a 15 day intensive awareness plan. Rallies were held at each block headquarters. Seminars and discussions were held. In each village the students took out rallies in the village raising literacy slogans. We then briefed the press and they covered each of the rallies in detail. In fact, the press when called upon by the Collector, responded to the extent of giving space in their newspapers daily for some article or contribution about literacy.

All India Radio also cooperated by covering every function and calling upon the Collector and his team to give talks on literacy. The Collector asked the people to send songs, articles and poems on literacy. Many came and best were selected and put in the form of a book. Many of these songs and poems were presented by All India Radio.

Yet, the most effective method was the use of street theatre. Voluntary groups were asked to come forward and they prepared a one-hour package on literacy. It was beautifully done. Teams were made at each block and were trained by these theatre groups. These teams then went from village to village giving their performances. The response was tremendous. Many villages formed their own version of plays and dance drama and began presenting it in and around their villages.

We also used a couple of video vans which showed a one-hour video on literacy mixed with entertainment in all the villages. The presentation was carefully done so that the programme was in local language and had messages which could be understood by our target audience–the illiterates.

Various other methods like puppet shows, song competitions and painting competitions were used to involve as many sections of society as possible with this campaign. Essays and debate competitions were also held.

We started a fortnightly newsletter on literacy in which we encouraged the village level volunteers to send their contributions. They responded and we published their poems or articles with their photographs–they felt a tremendous sense of recognition. We wanted them to work voluntarily and the only motivation we could offer them was recognition. In fact, we called all our volunteers 'soldiers for literacy' and gave them a badge to this effect. Functions were held repeatedly to honour volunteers by praising their role in public.

One tremendous event was to have a human chain for literacy. This chain was about 8 km long and people from all walks of life and even school-children participated in this. The impact of this could be felt throughout the district. The Collector did the initial planning for environment building but thereafter he gave a free hand to people and they responded with really innovative methods of spreading the message of literacy and ensuring participations of all.

The pramukhs, pradhans and other local leaders were all skeptical of this programme. In the initial block level functions held, these people spoke about their misgivings and in essence criticized the programme. The Collector had to personally attend and in his speech he gave a rebuttal and tried to convince them about the genuineness of the campaign. Gradually, they changed their attitude and became supporters of the programme. Once again, the role of Collector was very important. The moment it was perceived that the Collector was giving literacy the highest priority they all began to support the programme actively. In fact, after that it became a practice that any pradhan or pramukh who would come to see me for some work would start by talking about his contribution to literacy hoping that he would win my goodwill by this.

Monitoring and Evaluation

With great fanfare and ceremony the classes were started but the most difficult part came after that as to how these classes, going on in over a thousand villages were to be monitored. Right at the beginning the problem was of fall-out amongst the volunteers, many of whom lost interest after a week. We then had to step up our awareness and motivation campaign in these areas and, in fact, had to take recourse to house to house campaigning. It took almost a month of sustained effort to finally stabilize the number of volunteers and to ensure that all the classes started.

It was once again the job of the Collector and his team to devise a system of monitoring and evaluation. The programme was to be that of the people. Yet it would lose its momentum if the Collector did not look after it and keep giving it the critical push.

We first formed the village level committees under the chairmanship of the pradhan and having a school teacher as its secretary.

Every Thursday these village level committees would meet and review the literacy movement. They were expected to call all the volunteers and listen to their problems and help them to exchange notes. Then every Friday there would be a nyay panchayat (ordinarily a cluster of about ten villages) level meeting. We had appointed on officer in-charge for each nyay panchayat. He would chair the meeting at the nyay panchayat level where all the pradhans and secretaries of village level committee would attend. It was open to volunteers to join this meeting.

The third tier was the block level committee where the block pramukh was the chairman and the BDO was the secretary. This meeting was attended by all the nyay panchayat incharges and full time workers. Now, this full time worker was an interesting innovation. We asked officers to opt for literacy for a year.

Many teachers and other employees did so. They would draw their salary from their parent department but work full-time for the cause of literacy. Each one of these full-time workers was allotted a group of villages. They visited the villages or mohallas, guided the volunteers and learners, attended the village level and nyay panchayat level meetings and then briefed the block level committee about the progress.

We had also made district level officers responsible for each block and they would attend these meetings. The Collector himself would attend these meetings at different blocks every week. In this way, total information about the functioning of centres was gathered, and motivation and guidance provided. All this information collected would then be discussed by the district level task force every Tuesday. Action for the next week about areas requiring more environment building, more motivation, etc were chalked out. We had seen that some areas were doing very well whereas others were lagging behind. Senior officers who were members of the core group would then visit these slow progress areas and guide them.

It was interesting to see how the Collector and his team acted as the catalyst and it soon became a people's programme moving with its own momentum. Yet, periodically the campaign had to be injected with energy. Slowly as achievement started coming, a spurt of competition amongst volunteers started. After a period of almost a year it was heartening to note that the district achieved the norms of a totally literate district as prescribed by Government of India. The evaluation team came from Government of India and it was a matter of great personal satisfaction to me when they declared Agra as the first totally literate district of Uttar Pradesh.

The above case study shows how the Collector can take up a difficult programme like literacy and if he provides the right leadership the whole district follows him and success is ensured.

The same concept is applied to projects like family welfare programmes. If the Collector gives importance to this programme then it will become a people's movement and quality achievement shall be possible. I remember in a district where as Collector I convened meeting of pradhans and gave them a list of target couples in their village. If they could motivate at least ten cases then the village would be eligible for special funds under the various development schemes. This worked very well. Of course, the promise about funds must be met.

The Collector has to get results from his team. Nothing is achieved by criticizing the quality of officers available. Through sufficient motivation and guidance one must bring out the best from all. It also does not help if the style of the Collector is abusive or arrogant. The officers may fear the Collector but they shall not follow him. It is best to carry the team with oneself and to build an atmosphere where each member of the team feels himself to be equally important and feels every achievement to be his own.

The district follows the lead given by the Collector. It is thus imperative for him to identify the felt needs of the people and design programmes and projects to meet them and then take the entire district with him in its implementation.

There is no denying that even today if the government wants something to be done or some scheme implemented on priority, it is the Collector/District Officer that they turn to. Inevitably any project which the Collector takes up and gives his personal attention and provides leadership succeeds. This clearly establishes that the role of the Collector as the leader has been greatly enhanced rather than diminished over the years.

Very recently the biggest programme of the Government was the Swatch Bharat Mission (SBM). All over the country millions of toilets were constructed within the stipulated time period and massive amount of awareness generation done to bring about behavioural change. This exercise was led by the

Collectors all over the country and it achieved success when India declared itself open defecation free (ODF) on 2nd October, 2019. This target was accomplished even in a diverse and huge state like UP. I have personal knowledge that since there was the political will of the Prime Minister and the Chief Ministers behind it the DM also accorded it the highest priority and this was the major reason behind this stupendous success. I recently read a book by Parmeswaran Aiyyar who as Secretary Government of India, department of drinking water and sanitation, was the architect of this success story. He outlines his strategy as being one where the PM/CM/DM model was used and it worked. In a similar vein the Jal Jeevan Mission (JJM) has been launched by the Government of India to provide tap water to each and every household by 2024. Once again they will have to work through the institution of the Collector to make this dream a reality.

The post of District Officer is one which offers great latitude to officers to innovate, create and implement. So many District Officers pick up projects which motivate them and with their effort they actually make a big difference. There was this Collector in UP who used the "Dalia Jalau" campaign to wage a frontal war against manual scavenging. The term "Dalia Jalau" literally means to burn the basket used by manual scavengers to carry human waste. In one year, this Collector created a sanitation revolution in his district and liberated hundreds of manual scavengers from a life of humiliation and indignity.

The eastern part of UP was affected by Japanese encephalitis and acute encephalitis syndrome (JE and AES). We wanted to spread awareness amongst the people that to prevent death of their child they have to rush him to the hospital at the earliest. We also had to convince the people that a vaccine for JE was available and all children must be vaccinated. We once again had to rely on the leadership of the institution of the District

Officer to implement and the result was that there was a dramatic decrease in the number of cases within a couple of years.

There are District Officers who focus on primary education. One collector regularly got the attendance of teachers checked and action was taken against the delinquent teachers. Teacher absenteeism was controlled in his district because of his personal commitment. Similarly, there have been District Officers who inspect schools from the point of view of assessing learning outcomes of the children and they are able to contribute significantly to the improvement of the quality of the education in the district. In the area of health also district hospitals began to look very neat, clean and adequately stocked with medicines once we emphasized upon the Collectors to carry out regular inspections. There is no doubt the leadership of the Collector is vital for the implementation of the development schemes of any department.

During my tenure as Chief Secretary there was this Collector of district Shravasti in UP who created a unique model of convergence in implementation of schemes related to health, nutrition, education and sanitation. Without seeking any extra funds from the government he was able to transform the impact of various schemes. He would make all workers converge in a village on a particular day and discuss and resolve issues related to the schemes and also generate awareness of them. This was so successful that it got labelled as the Shravasti model and we had to direct every District Officer to replicate this.

The leadership qualities of the District Officers are evident at the time of crises. It could be a law and order issue or natural calamity or even conduct of elections. The calmness and coolness with which the Collector leads his team is the key to successful handling of any emergent situation.

The District Officers, then, learn and develop qualities of leadership. Personally traits and working style determine the leadership of a District Officer rather than his physical attributes and academic brilliance. The District Officer has to lead from the front through his example. He has to show the way and only then would others follow him. He is the captain of the team and has to inspire and motivate each member of his team to perform. He has to maintain a delicate balance between going in to too much detail vis-à-vis keeping in touch with a larger vision.

How much should he delegate? To what extent should he be "hands on"? These things depend upon the particular situation and the working style of the District Officer. His leadership style has to be such as to enable him to deliver outcomes. Taking a very broad spectrum the District Officer can have one of the two main leadership's styles–he could be democratic or authoritarian. Since, his role is to coordinate between various departments the authoritarian style does not suit the District Officer. He has to carry the entire team with him and he has very little direct authority over officers of other departments. Even otherwise an authoritarian style of leadership which implies forcing your will on others is basically coercive and is often accompanied by arrogance, rudeness and intemperate behaviour. These are not desirable traits to any leader. However, I have found that many District Officers become so obsessed with their sense of power that they lead by throwing their weight around. Actually, the post of the District Officer carries tremendous powers with it and has a very high status in the society. Everybody who comes into contact with him speaks with a lot of respect and this can quite easily go to the head. This is the reason why many departmental officers resent the behaviour of the District Officer and may listen to him out of a sense of fear but rarely respect him and are never loyal to him.

A District Officer must realize that a leadership role has been literally thrust upon him by the virtue of his post and he does not have to exhibit behaviour which will antagonize the other officers. He has to command the respect of others and this is best done if he leads by his example of hard work, sense of balance, maturity, calmness, control, positivism and result orientation. The other officers should follow him out of respect for his abilities and commitment to excellence.

There are situations where a coercive style has to be adopted. A Collector cannot afford to be too democratic in the event of a natural calamity like floods, droughts, fires or earthquakes or any other disaster. In such situations he has to take the command and after assessing the situation assign clear roles to all officers and give them specific instructions. However, even then abrasiveness or boorish behaviour is not to be encouraged. Every district has a disaster management plan and the job of the District Officer is to see that it is implemented to the last detail.

Elections are another area where complete powers are vested in the Collector by the laws relating to elections. He has to be tough and rule bound while he conducts the election process. He can requisite vehicles of any departments, assign magisterial, sector officer or polling party duties to officers of any department. None can refuse him as he is in complete command and law regarding elections prescribes very tough penalties for those who do not conduct their election duties in a responsible manner. However, even when vested with such complete authority the District Officer as a leader would do well to use his common sense. His actions cannot be arbitrary and must appear to be fair to all concerned. For instance, a District Officer has to see the seniority level of officers of various departments before assigning them specific duties otherwise it creates unnecessary discord and unpleasantness.

All recent studies of managerial performance have shown that EQ (emotional quotient) which is a measure of emotional intelligence is far more relevant than IQ (intelligence quotient). Study has shown that 90% of good performers are people with high EQ. It is also empirically borne out that there is a clear relationship between high EQ and performance even though the IQ of a person may be average. On the other hand, those with high IQ and average EQ generally tend to underperform. All IAS officers who are posted as District Officers/Collectors have good IQ because without this they cannot succeed in the competitive examination. However, to succeed they have to be good leaders and for this in addition to IQ a very high level of EQ is required. A major part of the job of the district officer is to handle and manage people. This requires qualities of understanding oneself, managing one's emotional responses, social awareness and relationship management. The District Officer has to be a considerate person who has empathy in good measure. A lot depends on how he responds to the people who meet him. The citizens meets the District Officer with respect to their grievances and expect the District Officer to give them a patient hearing, courtesy, politeness and a positive response to their problems. Even the smiling face of a District Officer sends a right message as opposed to a rough, rude and egotistical demeanor. Ultimately, the reputation of a District Officer is built on what the people in the district perceive about him. If they feel that he is positive, has a problem-solving approach, is accessible and has genuine concern for their problems then they respect the District Officer and there is a general feeling of well being in the district. The personality of District Officer has to be such that people want to come to him with their problems. The effort of the District Officer should be to see that anybody who comes to meet him with a problem goes out of his office with a smile and with faith and belief in the officer and the system.

Emotional intelligence (EI) is essential to allow the District Officer to function as the principle coordinator. Rather than raising his voice and being abrasive the District Officer gets much more support and cooperation if he shows maturity and an understanding behaviour. In order to achieve this state the District Officer must be able to manage his own emotions. He should not give in to stress and even in the most difficult of circumstances he should exhibit a calm exterior and should be able to take decisions based on logic and analysis rather than letting his emotional responses take control of his rational thinking. These are the qualities of a leader and the officers shall follow the District Officer when they witness these qualities in him.

As a leader, the District Officer must know his team members. He should be able to analyze the strengths and weaknesses of each officer and use him accordingly. Different approaches motivate people differently. He has to choose the right approach for each and every officer and he must be an excellent judge of men. The district administration is like a living organism which begins to perform at a higher level if each one of its constituent units is functioning well and all together are moving in the same direction. It is the District Officer who builds a team. I do recall with some satisfaction that both as DM Agra and DM Allahabad people praised my tenure and also said that I had a very good team. I was happy that I was able to build the team and it showed that the same bunch of officers can be excellent members of a team if they are handled properly and are motivated otherwise they can became dysfunctional. If you are a poor leader you always blame the team you have. A good leader is able to mould all officers into a performing team. There are times when officers are in conflict with one another and the Collector has to play a balancing role. Two of my additional District Magistrates in a district did not like each other but I was fair and neutral and did not encourage gossip and the result was that the both performed effectively. The best part was that both of them felt that I was very close to them. This is how all officers should feel about the District Officer.

A leader is determined by the way he shoulders responsibility. If the District Officer is constantly criticizing his officers and complaining against them or instituting inquiries against then he will never get the loyalty and support of his team members. A District Officer as a leader should have the courage and ability to take decisions and also be accountable for them. An indecisive District Officer will never get the respect of his team. Every decision has a repercussion. Sometimes officers take credit if everything works out but are quick to disown the members of the team if there are problems. There was a Collector in UP in the pre-mobile days who would drive off to the western part of the district if there was a law and order problem and the eastern part and return after several hours. Then if the problem had been handled properly by his team he would take all the credit and send a report accordingly to the government. If, one the contrary, the situation has not been controlled he would blame his team members and write against them to the government and threaten action. He could never command the respect of his team who had only bad words for him in their private conversations. The leader should take responsibility and never try to pull down his team members. The District Officer has to be very careful about this aspect of his personality. The District Officer should also not shout and insult other officers in front of others. Negative feedback is best given in private.

A word of praise, a letter of appreciation go a long way in motivating the team. The District Officer is working in a government setup where instant rewards are not possible as incentives. However, praise can do wonders. Every officer likes his work to be recognized and puts in double the effort if the District Officer gives him a special good performance appraisal or writes to the government in his favour. I was a young Collector in a hill district and the government had just decided to introduce the district planning process. We worked very hard to prepare the district plan of the district and my district statistics officer really applied himself. In the meeting before the commissioner our district plan was rated as the best and the commissioner complimented me. I stood up and thanked him but also added that all this was possible only because of the effort put in by the district statistics officer. The concerned officer was also present in the room. He was absolutely overwhelmed and when met me later there were tear in his eyes. He later on worked with even more dedication. This is just an example to show how if the District Officer recognizes the work of his team members he would be able to motivate them to perform at the next level.

It is, thus, the democratic style of leadership which encourages participation that is more appropriate for the District Officer. The democratic style does not mean that he should be easy going and that officers get a free run to do what they want. In such a situation there would be anarchy all around and performance would be poor. It also does not mean that he is democratic to the extent of being indecisive. He should be able to guide and control any discussion or debate and channelize it in the right direction. The goal should be clear; the priorities shared by all and all participation should be in that direction. Once again the District Officer as the leader has to decide how democratic he should be in which situation. Being too democratic in a law and order situation could lead to a catastrophe. Similarly, in conducting elections District Officer has to often resort to the coercive style of leadership.

The District Officer as a leader has to lead by example and by virtue of his command over the district and integrity and capacity for hard work and dynamism. His personality has to be such that the other officers in the district listen to him with respect. They would not respect the chair for too long if the incumbent is much smaller than the chair. They look up to a leader who adorns the chair he sits on and gracefully exudes power and authority.

The District Officer as a leader has to be an excellent communicator. He should be able to inspire and motivate his team with his words and the way he speaks. It is always better if he is a good public speaker because a District Officer is asked to address a number of gatherings and these give him the right platform to generate awareness for government schemes and also make people accept the schemes. The Swatch Bharat Mission would never have succeeded without the leadership provided by the District Officer.

A District Officer is remembered for long after he has left a district provided he has built a rapport with the people and has genuinely tried to resolve their problems. People in a district always remember a good District Officer with fondness and keep visiting him year after year even after he has left the district. I still find people from my districts coming to visit me even though I have retired and almost three decades have gone by. There are a number of examples of District Officer who had to be sent back to a district to calm down a law and order disturbance and they had such rapport with the people that they could bring about peace just by their presence. To attain the high ideal the District Officer must be extremely accessible. People should be able to meet him without going through petty officials. He should listen to their problems and try to resolve them. His attitude must always be positive. His tenure at the district must bring about some transformational change in the development of the district. Even small things matter like significant improvement in sanitation, street lights or power supply or removal of encroachments. He is seen as an agent of change for the better.

The role of Collector/District Officer has changed a lot over time. He does not have direct authority over officers in the district but he still is the representative of the government at the district level. He is a leader in a greater sense now because the scope of his work has been enhanced several times. He has to plan, coordinate and execute. The institution of the District Officer is still the fulcrum of district administration and it is his leadership qualities which make a difference on how a district is govern and developed.

The Collector's Social Life and the District

The Collector is considered by the people as the central figure of the district and they like to relate to him socially. The Collector cannot shut himself up. He has to participate in the social and cultural life of the district and here again everything begins to revolve around him. The Collector however has to maintain a certain distance which is necessary for him to carry out his official duties in an impartial manner. This situation requires delicate balancing, and once again, the Collector should pay special attention to this.

Official Calls

First comes the issue of calling on officers. The protocol for this has been well laid out and should be followed. The Collector is the head of the district but the protocol is that if he comes to the district after the district judge then he will call on him. If the district judge joins later then he would call on the DM. The Superintendent of Police and all other officers of the district call on the Collector. There should be no problem or ego felt by anybody in this and often the relations between officers get sour only on this issue.

The Commissioner is the direct boss of the Collector and the Collector must call on him officially and socially on joining a district. The Collector and his wife must encourage other officers of the district to call on them socially. These traditions go a long way in building bonhomie.

Relations with Defence

Excellent relations have to be maintained with defence personnel. In larger districts there is a senior officer of the Army posted and at some places of Air Force also. The Collector can develop tremendous goodwill by calling on them. This comes in handy at time of aid to civil authority. The army is ready to come to your assistance without raising too many questions or insisting on too much procedure. Also at times of disasters and major accidents you require some assistance from the armed forces which is forthcoming if the relations are good. I recall the case where an excellent project for a park was planned but it was soon discovered that the land belonged to the army. However, since the relations with the armed forces were good, once the project was explained to the sub-area commander, he took it upon himself to have the land leased to us. It was because of this support and enthusiasm that the park eventually came up.

In another situation of law and order we did not want to requisite the army but at the same time wanted to create terror in the hearts of communal and anti-social elements. I called on the sub-area commander and he gave us the required help. He sent a couple of open army jeeps with armed jawans mounted on them for a 'reconnaissance' of the affected areas. We added police and PAC vehicles to this and went around the town. The effect was tremendous. Without calling the army we had achieved our results.

All the above can be managed easily if the social relations are good. After the official call the Collector and his wife can make social calls on the army or air force commanders and their wives. Thereafter, the defence people are most cordial and always invite for their social functions. As far as possible one should attend also in return call them over for social functions held by the Collector.

In the same vein if there is a High Court in the district one must call on the Chief Justice. If there is a university then one must call on the Vice-Chancellor and if there are any major union government offices, e.g., the office of the accountant general, one must call on their senior most officers. The same applies to railways. Good relations with DRM can ensure that he goes all the way to help you when you need reservations for VIPs.

The Collector must be very particular about things like returning calls and telephone calls. Most of the orderlies of Collectors do not maintain a list of people who ring up while the Collector is away. This upsets people. Whereas if a Collector on returning from a tour rings back people, they feel happy and a reputation is built up. Same is true for social calls–the Collector should try and find time to return these calls. He is always hard-pressed for time but this is an important aspect of his job and if he tries hard enough there is no reason why he would not get time.

The Collector's Wife

The wife of the Collector plays an extremely important role in the running of a district. She is also the number one lady of the district and her attitudes and reactions are also the topic of attention among people. Very often they get carried away by the status accorded to them and tend to behave in a haughty manner. In fact, many a conflict among officers especially that between the DM and the SP tend to start with tension between the wives.

But most often the Collector's wife can play a very important role in holding the district together. I recall my first change as Collector of a very backward district. The only company that the officers could have was that of each other. However, these very circumstances led to the building up of groups and there were constant tensions and rivalries. These tensions were spilling on to the work place and affecting the performance. Soon after my joining, my wife started a ladies club in which she made all the wives of the officers as members. They would meet regularly. Then they started having functions in which officers were also invited. Interesting functions like 'husband evening', etc, were held where everyone participated in party games and there was a lot of fun and gaiety. Then almost every quarter a cultural programme was organized where the officers, their wives and children participated and gave expression to their talent. Then again the ladies organized picnics, fetes and several such get-togethers where everybody joined in an informal atmosphere. The result was to be seen to be believed. The tensions between various offices vanished–excellent relations with judiciary, police and technical departments were the result. In fact, when the wives become close and they have functions involving the husbands a spirit of camaraderie and oneness is built up which leads to tension-free working atmosphere and high quality of performance.

There are a lot of programmes specially those relating to health and education where if the Collector's wife is involved she can rally around the ladies of the district and make significant impact. I recall in a district my wife took up immunization programme for children. She and other ladies acted as a voluntary group and adopted certain villages. They visited the villages, spoke to the ladies and convinced them about the advantage of the programme. This ensured 100% achievements in these villages. The most startling success was in the achievement of total literacy in a district. We were having problems with women-illiterates who were not coming forward to learn. My wife and the other ladies organized themselves into a group and went to talk to the ladies. The women did not want to become literate as they could see no tangible benefit accruing to them. It was then that the ladies told them that if they learnt how to read and write then they could write letters to their children. This appealed so much to the women that they enthusiastically joined the literacy programme. The point I want to emphasize from these anecdotes is that the role of Collector's wife is very important in a district and she can be a great asset to her husband if she participates equally with him in the problems of the district.

Cultural and Sports Activities

The Collector can prove leadership in the cultural and sport activities of a district. He is expected to inaugurate poetry recitation (mushairaas) meets, sports championships, etc. Actually the organization of all these require funds which can be collected best if the Collector takes personal interest in the matter. Organizing such functions not only helps in building a creative and constructive atmosphere; it infuses a certain enthusiasm and it helps in his being projected as a true leader of the district. Long after the Collector has been transferred it is these contributions which are remembered the most.

As district Collector of Agra, my wife and I organized the Taj Mahotsav. It included a fifteen day craft bazaar with continuous programmes of folk dance and folk music representing various regions of the country. This was all done at a site called Shilpagram which was designed in a manner that it looked like a real village. In addition there were live evenings of top class classical music and dance. We did not have any funds–we raised resources locally and had a committee of non-official people who, with my wife as chairperson, organized the entire programme. In fact my wife spent several sleepless nights designing the layout and structure of the programme site to give it the ambience of a village. It became the talking point of the district and also helped improving the tourism prospects of the city. Ever since then Taj Mahotsav has been held on the same days in the month of February and it has became a part of the International tourism calendar. Substantial funding is now received from the Government.

Every district has some activity that people are fond of. If this is recognized and the Collector and his wife actively encourage such activities then they can really galvanize the social and cultural life of the district. In one district the people were very fond of wrestling so the Collector organized a major wrestling championship and called Dara Singh and others. In another, it was the love for Urdu poetry and the Collector assisted in organizing an excellent mushaira. In a district like Allahabad one realized that classical music was a great tradition but over the years no proper festival had been held. My wife and I organized a Prayag Mahotsav which brought top artists in classical vocal, instrumental music and dance to Allahabad. The programme was a roaring success and it brought to life the cultural taste of the people of Allahabad.

All this goes to show that the Collector must understand his district and take a lead in its social and cultural life. This helps him in his job also as he wins tremendous support of the people and develops contacts which help him tackle difficult situations. This aspect of a Collector's life at the district should not be overlooked by any officer. He must find the time and energy for this.

So many people would be wanting to invite the Collector for dinner or other functions. Here, he should be reserved. Most people calling him for dinner can approach him the next day asking for some favour which may not be strictly legal. People tend to take advantage if the Collector dines with them or visits their house too often. Not only this, but certain people have a bad reputation in the district and if the Collector goes to their house he acquires a bad reputation also. The advent of the mobile has created another problem as everyone now wants to take a selfie with the Collector and make it viral. This creates problems if the Collector is caught in a selfie frame with a person having a dubious reputation.

The necessity to remain impartial involves the fact that the Collector shall have to be very selective in where he goes out and which functions he attends. The British had an excellent system of writing the district gazetteer and charge handover notes. In these they specifically mentioned the people with whom a Collector can maintain social contacts. One should be selective but not withdrawn. The Collector and his wife can be the social leader in a district and make the atmosphere lively. I remember that our first posting was in the backwaters of eastern UP in a district called Ghazipur. There was no source of entertainment there as at that time the T.V. had just made an appearance and there was no internet or mobiles. Yet my wife and I coordinated and initiated so many social and cultural activities that time sped by without our realizing. Even today, all the officers posted at Ghazipur at that time have fond memories of that period which was truly enjoyable.

A large proportion of the Collector's time is taken away by being invited for inaugurations, foundation stone laying, closing ceremonies, ceremonial function, etc. Whereas this is a necessary part of a Collector's job it is time-consuming and as such needs to be controlled. If a Collector does not learn to say 'no' to such invitations he would spend half his time in such unproductive activities.

However, there is a positive side to these functions. When a Collector visits a village for any function a lot of development work in the village gets done by itself. Also, it is a great opportunity for a Collector to know the people of his District and get genuine feedback and see ground realities for himself. There is no doubt that the social and cultural life of the district revolves around the personality of the Collector.

Nothing can be more gratifying than the respect of the people earned by the Collector and it is a great feeling when citizens from a district keep meeting you, years after you have left the district, with love and affection. The period spent in the district is the happiest and most rewarding of one's service life and it is the most satisfying and exhilarating job that you can get.

Conclusion

We have discussed the various functional aspects of the job of a Collector. Hard work and knowledge about one's work are essential for success but there can never be any ready-made solution to any problem. What is more important is to be clear about one's goals and to have a problem-solving approach. The buck always ends at the Collector and to be effective he had to decide and be prompt in his decision-making. He has to ensure the implementation of his decisions and to face the reactions of the people. There is no running away from a situation for a Collector. He has to be at the place of action interacting continuously with situations and people.

It is said that the chief executive of any organization is a lonely person. He has to take decisions alone and face things personally. This is absolutely true for a Collector. Despite all the trappings of power and halo of authority he remains essentially a lonely person. He cannot delegate this crucial decision-making to anyone. He is vulnerable from all sides. He cannot open his mind to anyone and he is aware of the fact that inferences can be drawn from not only his actions but gestures as well.

This, undoubtedly, means that the Collector would always be under a lot of stress. One of the first requirements of a good Collector is his ability to manage stress. An ever-smiling face, a calm demeanour, a confident approach go a long way in earning respect for the officer and making him successful. Temper should never be lost. Whenever anger comes in rationality suffers and this opening is enough for criticism to start. This does not mean that politeness at all times should be adhered to. There are occasions where a 'roar' is required but this should be done consciously and in a controlled manner. The officer must be able to control the length and intensity of his 'roar'.

Law and order situations can only be tackled by a cool approach because it is important for the officer to think and plan. It is necessary for his team to feel confident and not nervous. Situation like a police firing or the outbreak of a riot need careful handling. One should never reach the spot and start picking faults with the officers on duty. There is no point in shouting, screaming and fixing responsibility at that time. It is best to show support for your team, give clear directions and by your coolness ensure that your team performs to the best of its ability.

Team Work

In fact, the route to success is team work. The Collector has to lead his team and solve the contradictions at his level. All the members of the team should be equal before the Collector. The worst situation comes when it is perceived that some officer or officers are closer than others. Regretfully many Collectors have started aligning themselves along the lines of caste and community. Thus is absolutely disastrous. The Collector would never be able to pull his officers together as a team. There are always conflicts and tensions between individual members of the team. The Collector should never encourage these conflicts and should persuade them to work in organizational interest. So often a Collector would find officers coming and speaking about one another. They will criticize the other person and try to show that they are close to the Collector. This should be discouraged at the very first instance and at an earliest opportunity the two concerned officers should be called and made to solve their differences.

The team at the disposal of the Collector is made up of various services. They have their own egos, insecurities, preconceived notions and it does not take long for a Collector to realize that they are all pulling in different directions. A subordinate officer can be obsequious in the presence of the Collector but may actually not be loyal to him and often tend to leave him alone at the time of a crisis.

The DM has to mould his team by sheer force of personality. Cardinal principles of a good manager should be adopted for doing this. One should never pull up one's subordinate in front of others. If he has to be admonished then it is best done alone. Even then the language used should never be rough or abusive. He should feel that your approach is to make him a better officer. At the same time praise should always be given in full view of others. But the important things about this aspect are that praise should be genuine and work based. It should not get perceived by other colleagues as favoritism. A good, specific appreciation letter after someone has really done a good job can encourage the person to perform to his level best. It should be clear to all officers that their evaluation shall strictly be on performance and not on some other personal issue.

Some officers believe that fear is necessary to get respect from people. They believe in hanging "dead crows" within the first few days of their joining. They would carry out surprise inspections and go on a spree of suspension and adverse entries. It is true that this approach shakes up the district and people start fearing this very 'strict officer' but by itself, does not ensure that results will come. A balanced consistent approach is better. It should be made clear that corruption, nepotism and willful staying away from work shall not be tolerated. At the same time, the DM should be perceived in the role of a parent rather than as a tyrant who is out to use his authority to subjugate the rest. In fact, in a government set-up there are many things that are not working as they should. Systems have to be devised for them. Mere fixing responsibility and taking action without listening to others and reforming the system tends to follow the law of diminishing returns.

A very important quality that the Collector must possess is to understand the strengths and weaknesses of his officers. One should be open-minded and have a broad view in this. For instance, an officer may be outstanding in implementing rule of law and maintaining law and order but could be rude in his behaviour. This weakness of his has to be taken into account and attempt should be made to counsel him on this. His strengths should be praised and he should be given assignment where his strengths would be used. This would ensure getting the best out of him.

The art is to get work out of everyone. Each officer has some individual quality and if he is given a task which corresponds to this then he does well. I recall the case of an officer who was never interested in files, could never take down proper minutes of a meeting, was unsure of the rules and regulations and generally had the reputation of being a waster. After sometime I observed that he had tremendous skill in organizing things and public relations but hated anything to do with paper. I picked him up and started entrusting him with full responsibility of organizing functions, etc. and dealing with the press. The man did an excellent job and from being one who avoided work he got totally immersed in his job.

Some officers are outstanding in law and order whereas some others are involved in their court work. Some carry out excellent field inspections, some are good at handling files, some are experts at VIP duties whereas others have the gift of the gab to talk their way out of any situation. The Collector has to constantly keep assessing this and choose the right man for the job. If he succeeds in doing this then his job is done. There is no point in lamenting over the team one has got. The team can never be as you want it. But by proper assessment and right assignment of tasks the Collector can mould his officers into a team and get the best results out of them.

Another method which pays rich dividends is to have faith and confidence in your subordinates and to give them the feeling of confidence. People have the ability to give results if they feel important and realize that their boss has faith in them. Once elections were round the corner and everybody was involved in elections work–a spate of VIPs were coming. A VVIP suddenly decided to come and address a public meeting–I had no officers to spare but felt that my young SDM should be able to handle it. I called him and discussed the arrangements with him. Then I told him that we all depended upon him and he should consider himself to be the DM and organize everything and if there was any major problem then he should inform me. The officer handled the VVIP visit very well and did not bother me even once. At the time of my farewell the same officer recounted this incident in his speech and I realized that my entrusting him with total responsibility and trust had such a motivational impact upon him. Most people respond positively when faith and trust is shown to them and they are given the independence to act.

To run a complex organization like a district, the Collector must be able to get all information, and view every situation from all possible angles. It is, thus, necessary for the Collector to allow his officers to express their views frankly. Some officers, in trying to project the image of being strict, do not allow their subordinates to discuss issues openly and attempt to force their will. They feel it is a sign of weakness if they are not able to impose their views on the others. In fact, in many a meetings one would observe a monologue taking place. The rest of the audience just listens and writes down something in diaries. This kind of situation never results in the organization becoming effective. No officer can carry out instructions about which he has doubts. It is the skill of the superior officer to convince his team about the proposed plan of action and hence carry their support with him. The District Officer must ensure that he does not create an atmosphere where his officers do not tell him the truth or unpleasant facts or even air divergent views. The district is such a complex organization that if the Collector does not keep all avenues of information open he is likely to commit mistakes and his effectiveness as an officer suffers.

In fact, very often if you want to introduce a new idea it is best to bring it into discussion dispassionately and not give the impression that it is being thrust upon others. Let it be debated and skillfully all the negative points thrown up should be ironed out. A decision by consensus would emerge.

During one election as District Officer I wanted to introduce the concept of sending ballot papers to polling booths in the morning of the poll day to reduce the chances of tampering at the village. The district being large in area had the traditions of sending polling parties two days in advance. Incidents of anti-social elements snatching and tampering the ballot papers at the village level had taken place earlier. I wanted to send the ballot papers on the day of the poll from the Tehsil through sector magistrates. I realized that this involved a total change of procedure and would never be accepted. I convened a meeting of all officers and posed the problem to them. Most of them responded by saying the problem was genuine but there was no solution to it. I persisted that as officers we must find a solution. After about fifteen minutes of discussion an officer said that the only way out was to send the ballot papers on the day of the poll but this was not possible. I quickly grabbed the point and asked the group to suggest whether this was possible. Slowly a consensus began to emerge and the group came out with the very solution I had in mind. I endorsed it and the system worked effectively.

The success came because all the officers felt that it was their idea and not thrust upon them by the Collector.

In essence, the Collector today has to encourage participation. He has to lead by involving everyone and encouraging them to come out with their best. If the Collector just keeps issuing orders then he is not likely to be obeyed. The results would not come. The Collector has to ensure that his decisions are implemented and taking action against defaulters is not the only way of doing this. He has to motivate his officers and carry them with him.

Performance Evaluation

One of the most important tasks before the DM is to appraise the performance of his team. The system at present involves giving of a performance sheet by the concerned officer at the close of the financial year and the Collector then records his report on this. In most cases this exercise is not done seriously. Often the reports are delayed for years and thereby lose their relevance and most often they are routine and stereotyped which do not reflect the actual assessment of an officer. In fact, a large number of officers ask their stenographers to put up a draft entry and get it signed. This makes the whole exercise farcical.

There is also this tendency among officers to write their own entries and catch the Collector in one of his good moments and request him to sign it. There are cases of officers who request for an 'outstanding' with folded hands and some go the extent of touching your feet for this.

Proper performance appraisal is essential to reward those who did well. This is the greatest motivating factor. It is the duty of a District Officer to actually apply his mind and record a factual and specific entry. However, the major drawback in this system is that it is like a post mortem. It does not in any way ensure improvement in the performance of an officer. Moreover, it is kept confidential except when adverse and is, hence, of no immediate use.

A better way for the District Officer is to have continuous evaluation. The method that can be used for this is to set to quarterly targets e.g. one can have targets for court work (number of cases to be disposed off), revenue collection, disposal of audit objection, contribution to national savings, etc. These targets should be fixed after discussing them with the officer concerned. There is no point in setting unrealistic goals. Then they should be reduced in writing and communicate to the officer.

At the end of three months the officer would give a report on all the tasks set for him and his achievements and reasons for success or failure. The officer can then be called for a personal audience. He should be complimented for the good performance but his weakness should also be pointed out. This can be done verbally. This process, if followed, can ensure development of the officer and spur him to greater efforts. Rather than having a post-mortem this continuous evaluation method ensures results. The end of the year report should then be based on these quarterly evaluations.

A proper and serious system of performance appraisal can certainly lead to the team performing well and to the expectation of the district officer.

Collector as a Trainer

Linked to this is the role of the Collector as a trainer, particularly in the case of young IAS probationers who come to the district for training. In the British days the joint magistrates would stay with the DM and be with him throughout learning the nuances of district administration. On the contrary, the young probationer of today finds that the Collector has no time for him and treats him as a hindrance. I recall my own days as probationer when my Collector told me that he wondered why I had been sent on training to his district. He nevertheless asked me to get in touch with the ADM (Executive). The ADM promptly asked the revenue assistant to draw up a programme. It was clear that I would have to plan my training myself. I started submitting daily diary to my Collector but he politely told me to send it to the ADM for perusal. After some time I wanted to do some independent work and I requested my DM but the officer connived to make me OC bills, a job which involved signing officer's salary bills.

The above is just to point out that many Collectors consider training a probationer as a burden, but it should be one of the priority jobs of a Collector. If proper care and concern is shown, and the Collector takes pains to guide the young officers, then the right attitudes are built in from the very beginning and it ensures that the trainees become successful and effective officers.

District administration is both an art as well as a science. One has to plan his work systematically and work according to principles. One has to manage one's time, manage the stress that is continuously upon him, and one has to clearly delineate the objectives and goals and then motivate his team to achieve them.

Time Management

There is always shortage of time for the Collector. At the end of the day he will always have a list of things which have not been taken up. The worst is the feeling that one has not been taken away by handling emergent situations. However, a conscious effort to control and manage one's time is required if any officer wants to be effective.

First of all there is the pressure of visitors. An open door policy is good and should be followed but if no time restrictions are imposed then one can merely go on meeting people from early morning till night. A system has to be developed and soon the people fall in time with this system. A Collector can keep four days in a week for meeting people. This should include Monday as the heaviest rush of visitors is on this day. Meeting the public should start at 10.00 am and it should be done preferably at the Collectorate. 10.00 am to 1.30 pm can set aside for this. During this period officers and employees with files should be discouraged from coming. If rigorously followed, this can meet the demands of visitors in most districts. Meeting people in the afternoon or evening should be discouraged. It has to be kept open for public representatives and members of the press. Refusing to see them when they come can take away more of your time and peace. However, most of them come after taking appointments and one can give time in the forenoon. Even then one would end up meeting people for some time during the evening also.

There are some professional touts in a district who would always come close and whisper that they have something very important to convey and would want time alone in the night. This should be refused. After some time they would understand the style of the officer.

In bigger districts where there are several additional Collectors, the Collector can reduce his meeting with the public to thrice a week. If he sits more, then no one goes to the ADMs and most of them sit idle. Work which can easily be tackled by them comes to the Collector and he simply marks it to the ADM.

The time that people take from you depends entirely upon your style. If you encourage them to talk then they would sit and not move. They will spend time praising the officer indulging in small talk and so on. Visitors should be welcomed with a smile but the attitude of the officer should be professional. This filters down to the people and they adjust by stating their work and leaving early. Any officer who likes to hear gossip can never control his time.

From 3.00 p.m. onwards there should be one hour for officers and officials who have to discuss files or issues. 4.00 p.m. onwards can be kept for meetings. A Collector has to preside over several meetings. Most of them are long, loose ended and do not result in anything. These meetings have to be effectively managed to make purposeful use of time. There should always be an agenda, minutes of previous meetings and their compliance. There is a habit in these meetings for officers to talk loosely and generally leading to fruitless discussion for hours. The Collector must lead the discussion and control it. As far as possible a decision or plan of action should be arrived at. This will reduce the time taken in meetings and also increase their output.

Decentralization of authority is the best way to manage time. A Collector who wants to dictate every letter himself, takes every decision at his own level, visits the site of every law and order occurrence himself can never find enough time for productive work. One should trust one's subordinates and delegate responsibility to them.

Also one has to have a clear sense of priorities. A draft letter put up may not be a piece of literature but if it meets the need or if it conveys the message then there is no need to spend time correcting the letter and retying it. One has to give more time to substantial issues rather than concentrate on issues which are not so important.

The Collector in a district is constantly being asked to attend functions, ceremonies, inaugurations, etc. These tend to make one popular but cost a lot of time. Every function starts off with the customary garlanding and welcome songs and is followed by inane speeches and at the end of a couple of hours one has not achieved anything. These ceremonial functions are best avoided. Time is too precious to be spent on activities that do not help in administering the district. This does not mean that a Collector should not participate in cultural or sports activities in a district. It is one of the aspects of a Collector's job to do so but there are many inaugurations and ceremonial functions which do no help in anyway. The crux of the problem is that the Collector should be very careful and choosy about giving time to such functions.

It is a fashion for officers to say that they work so hard that they have no time for their family or for their health. This shows poor time management again. It is essential to perform much better at your job. Time can certainly be found and one can be very stingy about one's time after 7.30 pm in the night. As far as possible one should spend a couple of hours with the family around this time.

Thirty minutes per day for walking or some other form of exercise is also essential, if one does not do it then health shall suffer and productivity shall go down. Time for this can be found after dinner. Normally a District Officer is so tired after the day's work that exercise suffers and this leads to putting on of weight and other related diseases.

Thus, as one can see, there are many aspects to the job of a Collector and time is the scarcest commodity for him. Time management, thus, is the topmost priority objective in a district officer's scheme of things. There is a direct correlation between a good time manager and an effective officer.

Administration is an art because every decision of the DM affects the people–it is related to human beings. It also involves constant interaction with people. One has thus, to satisfy them without trespassing rules and regulations. Administration at the district level is essentially management of human beings.

Things have changed. The glory and the glamour of the post have receded. The Collector is no longer independent and not really 'the monarch of all he surveys'. Even then the assignment is still one of the most challenging and rewarding in the service. It is one job which gives a tremendous opportunity to do something for the people. One can really understand the problems of the people and the solution is with you. The increasing complexities of the job have made it all the more interesting and there is tremendous scope for creativity and personal initiative. In fact, a district is almost like a living organism which responds to the touch of the personality and style of a Collector. There is a constant interaction between the DM and his district, and the people instantaneously judge the performance of a Collector. The greatest satisfaction comes if the people are happy, and perceive the administration as one that cares for them and it is this goal that one has to strive for.